Leaving Certificate
Ordinary Level Paper 2

Mathematics

Tom Healy

The Educational Company of Ireland

Edco

Published 2015

The Educational Company of Ireland
Ballymount Road
Walkinstown
Dublin 12

www.edco.ie

A member of the Smurfit Kappa Group plc

© Tom Healy, 2015

ISBN: 978-1-84536-644-5

Book design: Liz White Designs

Cover design: Identikit

Layout: Compuscript

Editor: Sam Hartburn

Illustrations: Compuscript

Proofreaders: Sam Hartburn, Martin Bates, Sally Vince

While every care has been taken to trace and acknowledge copyright, the publishers tender their apologies for any accidental infringement where copyright has proved untraceable. They would be pleased to come to a suitable arrangement with the rightful owner in each case.

Web references in this book are intended as a guide for teachers. At the time of going to press, all web addresses were active and contained information relevant to the topics in this book. However, The Educational Company of Ireland and the authors do not accept responsibility for the views or information contained on these websites. Content and addresses may change beyond our control and students should be supervised when investigating websites.

CONTENTS

Introduction

This book covers the material required for Paper 2 of the Leaving Certificate Ordinary Level mathematics examination. Paper 2 is dominated by strands 1, 2 and 3·4 (Statistics, Probability, Synthetic Geometry, Co-ordinate Geometry of the Line and of the Circle, Trigonometry and Length, Area and Volume).

Each chapter ends with three sets of exercises followed by detailed solutions. Exercise A contains straightforward questions, designed to build confidence and to reinforce basic skills. Exercise B contains more progressive questions. Exercise C contains examination questions from past papers.

This book is designed to help students of all abilities. I have aimed to provide enough support for a student working hard towards obtaining a grade D and enough challenge for a student aiming for a grade A.

If you are experiencing difficulties with maths in general, I'd suggest that you work through the notes in each chapter and concentrate on mastering Exercise A in each chapter before going on to the more challenging exercises. If, on the other hand, you have no problems with a particular section, feel free to skip ahead. It is important to pick and choose work according to your individual needs.

However, every student should, after sufficient preparation, pay careful attention to Exercise C at the end of each chapter. Year after year, the Chief Examiner's Report has pointed out that students who achieve the highest grades have extensively practised examination questions.

If you cannot solve a question relatively easily, it is vital to go over it again. The appendix contains record sheets for such practice. You should write the page number and question number of any question causing you problems. Tick a box every time you practise the question. After five ticks you should be a lot more fluent in that area. It amazes me how often students spend time studying things they already know. This method focuses on learning the things you *don't*, which is far more efficient.

In the Project Maths syllabus, any topic can appear in any question. It is important to be aware that material usually associated with Paper 1 can be examined in Paper 2. For example, an algebra question, e.g. one on solving quadratic equations, could easily be part of a trigonometry or length, area and volume question. A complex number question could be part of a co-ordinate geometry question, and so on.

Another theme in Project Maths is that there is more than one way to solve a problem. In the solutions in this book you will frequently find a number of methods. Understanding the concepts behind different methods promotes a flexible approach to problem solving.

In the examination itself, you *must* answer all questions. There is no choice. This simplifies matters to a certain extent. Each paper lasts two and a half hours, with a maximum of 300 marks available. That is, you have 150 minutes to get up to 300 marks. This gives an average of 2 marks a minute.

Every question will have the number of marks it is worth written clearly beside it. If a question is worth 50 marks you *must not* spend more than 25 minutes on it. If such a question has five parts, that's a maximum of five minutes for each part. When you've used up the allotted time you *must* move on. On no account allow yourself to run out of time.

An examination question is an opportunity to demonstrate knowledge. Show what you know. Don't skimp. Write your answers in reasonable detail. You won't win any prizes for saving ink!

Do not leave the examination hall early no matter how finished you think you are. Check all your arithmetic again with your calculator. Re-read questions to check that you have answered what was actually asked. Have you written any required units after your answers? If you've drawn a graph, have you labelled it properly? Have you rounded your answers to the required number of decimal places or significant figures?

Never leave a question completely unanswered.

If a question seems too difficult, find something to write down.

- Highlight keywords. Is there any relevant formula or fact you can write down?

- Have a look in the relevant section of the *Formulae and Tables* booklet.

- Do a calculation, no matter how simple. Will trial and improvement work? Can you make a table or draw a graph or diagram? Define one of the keywords in the question.

You'd be surprised how many marks you can get for just trying.

Remember: it's a *written* examination. You can *only* get marks by writing things down or by drawing diagrams or tables.

It is essential to bring a geometry set for Paper 2. (I'd recommend having one for Paper 1 as well.)

Buy a good calculator well in advance of the examinations. Make sure that your calculator has natural display. It makes a huge difference if you can type an expression like $\sqrt{(1{\cdot}5)^2 + (3\sqrt{7})^2 - 2(1{\cdot}5)(3\sqrt{7})\cos(48{\cdot}6°)}$ and it looks the same on the screen as it does on the page.

Read the manual! Many students throw this valuable document away with the packaging. Do you know how to calculate the mean of a frequency distribution using your calculator? Can you reliably calculate powers of ten,

e.g. $\dfrac{1\!\cdot\!5 \times 10^3 + 2\!\cdot\!6 \times 10^4}{2\!\cdot\!5 \times 10^2} = 110$? Can you use the hours, minutes and seconds button? Know how to change the setup of your calculator for scientific notation, statistics, normal mode, etc. Having good calculator skills is a big plus. If you've lost the manual, download it and read it carefully at least twice. This is *really* important.

I recommend two calculators in particular: the Casio *fx*-83GT PLUS and the Sharp WriteView EL-W531. Both of these have natural display and advanced DAL (direct algebraic logic).

A word of warning: the Sharp EL-531X does not have natural display. Make sure that the code has a 'W' and not an 'X' if you decide to buy the Sharp model recommended above.

Don't buy an unfamiliar calculator the day before the exam. You need a friend you can rely on, not alien technology.

How old is your calculator? After two or three years, the battery or the screen can fail. Nobody wants this to happen in an exam. Have a good-quality back-up calculator, just in case.

It's worth buying a copy of the *Formulae and Tables* booklet. There is a wealth of information there and you need to be familiar with it. Students who use this booklet regularly have a decided advantage over those who don't.

Be as active as you can when studying maths. Work through examples as you read them, do all the calculations. Cover the solution and try to work it out yourself. Be efficient, but don't rush. You know when you are learning and when you are not. Whatever your method of study, make sure that you *are* actually learning. There is no substitute.

Good luck!

Tom Healy

Probability

Learning objectives

In this chapter you will learn how to:

- Understand terms such as *experiment*, *sample space*, *event*, *experimental* and *theoretical probability*

- Calculate probabilities for experiments involving cards, coins, dice, etc.

- Place events on a probability scale

- Solve problems using tables, Venn diagrams and tree diagrams

- Apply the fundamental principle of counting

- Calculate factorials and permutations (arrangements)

- Calculate expected values and use them to say if a game is fair or not

- Define Bernoulli trials

- Calculate the probability of a success for the first time on the nth Bernoulli trial.

Basic concepts

Probability is the mathematics of chance. A probability **experiment**, or **trial**, is an activity where the outcome cannot be predicted.

A **sample space**, S, is the set of all possible outcomes, e.g. {H, T}, {1, 2, 3, 4, 5, 6}. An **event**, E, is a subset of a sample space S. $E \subset S$.

The probability that an event E will occur is written $P(E)$.

Examples

(a) List four examples of a probability experiment.

(b) List the sample space if **(i)** a die is thrown **(ii)** a coin is tossed.

(c) A coin is tossed. List all the possible events.

Solutions

(a) Tossing a coin, throwing a die, picking a card from a standard deck, spinning a spinner.

(b) (i) $S = \{1, 2, 3, 4, 5, 6\}$ **(ii)** $S = \{H, T\}$

(c) The possible events can be listed as getting a head, getting a tail, getting a head or a tail, getting neither.

In set notation, the four possible events are $\{H\}, \{T\}, \{H, T\}, \{\ \}$.

Note that the last event, the null event, represents an impossible outcome, e.g. the coin turns into a winged horse and flies away. Based on experience, this event has a probability of zero.

Also note that $P(S) = P(\{H, T\}) = 1$, a certainty.

The probability scale

Probabilities are numbers between zero and one. If the probability of an event is zero it can never occur. If the probability of an event is one it is certain to occur.

A probability can be written as a decimal, a percentage or a fraction, e.g. 0·5, 50% or $\frac{1}{2}$.

Probabilities can be arranged on a scale, as in the diagram below.

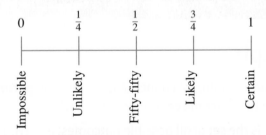

Point to note

The theoretical probability, $P(E)$, of an event, E, where the outcomes are equally likely, is given by

$$P(E) = \frac{\text{the number of outcomes of interest}}{\text{the number of possible outcomes}} = \frac{\#E}{\#S}.$$

Example

A fair die is thrown.

(a) What is the probability that it lands on a four?

(b) Suppose that the die is thrown three hundred times. How many fours would you expect?

Solution

(a) $P(4) = \dfrac{\#\{4\}}{\#\{1, 2, 3, 4, 5, 6\}} = \dfrac{1}{6}$

(b) $\dfrac{1}{6} \times 300 = 50$

Experimental probability

Experimental probability is based on observation. It is calculated using relative frequency. The experimental probability, $P(E)$, of an event, E, is given by

$$P(E) = \frac{\text{the number of trials where } E \text{ occurs}}{\text{the total number of trials}}.$$

Example

Philip tosses a coin ten times, twenty times, thirty times and two hundred times and records the results in a table.

Number of tosses	10	20	30	200
Number of heads	3	14	12	102

(a) Calculate the experimental probability of getting a head in each case.

(b) Comment on how the experimental probabilities change as the number of trials increases.

Solution

(a)

Number of tosses	10	20	30	200
Number of heads	3	14	12	102
Relative frequency or experimental probability	$\dfrac{3}{10} = 0.3$	$\dfrac{14}{20} = 0.7$	$\dfrac{12}{30} = 0.4$	$\dfrac{102}{200} = 0.51$

(b) As the number of trials increases, the experimental probability gets closer to the theoretical probability, 0·5.

A deck of cards

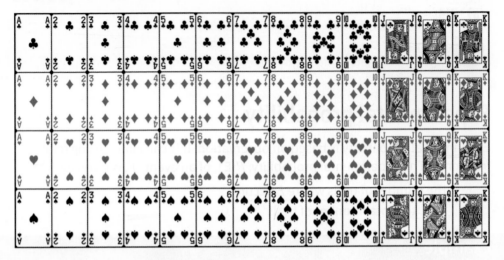

A standard deck has 52 cards. The four suits are shown here in the order clubs, diamonds, hearts and spades.

Each suit contains 13 cards.

There are 12 picture cards: four jacks, four queens and four kings. There are 26 red cards and 26 black cards.

Note that, on our course, a standard deck does *not* contain jokers.

Types of number that may appear in questions

Factors are numbers that divide a given number evenly. For example, the factors of 8 are {1, 2, 4, 8}.

Prime numbers have exactly two factors, e.g. 7 = 7 × 1. The prime numbers less than twenty are 2, 3, 5, 7, 11, 13, 17 and 19.

Composite numbers have more than two factors, e.g. 12 = 12 × 1 = 6 × 2 = 3 × 4.

The number 1 is neither prime nor composite.

A **multiple** of a number is the product of that number and any other natural number. For example, 3, 6, 9, 12, 15, … are multiples of 3.

Square numbers look like squares when drawn as dot-diagrams.

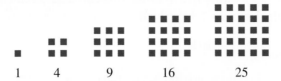

1   4   9   16   25

Example

A shop sells shirts in 5 different sizes, 8 different colours and 3 different styles. How many different types of shirt does it sell?

Solution

$5 \times 8 \times 3 = 120$

Example

A fair coin is tossed three times.

(a) Draw a tree diagram showing all the possible outcomes.

(b) Calculate the probability of getting:

    (i) three heads   (ii) exactly two heads   (iii) at least two tails.

Solution

(a)

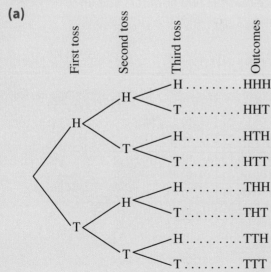

(b) Notice that there are 8 outcomes in total. This can also be calculated using the counting principle, i.e. $\#S = 2 \times 2 \times 2 = 8$.

(i) $P(\text{Three heads}) = \dfrac{\#\{HHH\}}{\#S} = \dfrac{1}{8}$

(ii) $P(\text{Exactly two heads}) = \dfrac{\#\{HHT, HTH, THH\}}{\#S} = \dfrac{3}{8}$

(iii) $P(\text{At least two tails}) = \dfrac{\#\{HTT, THT, TTH, TTT\}}{\#S} = \dfrac{4}{8} = \dfrac{1}{2}$

Top Tip

Don't just give your answer to a probability question as a number with no supporting work. List outcomes, draw a table or tree diagram. You will lose marks if you don't support your answer. Think of it like a court case. A lawyer can't just say 'My client is not guilty' and expect them to be let off. No matter how convinced they are of their client's innocence, they still have to give evidence.

Example

A fair die is thrown twice.

(a) Construct a table to illustrate the sample space.

(b) Find the probability that you get a six on one or both throws.

(c) Find the probability that the numbers thrown add up to eight.

(d) Is it true that there is a 50 : 50 chance that the two numbers add up to a prime number?

Solution

(a)

			Second throw			
		1	2	3	4	5	6
First throw	1	(1, 1)	(1, 2)	(1, 3)	(1, 4)	(1, 5)	(1, 6)
	2	(2, 1)	(2, 2)	(2, 3)	(2, 4)	(2, 5)	(2, 6)
	3	(3, 1)	(3, 2)	(3, 3)	(3, 4)	(3, 5)	(3, 6)
	4	(4, 1)	(4, 2)	(4, 3)	(4, 4)	(4, 5)	(4, 6)
	5	(5, 1)	(5, 2)	(5, 3)	(5, 4)	(5, 5)	(5, 6)
	6	(6, 1)	(6, 2)	(6, 3)	(6, 4)	(6, 5)	(6, 6)

(b) $P(6) = \dfrac{\#\{(6,1),(6,2),(6,3),(6,4),(6,5),(6,6),(1,6),(2,6),(3,6),(4,6),(5,6)\}}{\#S}$

$\qquad = \dfrac{11}{36}$

(c) $P(\text{Add to 8}) = \dfrac{\#\{(6,2),(5,3),(4,4),(3,5),(2,6)\}}{\#S} = \dfrac{5}{36}$

(d) The sum of the two scores is between 2 and 12 inclusive. The only possible prime numbers in this range are 2, 3, 5, 7, 11. The outcomes that match these values are highlighted in the table below.

		Second throw					
		1	2	3	4	5	6
First throw	1	(1, 1)	(1, 2)	(1, 3)	(1, 4)	(1, 5)	(1, 6)
	2	(2, 1)	(2, 2)	(2, 3)	(2, 4)	(2, 5)	(2, 6)
	3	(3, 1)	(3, 2)	(3, 3)	(3, 4)	(3, 5)	(3, 6)
	4	(4, 1)	(4, 2)	(4, 3)	(4, 4)	(4, 5)	(4, 6)
	5	(5, 1)	(5, 2)	(5, 3)	(5, 4)	(5, 5)	(5, 6)
	6	(6, 1)	(6, 2)	(6, 3)	(6, 4)	(6, 5)	(6, 6)

$P(\text{Add to 2, 3, 5, 7 or 11}) = \dfrac{1+2+4+6+2}{36} = \dfrac{15}{36} \approx 0.42$. This is less than a 50:50 chance.

Note that highlighting the relevant outcomes in the table is an efficient way to count them.

Factorials and permutations

The number of ways of arranging n objects in order is given by $n!$ (**n factorial**) where $n! = n(n-1)(n-2) \ldots 3 \times 2 \times 1$.

The number of ways of arranging r objects from n distinct objects is given by ${}^nP_r$.

The letter P stands for **permutation**. There is a button on your calculator for ${}^nP_r$. Make sure you know how to use it. Download the manual for your calculator if necessary.

Examples

(a) How many five-letter arrangements can be made from the letters in the word MATHS?

(b) There are twelve dogs in a dog show. A prize is given for first, second and third place. How many possible outcomes are there?

Solutions

(a) Method 1   The fundamental principle of counting

There are five choices for the first letter, four for the second, etc. This gives $5 \times 4 \times 3 \times 2 \times 1 = 120$ arrangements.

Method 2   Use the factorial button on the calculator

$5! = 5 \times 4 \times 3 \times 2 \times 1 = 120$

On the *Casio fx-83GT PLUS* calculator, type `5` then `SHIFT` then `x⁻¹` then `=`.

On the *Sharp WriteView EL-W531* calculator, type `5` then `2nd F` then `4` then `=`.

(b) Method 1   The fundamental principle of counting

Any of the 12 dogs could win first place. Any of the remaining 11 could win second place and any of the remaining 10 could win third place. This gives $12 \times 11 \times 10 = 1320$ possible outcomes.

Method 2   Use the permutation button on the calculator

$^{12}P_3 = 1320$

On the *Casio fx-83GT PLUS* calculator, type `12` then `SHIFT` then `×` then `3` then `=`.

On the *Sharp WriteView EL-W531* calculator, type `12` then `2nd F` then `6` then `3` then `=`.

Probability and set notation

In the diagrams below, the shaded area represents the indicated set.
In probability the universal set, U, is the sample space, S.

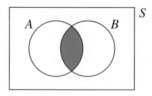

A intersection B: $A \cap B$. The probability that A *and* B occur is equal to $P(A \cap B)$.

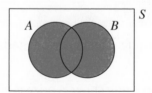

A union B: $A \cup B$. The probability that *either A or B* (or both) occurs is equal to $P(A \cup B)$.

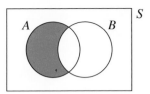

A less B: $A \setminus B$.

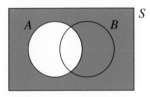

The complement of A, denoted A' or A^C.

Note that A' is also called not-A. The events A and A' cannot occur at the same time. They are **mutually exclusive**. Here, $P(A') = 1 - P(A)$.

Any two events with a null intersection are mutually exclusive.

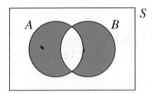

In the above diagram, the events $A \setminus B$ and $B \setminus A$ are mutually exclusive.

 Point to note

Two events, E and F, are mutually exclusive if they cannot occur at the same time. That is, $E \cap F = \varnothing$, their intersection is the null set.

Example

The diagram shows the sample space, S, of an experiment with equally likely outcomes. The outcomes are represented by dots.

Find the experimental probability of each of the following events:

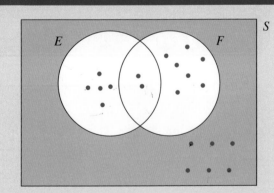

(a) S (b) $\varnothing$ (c) E

(d) $E \setminus F$ (e) $E \cap F$ (f) F'.

Solution

$\#S = 5 + 2 + 7 + 6 = 20$

(a) $P(S) = \dfrac{\#S}{\#S} = \dfrac{20}{20} = 1$

(b) $P(\varnothing) = \dfrac{\#\varnothing}{\#S} = \dfrac{0}{20} = 0$

(c) $P(E) = \dfrac{\#E}{\#S} = \dfrac{7}{20}$

(d) $P(E\backslash F) = \dfrac{\#(E\backslash F)}{\#S} = \dfrac{5}{20} = \dfrac{1}{4}$

(e) $P(E \cap F) = \dfrac{\#(E \cap F)}{\#S} = \dfrac{2}{20} = \dfrac{1}{10}$

(f) $P(F') = \dfrac{\#F'}{\#S} = \dfrac{5+6}{20} = \dfrac{11}{20}$

Note that $P(F') = 1 - P(F) = 1 - \dfrac{9}{20} = \dfrac{11}{20}$

Expected value

Multiply each probability by the number + add all your answers.

The **expected value**, E, is the probability-weighted mean of the outcomes when a random experiment is repeated a large number of times.

> **Point to note**
>
> (For those who like formulae.)
>
> Recall the formula for the mean of a frequency distribution $\mu = \dfrac{\Sigma fx}{\Sigma f}$ (*Formulae and Tables* booklet page 33).
>
> Replacing the frequency, f, with the probability, $P(x)$, and the mean with expected value, $E(x)$ we get:
>
> $$E(x) = \frac{\Sigma xP(x)}{\Sigma P(x)} = \frac{\Sigma xP(x)}{1} = \Sigma xP(x).$$

> **Remember**
>
> To calculate the expected value:
>
> 1. Multiply each outcome by its probability.
> 2. Add the answers.
>
> The mean is the average of what *has happened*. The expected value is the average of what *is going to happen* in the long run.

You might ask, what is the point of the expected value? This is a valid question. It is used, for example, to calculate how much an insurance company should charge a customer while still making a profit. Casinos also use it to calculate how much a customer should pay. It can also be used to check if a game is fair or not.

Example

(a) Ann throws a die 500 times. She adds up all 500 outcomes and gets a total of 1760. Find the mean of these outcomes.

(b) Find the expected value, E, if a fair die is thrown.

(c) Compare the answers to parts (a) and (b).

Solution

(a) Mean $= \dfrac{\text{total}}{\text{number of throws}} = \dfrac{1760}{500} = 3{\cdot}52$

(b) The sample space is $S = \{1, 2, 3, 4, 5, 6\}$. Each outcome has a probability of $\frac{1}{6}$.

Multiplying each outcome by its probability and adding the answers we get

$E = 1 \times \dfrac{1}{6} + 2 \times \dfrac{1}{6} + 3 \times \dfrac{1}{6} + 4 \times \dfrac{1}{6} + 5 \times \dfrac{1}{6} + 6 \times \dfrac{1}{6} = 3{\cdot}5$

The fact that you can't throw a 3·5 with a standard die shows that the expected value does not have to be one of the outcomes.

(c) The mean of a large number of throws is very close to the expected value.

Bernoulli trials

A **Bernoulli trial** is an experiment where the outcome is random and can be either of two possibilities, 'success' or 'failure'. The probability of success or failure does not change from trial to trial.

Example

John is playing a game with a fair die. He only stops throwing the die when he gets a six. What is the probability that he will stop after:

(a) one throw   (b) two throws   (c) four throws?

Solution

Let S be the event that he throws a six (success), and F be the event that he doesn't throw a six (failure). Note that $P(S) = \frac{1}{6}$ and $P(F) = \frac{5}{6}$.

(a) $P(S) = \frac{1}{6}$

(b) $P(FS) = \frac{5}{6} \times \frac{1}{6} = \frac{5}{36}$

(c) $P(FFFS) = \frac{5}{6} \times \frac{5}{6} \times \frac{5}{6} \times \frac{1}{6} = \frac{125}{1296}$

Exercise A

Q1 According to the weather report, there is a 20% chance of rain tomorrow. Which of the following statements would be appropriate?

    (a) It will rain on one of the next five days.

    (b) Rain will fall for 4·8 hours of the next 24 hours.

    (c) Of past days when conditions were similar, one out of five had some rain.

    (d) It will rain on 20% of the area of the country.

Q2 (a) What is meant by the terms   **(i)** sample space   **(ii)** event?

    (b) List the elements of the sample space for each of the following experiments:

      (i) a fair coin is tossed three times

      (ii) the following spinner is spun twice (all sectors are equal in size and shape).

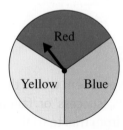

    (c) A fair die is thrown five times. Calculate the size of the sample space.

Q3 Which of the following best describes how likely it is that each of the following events occurs? Write the letter corresponding to the correct answer in the box in the table.

A. Impossible or almost impossible.

B. Not very likely.

C. About 50% likely.

D. Very likely.

E. Certain or almost certain.

Event	How likely
A baby will be born in Ireland tomorrow.	
If you pick one card from an ordinary pack of cards you will pick the queen of hearts.	
There will be 400 days in the year 2050.	
If a fair coin is tossed you will get a head.	
It will not rain in Ireland during the month of November.	
If two ordinary dice are thrown, the sum of the numbers will be 1.	

Q4 (a) A card is picked at random from a standard deck. What is the probability that it is:

    (i) the ace of hearts

    (ii) a three

    (iii) a picture card

    (iv) a diamond or a picture card?

  (b) Two cards are picked at random from a standard deck. What is the probability that:

    (i) they are both queens

    (ii) they are both red?

Q5 (a) Sophie tosses a fair coin 19 times. She gets 19 heads. What is the probability that she will get a head on the twentieth toss?

  (b) Daniel says that there are six outcomes when a die is tossed. Thus, there will be 12 outcomes when two dice are tossed. Do you agree? If not, say how many outcomes you think there are.

  (c) Charlie says that if you toss two coins there are three outcomes: two heads, two tails or a head and a tail. Do you agree? Justify your answer.

Q6 A café has the following menu:

Sandwich: chicken, ham, tuna, beef, cheese.

Soup: tomato, chicken, vegetable.

Dessert: ice-cream or fruit salad.

Drink: tea, coffee, orange juice, lemonade.

Lunch consists of a sandwich, soup, a dessert and a drink. How many possible lunches are there?

Q7 Mary surveyed 150 students to find which social networking sites they use. Some of the results are shown in the Venn diagram below.

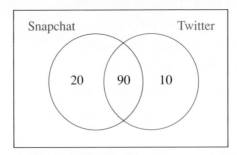

(a) Find the number of students who use neither of the two sites.

(b) One student is chosen at random from those surveyed. Find the probability that the student uses both sites.

Q8 (a) How many ways are there of arranging six different objects in a row?

(b) How many ways are there of arranging four objects selected from ten distinct objects?

(c) Ann has a collection of DVDs. There are over three million ways of arranging them in order. What is the smallest number of DVDs that Ann could have?

Q9 A fairground game costs €2 to play. Three coins are thrown. You get €1 for every head that appears.

(a) Write down the sample space for tossing the three coins.

(b) Copy and complete the table:

Number of heads	0	1	2	3
Probability				

(c) (i) Find the expected value for the number of heads.

(ii) Is this a fair game? Justify your answer.

Q10 Molly has a probability of $\frac{7}{10}$ of scoring from a penalty. In a match she takes three penalties. What is the probability that she scores for the first time from:

(a) the first penalty   (b) the second penalty   (c) the third penalty?

Exercise B

Q1 A fair coin is tossed four times.

   (a) Calculate the size of the sample space.

   (b) Draw a tree diagram illustrating all the possible outcomes.

   (c) Find the probability of getting exactly one head from the four tosses.

   (d) Find the probability of getting at least one head.

   (e) Emma says that the chances of getting exactly two heads are 50:50. Do you agree? Justify your answer.

Q2 A die was rolled 60 times, with the following results recorded.

Outcome	1	2	3	4	5	6
Frequency	10	9	10	12	8	11

Find the experimental probability of:

   (a) getting a 4

   (b) getting an odd number

   (c) getting a number greater than 3.

Q3 Brianna throws a fair six-sided die and spins a fair spinner numbered 1 to 4 as shown.

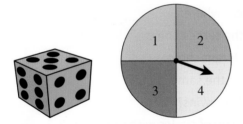

The results are multiplied.

   (a) Copy and complete the table to illustrate the sample space.

	Spinner			
×	1	2	3	4
1				
2				
3		6		
4				
5			15	
6				

(Die)

(b) How many outcomes are there?

(c) What is the probability of getting:

    (i) 12   **(ii)** 20% of 25   **(iii)** a multiple of 9?

Q4 The probability that John will be on the school football team is 0·6. The probability that he will be on the school hurling team is 0·5 and the probability that he will be on both the football team and the hurling team is 0·3.

John's father says that he will buy John a bicycle if he represents the school in either of the above sports.

(a) Draw a Venn diagram to represent the above data.

(b) What is the chance that John gets the bicycle from his father?

Q5 (a) In how many ways can the letters of the word IRELAND be arranged if each letter is used exactly once in each arrangement?

(b) In how many of these arrangements do the vowels come together?

(c) In how many arrangements do the vowels not come together?

Q6 Aleksandra, Chloe and Dara play rock-paper-scissors for three players.

Aleksandra wins if *all three* players make the same choice.

Chloe wins if each player makes a *different* choice.

Dara wins if exactly *two* players make the same choice.

(a) How many possible outcomes are there?

(b) How many outcomes are there where:

    (i) all three players make the same choice

    (ii) each player makes a different choice

    (iii) exactly two players make the same choice?

(c) What is the probability that Dara wins?

Q7 The dartboard illustrated is made up of circles with radii of 1, 2, 3, and 4 units.

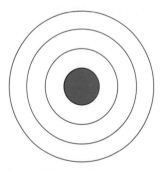

A dart hits the target randomly. What is the probability that the dart hits the bullseye?

Q8 There are four main blood groups: Group O, Group A, Group B and Group AB. The blood in each group is further classed as either rhesus positive (+) or rhesus negative (−).

In Ireland, the percentage of the population in each blood group is given in the following table:

Blood group	O		A		B		AB	
Rhesus positive (+) or Rhesus negative (−)	O^+	O^-	A^+	A^-	B^+	B^-	AB^+	AB^-
Percentage	8	47	5	26	2	9	1	2

(a) **(i)** Find the percentage of the population in blood group O.

(ii) Find the percentage of the population with rhesus positive blood.

(b) The table below has statements about a person's blood group. A person is picked at random from the population. In each case, find the probability that the statement is true for that person.

Statement	Probability
Is in blood group A^+	
Is in blood group AB	
Is in blood group A or B	
Has blood which is rhesus negative	
Not in blood group O	

(c) Over a period, 8000 people donate blood at a clinic. How many of these 8000 people would you expect to donate:

(i) type AB blood

(ii) rhesus negative blood

(iii) rhesus positive blood?

A die is thrown twice. The results are added.

(a) Copy and complete the table below to illustrate the sample space for the experiment.

		Second throw					
		1	2	3	4	5	6
First throw	1	2					
	2						
	3		5				
	4						
	5						
	6						12

(b) What is the probability of getting a sum of 4?

(c) What is the probability that the sum will be a multiple of 6?

(d) What is the probability that the sum will be a square number?

(e) Find x where $P(x) = P(11)$, where $x \neq 11$.

Q10 For a particular age group, statistics show that the probability of dying in any one year is 1 in 1000 people and the probability of suffering some sort of disability is 3 in 1000 people.

The Hope Life Insurance Company offers to pay out €20 000 if you die and €10 000 if you are disabled. What profit is the insurance company making per customer based on the expected value if it charges a premium of €100 to its customers for the above policy?

Q11 A basketball player has made 80% of his foul shots during the season. Assuming the shots are independent, find the probability that in tonight's game he:

(a) misses for the first time on his fifth foul shot,

(b) makes his first basket on his fourth foul shot,

(c) makes his first basket on one of his first 3 foul shots.

Q12 This is a true story.

A teacher gave her class a test where they had to write 'true' or 'false' to answer each question. She saw one boy tossing a coin. He said that he hadn't studied and decided to leave it to chance. Long after the others had finished, the boy was still tossing a coin.

'What are you doing?' asked the teacher.

'I'm checking my answers,' he replied.

(a) What percentage of questions would you expect the boy to get right?

(b) What is wrong with his method of checking his answers?

Exercise C

Q1 A plastic toy is in the shape of a hemisphere. When it falls on the ground, there are two possible outcomes: it can land with the flat side facing down or with the flat side facing up. Two groups of students are trying to find the probability that it will land with the flat side down.

(a) Explain why, even though there are two outcomes, the answer is not necessarily equal to $\frac{1}{2}$.

(b) The students estimate the probability by experiment. Group A drops the toy 100 times. From this, they estimate that it lands flat side down with probability 0·76. Group B drops the toy 500 times. From this, they estimate that it lands flat side down with probability 0·812.

　(i) Which group's estimate is likely to be better, and why?

　(ii) How many times did the toy land flat side down for Group B?

　(iii) Using the data from the two groups, what is the best estimate of the probability that the toy lands flat side down?

(2011)

Q2 Peter and Niamh go to a large school. One morning, they arrive early. While they are waiting, they decide to guess whether each of the next three students to come in the door will be a boy or a girl.

(a) Write out the sample space showing all the possible outcomes. For example, BGG is one outcome, representing boy, girl, girl.

(b) Peter says these outcomes are equally likely. Niamh says they are not. What do you need to know about the students in the school to decide which of them is correct?

(c) If all the outcomes are equally likely, what is the probability that the three students will be two girls followed by a boy?

(d) Niamh guesses that there will be at least one girl among the next three students. Peter guesses that the next three students will be either three boys or two boys and a girl. Who is more likely to be correct, assuming all outcomes are equally likely? Justify your answer.

(2012)

Q3 (a) In the Venn diagram below, the universal set is a normal deck of 52 playing cards. The two sets shown represent clubs and picture cards (kings, queens and jacks). Show on the diagram the number of elements in each region.

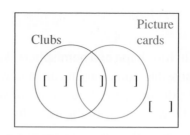

(b) (i) A card is drawn from a pack of 52 cards. Find the probability that the card drawn is the king of clubs.

   (ii) A card is drawn from a pack of 52 cards. Find the probability that the card drawn is a club or a picture card.

   (iii) Two cards are drawn from a pack of 52 cards. Find the probability that neither of them is a club or a picture card.
Give your answer correct to two decimal places.

(2012)

Q4 Katie tossed a coin 200 times and threw 109 heads. Joe tossed the same coin 400 times and threw 238 heads. Lucy tossed the same coin 500 times and threw 291 heads. Katie, Joe and Lucy now think the coin may be biased.

(a) Give a reason why they think that the coin may be biased.

(b) Lucy uses all the above data and calculates that the best estimate of the probability of throwing a head with this coin is 0·58. Show how Lucy might have calculated this probability.

(c) Joe agrees with Lucy's estimate of 0·58 as the probability of throwing a head with this coin.

He claims that the probability of throwing 3 successive heads with this coin is less than the probability of throwing 2 successive tails. Calculate the probability of each event and state whether Joe's claim is true or not.

(2013)

Q5 An unbiased circular spinner has a movable pointer and five equal sectors, two coloured green and three coloured red.

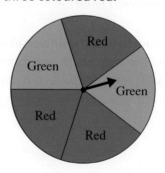

(a) **(i)** Find the probability that the pointer stops on green for one spin of the spinner.

(ii) List all the possible outcomes of 3 successive spins of the spinner.

(b) A game consists of spinning the spinner 3 times. Each time the spinner stops on green the player wins €1; otherwise the player wins nothing. For example, if the outcome of one game is 'green, red, green' the player wins €2.

Copy and complete the following table.

Player wins	€0	€1	€2	€3
Required outcomes				

(c) **(i)** Is one spin of the spinner above an example of a Bernoulli trial?

(ii) Explain what a Bernoulli trial is. (2013)

Q6 (a) State the fundamental principle of counting.

(b) How many different ways are there to arrange five distinct objects in a row?

(c) Peter is arranging books on a shelf. He has five novels and three poetry books. He wants to keep the five novels together and the three poetry books together. In how many different ways can he arrange the books?

(SEC Sample Paper 2014)

Q7 A biased die is used in a game. The probabilities of getting the six different numbers on the die are shown in the table below.

Number	1	2	3	4	5	6
Probability	0·25	0·25	0·15	0·15	0·1	0·1

(a) Find the expected value of the random variable X, where X is the number thrown.

(b) There is a game at a funfair. It costs €3 to play the game. The player rolls a die once and wins back the number of euro shown on the die. The sentence below describes the difference between using the above biased die and using a fair (unbiased) die when playing this game. By doing the calculations required, complete the sentence.

'If you play the game many times with a fair die, you will win an average of _____ per game, but if you play with the biased die you will lose an average of _____ per game.'

(SEC Sample Paper 2014)

Q8 A garage has 5 black cars, 9 red cars and 10 silver cars for sale.

    (a) A car is selected at random. What is the probability that:

        (i) the car is black   **(ii)** the car is black or red?

    (b) A car is selected at random. Then a second car is selected at random from those remaining. What is the probability that: **(i)** the first car is silver and the second car is black   **(ii)** one of the selected cars is red and the other is black?

    (c) Three of the black cars, two of the red cars and four of the silver cars have diesel engines. One car from the garage is again selected at random. What is the probability that it is a red car or a diesel car?

                                                                    (2014)

Q9 When taking a penalty kick, the probability that Kevin scores is always $\frac{3}{4}$.

    (a) Kevin takes a penalty. What is the probability that he does not score?

    (b) Kevin takes two penalties. What is the probability that he scores both?

    (c) Kevin takes three penalties. What is the probability that he scores exactly twice?

    (d) Kevin takes five penalties. What is the probability that he scores for the first time on his fifth penalty?   *(2014)*

Solutions to Exercise A

Q1 (a) No. The probability refers to tomorrow, not the next five days.

    (b) No. There is a 20% chance of rain. It isn't specified how long it will rain for.

    (c) This is the most appropriate statement. The probability of 20% is based on past experience of similar conditions.

    (d) No. This is replacing a probability statement with one that is certain, i.e. that it *will* rain on a particular area.

Q2 (a) **(i)** A sample space is the set of all possible outcomes.

        (ii) An event is a subset of the sample space.

    (b) **(i)** {HHH, HHT, HTH, HTT, THH, THT, TTH, TTT}

            Note that if the coin was tossed twice the sample space would be {HH, HT, TH, TT }. Write these with a H in front, then with a T in front to list all the outcomes for three tosses.

        (ii) {RR, RB, RY, BR, BB, BY, YR, YB, YY}

(c) There are 6 possible outcomes for each throw. By the fundamental principle of counting, this gives $\#S = 6 \times 6 \times 6 \times 6 \times 6 = 7776$ for five throws.

Note that you don't have to list the outcomes here, just count them.

Q3

Event	How likely
A baby will be born in Ireland tomorrow.	E
If you pick one card from an ordinary pack of cards you will pick the queen of hearts.	B
There will be 400 days in the year 2050.	A
If a fair coin is tossed you will get a head.	C
It will not rain in Ireland during the month of November.	B
If two ordinary dice are thrown, the sum of the numbers will be 1.	A

Note that the letter D is a distracter. It does not appear in the answer.

Q4 (a) (i) $P(\text{ace of hearts}) = \dfrac{1}{52}$

(ii) $P(\text{three}) = \dfrac{4}{52} = \dfrac{1}{13}$

(iii) $P(\text{picture card}) = \dfrac{12}{52} = \dfrac{3}{13}$

(iv) There are 13 diamonds, 3 of which are picture cards. There are 9 other picture cards. Thus $13 + 9 = 22$ cards match the description.

$$P(\text{diamond or picture card}) = \dfrac{22}{52} = \dfrac{11}{26}$$

(b) (i) $P(QQ) = \dfrac{4}{52} \times \dfrac{3}{51} = \dfrac{1}{221}$

(ii) $P(RR) = \dfrac{26}{52} \times \dfrac{25}{51} = \dfrac{25}{102}$

Q5 (a) The probability of getting a head on the twentieth throw is $\dfrac{1}{2}$. The twentieth toss is independent of the first nineteen.

(b) Daniel is wrong. By the fundamental principle of counting there are $6 \times 6 = 36$ outcomes, not 12.

(c) Charlie is wrong. There are four outcomes, {HH, HT, TH, TT}, since there are two ways of getting a head and a tail.

Q6 $5 \times 3 \times 2 \times 4 = 120$ lunches

Q7 (a) $150 - (20 + 90 + 10) = 30$

(b) $P(\text{uses both}) = \dfrac{90}{150} = \dfrac{3}{5}$

Q8 (a) $6! = 6 \times 5 \times 4 \times 3 \times 2 \times 1 = 720$

(b) $^{10}P_4 = 10 \times 9 \times 8 \times 7 = 5040$

(c) Use trial and improvement.

$8! = 40\,320$, $9! = 362\,880$, $10! = 3\,628\,800$. Thus Ann has at least ten DVDs.

Q9 (a) $S = \{\text{HHH, HHT, HTH, HTT, THH, THT, TTH, TTT}\}$

(b)

Number of heads	0	1	2	3
Probability	$\frac{1}{8}$	$\frac{3}{8}$	$\frac{3}{8}$	$\frac{1}{8}$

(c) (i) $E = 0 \times \frac{1}{8} + 1 \times \frac{3}{8} + 2 \times \frac{3}{8} + 3 \times \frac{1}{8} = 1 \cdot 5$ heads.

(ii) The game is not fair. A player pays €2 to win €1·50 on average per game. That is, they will lose 50c on average per game.

Q10 The probability of success is $P(S) = 0 \cdot 7$ so the probability of failure is $P(F) = 0 \cdot 3$.

(a) $P(S) = 0 \cdot 7$

(b) $P(FS) = 0 \cdot 3 \times 0 \cdot 7 = 0 \cdot 21$

(c) $P(FFS) = 0 \cdot 3 \times 0 \cdot 3 \times 0 \cdot 7 = 0 \cdot 063$

Solutions to Exercise B

Q1 (a) According to the fundamental principle of counting

$\# S = 2 \times 2 \times 2 \times 2 = 16$.

(b)

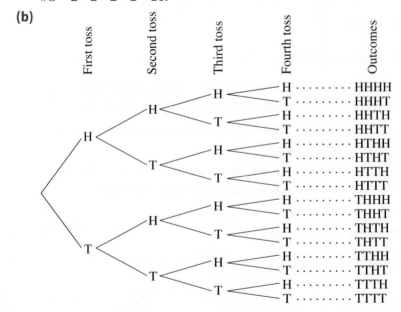

(c) $P(\text{one head}) = \dfrac{\#\{\text{HTTT, THTT, TTHT, TTTH}\}}{16} = \dfrac{4}{16} = \dfrac{1}{4}$

(d) Getting at least one head is the same as getting everything except TTTT.
Thus $P(\text{at least one head}) = \dfrac{15}{16}$.

(e) Emma is wrong. $P(\text{two heads}) = \dfrac{6}{16} = \dfrac{3}{8}$, which is less than $50:50$.

Q2 (a) $\dfrac{12}{60} = \dfrac{1}{5}$

(b) $\dfrac{10 + 10 + 8}{60} = \dfrac{28}{60} = \dfrac{7}{15}$

(c) $\dfrac{12 + 8 + 11}{60} = \dfrac{31}{60}$

Q3 (a)

		Spinner		
×	1	2	3	4
1	1	2	3	4
2	2	4	6	8
3	3	6	9	12
4	4	8	12	16
5	5	10	15	20
6	6	12	18	24

(rows labelled by Die: 1–6)

(b) There are $6 \times 4 = 24$ outcomes.

(c) **(i)** $P(12) = \dfrac{3}{24} = \dfrac{1}{8}$

(ii) 20% of 25 is 5, $P(5) = \dfrac{1}{24}$

(iii) $P(\text{a multiple of } 9) = P(9 \text{ or } 18) = \dfrac{1 + 1}{24} = \dfrac{2}{24} = \dfrac{1}{12}$

Q4 (a) The probability of playing both games is 0.3.

Thus, the probability of playing football but not hurling is
$0.6 - 0.3 = 0.3$.

Similarly, the probability of playing hurling but not football is
$0.5 - 0.3 = 0.2$.

Since the sum of all the probabilities is 1, the probability of playing
neither game is $1 - 0.3 - 0.2 - 0.3 = 0.2$.

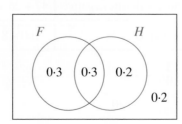

(b) The probability he will get a bicycle is $0.3 + 0.3 + 0.2 = 0.8$.

Q5 (a) $7! = 7 \times 6 \times 5 \times 4 \times 3 \times 2 \times 1 = 5040$

(b) Treat the three vowels as a block. There are $3! = 3 \times 2 \times 1 = 6$ ways they can be arranged together. This block and the other four letters make five objects.

There are $5! = 5 \times 4 \times 3 \times 2 \times 1 = 120$ ways these five objects can be arranged.

Remember that possibilities multiply. Thus there are $5! \times 3! = 120 \times 6 = 720$ ways that all the letters can be arranged where the vowels come together.

(c) $5040 - 720 = 4320$

Q6 (a) Number of outcomes $= 3 \times 3 \times 3 = 27$

(b) **(i)** They all make the same choice. The first player can pick any of rock, paper or scissors, leaving the other two players with only one choice. $3 \times 1 \times 1 = 3$.

(ii) Each player makes a different choice. The first player can pick any of the three, this leaves two choices for the second player and only one for the third. $3 \times 2 \times 1 = 6$.

(iii) Exactly two players make the same choice. So, of the 27 possible outcomes, there are only 18 left: $27 - 3 - 6 = 18$.

(c) $P(\text{Dara wins}) = \dfrac{18}{27} = \dfrac{2}{3}$

Q7 $P(\text{hitting bullseye}) = \dfrac{\text{area of bullseye}}{\text{area of board}} = \dfrac{\pi(1)^2}{\pi(4)^2} = \dfrac{\pi}{16\pi} = \dfrac{1}{16}$

Q8 (a) **(i)** $8 + 47 = 55\%$

(ii) $8 + 5 + 2 + 1 = 16\%$

(b)

Statement	Probability
Is in blood group A^+	5%
Is in blood group AB	$1 + 2 = 3\%$
Is in blood group A or B	$5 + 26 + 2 + 9 = 42\%$
Has blood which is rhesus negative	$47 + 26 + 9 + 2 = 84\%$
Not in blood group O	$100 - 8 - 47 = 45\%$

(c) **(i)** $8000 \times \dfrac{3}{100} = 240$

(ii) $8000 \times \dfrac{84}{100} = 6720$

(iii) $8000 - 6720 = 1280$

Q9 (a)

		Second throw					
First throw	+	1	2	3	4	5	6
	1	2	3	4	5	6	7
	2	3	4	5	6	7	8
	3	4	5	6	7	8	9
	4	5	6	7	8	9	10
	5	6	7	8	9	10	11
	6	7	8	9	10	11	12

(b) $P(4) = \dfrac{3}{36} = \dfrac{1}{12}$

(c) $P(6 \text{ or } 12) = \dfrac{5+1}{36} = \dfrac{6}{36} = \dfrac{1}{6}$

(d) $P(4 \text{ or } 9) = \dfrac{3+4}{36} = \dfrac{7}{36}$

(e) $P(11) = \dfrac{2}{36} = \dfrac{1}{18}$ and $P(3) = \dfrac{2}{36} = \dfrac{1}{18}$, so $x = 3$.

Q10

Outcome	x	$P(x)$	$xP(x)$
Dying	€20 000	$\dfrac{1}{1000}$	€20
Disability	€10 000	$\dfrac{3}{1000}$	€30
Neither	0	$\dfrac{996}{1000}$	0
Expected value			€50

Since the company charges €100 per customer, they expect to make a profit of €100 − €50 = €50 per customer, in the long run.

Q11 The probability of success is $P(S) = 0{\cdot}8$, thus the probability of failure is $P(F) = 1 - 0{\cdot}8 = 0{\cdot}2$.

(a) $P(SSSSF) = 0{\cdot}8 \times 0{\cdot}8 \times 0{\cdot}8 \times 0{\cdot}8 \times 0{\cdot}2 = 0{\cdot}08192$

(b) $P(FFFS) = 0{\cdot}2 \times 0{\cdot}2 \times 0{\cdot}2 \times 0{\cdot}8 = 0{\cdot}0064$

(c) Note that the player stops after making a basket. That is, he (i) makes the first attempt and stops, (ii) misses the first but makes the second attempt and stops or (iii) misses both first and second and makes the third.

$P(S) + P(FS) + P(FFS) = 0{\cdot}8 + 0{\cdot}2 \times 0{\cdot}8 + 0{\cdot}2 \times 0{\cdot}2 \times 0{\cdot}8 = 0{\cdot}992$

Q12 (a) Since the questions are all either true or false, I would expect him to get 50% right.

(b) It is very unlikely that the second sequence of tosses would be the same as the first.

Solutions to Exercise C

Q1 (a) One side of the toy is flat and the other is hemispherical. The two outcomes are not necessarily equally likely.

(b) (i) Group B's estimate is likely to be better. Group B conducted 500 trials. The higher the number of trials, the better the estimate of the true probability is likely to be.

(ii) $0.812 \times 500 = 406$ times.

(iii) For Group A the toy landed flat side down $0.76 \times 100 = 76$ times.

Combining both results:

$$P(\text{toy lands flat side up}) = \frac{406 + 76}{500 + 100} = \frac{482}{600} = 0.803$$

Q2 (a) BBB, GGG, BBG, BGB, GBB, GGB, GBG, BGG.

Top Tip

Use the fundamental principle of counting to check your answer when listing outcomes. Here there are $2 \times 2 \times 2 = 8$ outcomes.

(b) The number of boys and the number of girls in the school.

(c) GGB represents only 1 outcome out of the 8 possibilities.

Thus $P(\text{GGB}) = \frac{1}{8}$.

(b) The only outcome where there are no girls is BBB. Thus the probability that Niamh is right is $\frac{7}{8}$.

Peter's guess allows for BBB, BBG, BGB or GBB. Thus the probability that Peter is right is $\frac{4}{8} = \frac{1}{2}$.

Niamh is more likely to be correct because of the higher probability, i.e. $\frac{7}{8} > \frac{4}{8}$.

Q3 (a)

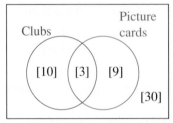

(b) (i) $P(\text{king of clubs}) = \frac{1}{52}$

(ii) $P(\text{club or picture card}) = \frac{10 + 3 + 9}{52} = \frac{22}{52} = \frac{11}{26}$

(iii) $P(\text{neither card is a club or a picture card}) = \frac{30}{52} \times \frac{29}{51} = \frac{145}{442} = 0.33$

Q4 (a) If the coin was unbiased there should be a 50% chance of throwing a head. All three of them threw more than 50% heads.

(b) $\dfrac{\text{Total number of heads}}{\text{Total number of throws}} = \dfrac{109 + 238 + 291}{200 + 400 + 500} = \dfrac{638}{1100} = 0{\cdot}58$

(c) $P(\text{HHH}) = 0{\cdot}58 \times 0{\cdot}58 \times 0{\cdot}58 = 0{\cdot}195112$

$P(\text{TT}) = (1 - 0{\cdot}58) \times (1 - 0{\cdot}58) = 0{\cdot}1764$

Joe's claim is not true.

Q5 (a) (i) $P(G) = \dfrac{2}{5}$

(ii) RRR, RRG, RGR, GRR, GGR, GRG, RGG, GGG

(b)

Player wins	€0	€1	€2	€3
Required outcomes	RRR	RRG RGR GRR	GGR GRG RGG	GGG

(c) (i) Yes.

(ii) A Bernoulli trial is an experiment whose results are random. There are only two possible outcomes. The probability of each outcome does not change from trial to trial.

Q6 (a) If there are m ways of doing something and n ways of doing something else, then there are mn ways of doing both. That is, possibilities multiply.

(b) $5! = 5 \times 4 \times 3 \times 2 \times 1 = 120$ ways.

(c) The five novels can be put together in $5! = 5 \times 4 \times 3 \times 2 \times 1 = 120$ ways.

The three poetry books can be put together in $3! = 3 \times 2 \times 1 = 6$ ways.

The two types of book can be put together in $2! = 2 \times 1 = 2$ ways, i.e. novels first or poetry books first.

This gives $120 \times 6 \times 2 = 1440$ ways.

Q7 (a) $E(X) = 1 \times 0{\cdot}25 + 2 \times 0{\cdot}25 + 3 \times 0{\cdot}15 + 4 \times 0{\cdot}15 + 5 \times 0{\cdot}1 + 6 \times 0{\cdot}1 = 2{\cdot}9$

(b) For a fair die, $E(X) = 1 \times \dfrac{1}{6} + 2 \times \dfrac{1}{6} + 3 \times \dfrac{1}{6} + 4 \times \dfrac{1}{6} + 5 \times \dfrac{1}{6} + 6 \times \dfrac{1}{6} = 3{\cdot}5.$

If you play the game many times with a fair die, you will win an average of €3·50 − €3·00 = €0·50 per game, but if you play with the biased die you will lose an average of €3·00 − €2·90 = €0·10 per game.

Q8 (a) $5 + 9 + 10 = 24$

(i) $P(\text{black}) = \dfrac{5}{24}$ **(ii)** $P(\text{black or red}) = \dfrac{5+9}{24} = \dfrac{14}{24} = \dfrac{7}{12}$

(b) (i) $P(1^{\text{st}} \text{ silver, } 2^{\text{nd}} \text{ black}) = \dfrac{10 \times 5}{24 \times 23} = \dfrac{25}{276}$

(ii) $P(\text{RB or BR}) = \dfrac{9}{24} \times \dfrac{5}{23} + \dfrac{5}{24} \times \dfrac{9}{23} = \dfrac{15}{92}$

(c) There are 9 red cars, two of which are diesel. There are $3 + 4 = 7$ other diesel cars.

Thus P(red or diesel) $= \dfrac{9 + 7}{24} = \dfrac{2}{3}$.

Q9 (a) P(no score) $= 1 - \dfrac{3}{4} = \dfrac{1}{4}$

(b) P(score, score) $= \dfrac{3}{4} \times \dfrac{3}{4} = \dfrac{9}{16}$

(c) P(scores exactly twice) $= P(\text{SSN}) + P(\text{SNS}) + P(\text{NSS})$

$$= \dfrac{3}{4} \times \dfrac{3}{4} \times \dfrac{1}{4} + \dfrac{3}{4} \times \dfrac{1}{4} \times \dfrac{3}{4} + \dfrac{1}{4} \times \dfrac{3}{4} \times \dfrac{3}{4} = \dfrac{27}{64}$$

(d) $P = \dfrac{1}{4} \times \dfrac{1}{4} \times \dfrac{1}{4} \times \dfrac{1}{4} \times \dfrac{3}{4} = \dfrac{3}{1024}$

Activity: Random art co-ordinates

Copy the grid below.

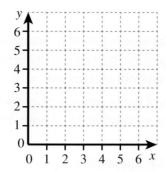

Throw a die. Say you get a 3. Throw it again. Say you get a 5. Plot the point $(3, 5)$.

Throw the die two more times. Say you get $(2, 4)$. Join the two points.

Repeat and join the new point to the previous one. Keep going. Colour in the final result.

You've made a piece of random art!

Statistics

In this chapter you will learn how to:

- Distinguish between types of data

- Understand samples and bias

- Represent data graphically with a line plot, bar chart, histogram, trend graph, stem-and-leaf diagram, pie chart, scatter plot

- Represent data numerically using measures of centre (the mean, mode, median) and measures of variability (the range, interquartile range, standard deviation)

- Describe the shape of a distribution using terms such as symmetric, non-symmetric, unimodal, bimodal, skewed to the right, skewed to the left, bell-shaped

- Distinguish between correlation and causation

- Appreciate that a correlation coefficient, r, is a number between −1 and 1, and match r with a given scatter plot and vice versa

- Apply the empirical rule to normal distributions

- Calculate the margin of error of a sample and use it to test hypotheses

- Be aware of how statistics can be used and misused.

Data types, populations, samples, bias

Statistics is the study of large amounts of data. To make sense of data on that scale, graphical and numerical summaries are prepared. Then hypotheses are proposed and tested.

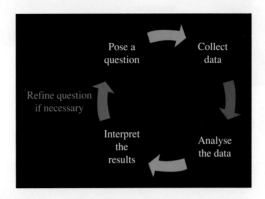

The data handling cycle

There are four important types of data: discrete numerical data, continuous numerical data, nominal categorical data and ordinal categorical data.

Numerical data is any data that can be represented by numbers. **Continuous numerical data** can take any value between two points, e.g. height, weight, time, speed, temperature. **Discrete numerical data** can only be whole numbers, e.g. number of people, number of cars.

Categorical data is any data that cannot be represented by numbers. **Nominal categorical data** doesn't have order, e.g. colours of cars, breeds of dogs, days of the week. **Ordinal categorical data** can be put in order, e.g. gold, silver and bronze medals, favourite three songs.

Data can also be **univariate** or **bivariate**. For example, data listing different people's annual income is univariate as there is only one variable, income. Data listing their income and the number of years they spent in education is bivariate, as there are two variables, income and years spent in education.

Note that the word 'data' is sometimes used as a plural word ('the data are …') and sometimes as a singular word ('the data is …'). There are convincing arguments for both uses.

Examples

State what type of data will be produced by the answers to the following questions:

(a) Are you male ☐ or female ☐?

(b) What is your height? ☐

(c) How many people are in your household? ☐

(d) In a typical week how often do you exercise?

Never ☐   Once or twice a week ☐   Several times a week ☐   Every day ☐

Solutions

(a) Nominal categorical data.

(b) Continuous numerical data.

(c) Discrete numerical data.

(d) Ordinal categorical data.

A **population** is the entire group about which information is wanted. A **sample** is a subset of the population.

It is time-consuming and expensive to survey large numbers of people. Surveying an entire population is usually out of the question. Information gathered from a representative sample allows us to make valid conclusions about the population.

A sample is **biased** if it favours some members of the population or excludes others. To avoid bias, members of a sample can be selected at random. Each name in the population, if available, can be given a number. A sample of numbered people can then be selected using a random number generator on a calculator or a computer.

There are two main methods of collecting data. **Primary data** is data you collect yourself. **Secondary data** is data which you use but someone else has collected.

One way to collect data is through an **observational survey.** In an observational study the researcher collects information without influencing events.

Another way to collect data is through a **designed experiment**. In a designed experiment the researcher deliberately changes the environment then tries to measure the effect of the change. The deliberate change is called the explanatory variable. The effect of the change is called the response variable.

Example

A company wishes to carry out a survey of its customers.

Give   (a)   the advantages   (b)   the disadvantages of each of the following methods:

(i)   face-to-face interview

(ii)   telephone interview

(iii)   postal questionnaire

(iv)   online questionnaire

(v)   observation.

Solution

(i) (a) Questions can be explained. (b) Expensive. Not random.

(ii) (a) Almost everyone has a phone. Questions can be explained.
   (b) Time-consuming.

(iii) (a) Not expensive. (b) Many people will not reply so answers may not be representative.

(iv) (a) Very low cost. Anonymity may encourage more honest answers.
   (b) May not be representative.

(v) (a) Low cost. Easy to carry out. (b) Only works for some types of survey.

Representing data graphically and numerically

Categorical data can be represented with a bar chart or a pie chart by graphing the frequencies in each category. A frequency table can also be drawn for numerical data. The range is broken up into different intervals.

A histogram can be drawn to illustrate the distribution. (A histogram is similar to a bar graph. One difference is that there are no gaps between the bars in a histogram.) One could also draw a stem-and-leaf diagram.

A trend graph shows how a quantity changes over time.

Measures of central tendency: mean, mode, median

Three common measures of central tendency are the mean, mode and median.

The **mean** of a set of values is equal to their sum divided by the number of values, N. The symbol for a sample mean is $\bar{x}$ (x-bar) and the symbol for the population mean is μ.

The **mode** of a set of values is the most frequent value.

The **median** of a set of values is the middle value when all the numbers are put in order.

	Advantages	Disadvantages
Mean	Uses all the data, easy to calculate	Affected by outliers
Mode	The only measure that can be used with nominal categorical data	A distribution may have many modes
Median	Not affected by outliers	Takes a long time to calculate for large amounts of data

An **outlier** is a value that is very different in size compared to the other values. Graphic representations make it easy to see outliers. Graphically, if the values lie on a line or curve, outliers will be points that are far away from the curve.

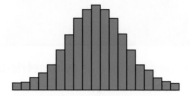

The above distribution is **symmetric, unimodal** and **bell-shaped**. In this case, mean = median = mode. The most commonly used measure of central tendency for a symmetric distribution is the mean.

When most of the data are located relatively close together but a few points are located in one direction far from the majority, the distribution of the data is said to be **skewed**.

If the points that are very different are located to the right of the majority, the distribution is said to be skewed to the right.

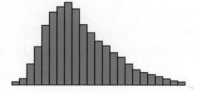

For a right-skewed distribution, mean > median.

If the points that are very different are located to the left of the majority, the distribution is said to be skewed to the left.

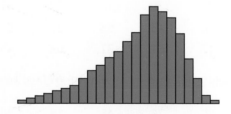

For a left-skewed distribution, mean < median.

> **Point to note**
>
> If a histogram is very asymmetric, i.e. skewed, the median is a better measure of central tendency than the mean, since the median is unaffected by extreme values.

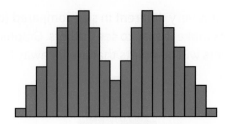

The above distribution can be described as **symmetric-bimodal**, since it has two clear peaks of equal height.

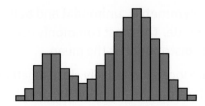

The distribution above can be described as **non-symmetric** and **bimodal**, since it has two clear peaks but they are not equal in height.

> ## Top Tip
>
> If you are asked to describe the shape of a distribution choose key words from this list: symmetric, non-symmetric, unimodal, bimodal, skewed to the right, skewed to the left, bell-shaped.

Example

The ages of the 30 people who took part in an aerobics class are as follows:

18	24	32	37	9	13	22	41	51	49
15	42	37	58	48	53	27	54	42	24
33	48	56	17	61	37	63	45	20	39

The ages of the 30 people who took part in a swimming class are as follows:

16	22	29	7	36	45	12	38	52	13
33	41	24	35	51	8	47	22	14	24
42	62	15	24	23	31	53	36	48	18

(a) Represent this data on a back-to-back stem-and-leaf diagram.

(b) Use your diagram to identify the median in each case.

(c) What other measure of central tendency could have been used when examining this data?

(d) Based on the data make one observation about the ages of the two groups.

Solution

(a)

```
        Aerobics class                              Swimming class

                      9 | 0 | 7  8
            8  7  5  3 | 1 | 2  3  4  5  6  8
         7  4  4  2  0 | 2 | 2  2  3  4  4  4 (9)
    (9)(7) 7  7  3  2 | 3 |(1) 3  5  6  6  8
 9  8  8  5  2  2  1 | 4 | 1  2  5  7  8
    8  6  4  3  1 | 5 | 1  2  3
          3  1 | 6 | 2
```

Key: For aerobics, $1\,|\,5$ means 51. For swimming, $5\,|\,1$ means 51.

(b) Since there are 30 people, the median age will be between the ages of the 15th and 16th person in each class (circled in red).

For the swimming class, the median $= \dfrac{29 + 31}{2} = \dfrac{60}{2} = 30$ years.

For the aerobics class, the median $= \dfrac{37 + 39}{2} = \dfrac{76}{2} = 38$ years.

(c) Another measure of central tendency that could be used would be the mean or the mode.

(d) The swimming class is younger since its median is 30 years compared with 38 years.

Example

Find **(a)** the mean and median of the numbers:
1·7, 2·9, 3·7, 4·5, 5·2

(b) the mean and median of the numbers:
1·7, 2·9, 3·7, 4·5, 52.

(c) Comment on your answers to parts (a) and (b).

Solution

(a) Mean $= \dfrac{\Sigma x}{n} = \dfrac{1\cdot7 + 2\cdot9 + 3\cdot7 + 4\cdot5 + 5\cdot2}{5} = \dfrac{18}{5} = 3\cdot6$

The median is the middle number of an ordered list. Since there are five numbers, the median is the third, 3·7.

(b) Mean $= \dfrac{\Sigma x}{n} = \dfrac{1\cdot7 + 2\cdot9 + 3\cdot7 + 4\cdot5 + 52}{5} = \dfrac{64\cdot8}{5} = 12\cdot96$

Again, the median is the third number, 3·7.

(c) The first distribution is fairly symmetric so the mean and median are close in value. The second distribution is right-skewed so the mean is greater than the median.

The outlier, 52, makes the mean quite unrepresentative of the majority of the numbers. The median is unaffected by the outlier.

Point to note

Page 33 of the *Formulae and Tables* booklet contains various statistics formulae.

The mean of a list is given as $\mu = \frac{\Sigma x}{n}$.

μ is the Greek letter 'mu' and denotes the mean.

Σ is the Greek letter 'sigma' and denotes the operation of adding, i.e. summing the data.

n is the number of values in the list.

The mean of a frequency table is given as $\mu = \frac{\Sigma fx}{\Sigma f}$. In this case, each value, x, is multiplied by its frequency, f, and the results are summed.

Both types of mean can be worked out using a calculator. Ensure that you read the manual for your calculator carefully and learn to use it to find the mean. Instructions are given for a Sharp or Casio calculator later in the chapter.

Measures of variability: range, interquartile range and standard deviation

Measures of variability tell you how spread out a distribution is. Hence, they are also called measures of spread (or scatter or dispersion).

The **range** of a set of values is the difference between the highest and lowest values. Since the range is calculated based on only two values, it tells you nothing about the values in between.

The **interquartile range** and the **standard deviation** are more sophisticated measures of variability.

Suppose you have a set of values, placed in order starting with the smallest. The **lower quartile**, Q_1, is less than or equal to the first quarter of the values in the set. The **upper quartile**, Q_3, is bigger than or equal to the first three quarters of the values in the set.

The **interquartile range**, IQR, is the difference between the upper and lower quartiles:

$$IQR = Q_3 - Q_1.$$

The interquartile range is not affected by extreme values. It gives the difference between the top and bottom values for the middle 50% of a distribution.

Given a set of values, the **standard deviation** is the square root of the mean of the squares of the differences between the values and the mean.

The symbol for the standard deviation of a sample is s. The symbol for the standard deviation of a population is σ.

Example

Find the mode, median, range, interquartile range, mean and standard deviation for the data 8, 5, 3, 8, 7, 6, 4, 8, 2, 9, 200.

Solution

It is often convenient to put the data in order: 2, 3, 4, 5, 6, 7, 8, 8, 8, 9, 200.

The mode is 8, since it is the most frequent value.

The median is 7, since it is in the middle. (Hint: cross off the first and last, the second and second last values, etc. until you are left with the middle value. That is, 2̶, 3̶, 4̶, 5̶, 6̶, 7, 8̶, 8̶, 8̶, 9̶, 2̶0̶0̶. If there are two values left, take their mean and this will be in the middle of the data set.)

The range = maximum − minimum = 200 − 2 = 198. (Note that the range is very large and gives no hint that most of the data are comparatively small.)

$$Q_1 \qquad Q_2 \qquad Q_3$$

2, 3,④, 5, 6,⑦, 8, 8,⑧, 9, 200

To find the IQR graphically, put the values in order, starting with the lowest.

For an odd number of values, circle the middle number. This is the second quartile, Q_2, or the median.

Then, the lower quartile, Q_1, is the median of the values to the left of the circle. The upper quartile, Q_3, is the median of the values to the right of the circle. Finally, $IQR = Q_3 - Q_1$.

In the present case, $IQR = Q_3 - Q_1 = 8 - 4 = 4$.

For an even number of values, draw a line dividing the values into two equal groups. Q_1 is the median of the values to the left of the line and Q_3 is the median of the values to its right. As before, $IQR = Q_3 - Q_1$.

To find the IQR numerically, first count the data. There are $n = 11$ values in this example.

To find the lower quartile, Q_1, multiply n by $\frac{1}{4}$ and round up if the result is not an integer: $\frac{1}{4} \times 11 = 2\cdot75 \approx 3$. Thus Q_1 is equal to the third value, 4.

To find the upper quartile, Q_3, multiply n by $\frac{3}{4}$ and round up if the result is not an integer: $\frac{3}{4} \times 11 = 8 \cdot 25 \approx 9$. Thus Q_3 is the ninth value, which is 8.

As before, the interquartile range, $IQR = Q_3 - Q_1 = 8 - 4 = 4$.

Notice that the IQR gives a much better sense of the scale of the values than the range of 198 does. The range is badly affected by the outlier, 200.

We will find the mean and standard deviation using a calculator. The list is: 2, 3, 4, 5, 6, 7, 8, 8, 8, 9, 200.

For a *Casio fx-83GT PLUS* calculator, follow these instructions:

Type MODE then 2 then 1 to get into statistics mode for univariate data.

Type 2 then = to input the first value.

Type 3 then = to input the second value. Repeat until all the values are inputted.

Press the AC button to exit the data screen.

Type SHIFT then 1 then 4 to access the mean and standard deviation screen.

Type 2 then = to get the mean: $\bar{x} = 23 \cdot 64$, correct to two decimal places.

Notice that the mean is considerably larger than the median, 7. This is due to the outlier, 200, which distorts the mean.

Again, type SHIFT then 1 then 4 to access the mean and standard deviation screen.

Type 3 then = to get the standard deviation: $\sigma = 58 \cdot 81$, correct to two decimal places.

Notice that the standard deviation is distorted by the outlier, 200, unlike the $IQR = 4$.

Finally, type MODE then 1 to exit statistics mode and return to normal. All statistics data is erased when you exit statistics mode on a Casio calculator.

For using a *Sharp WriteView EL-W531* calculator, follow these instructions.

Type MODE then 1 then 0 to get into statistics mode for univariate data.

Type 2nd F then CA to clear the memory. (This is vital, otherwise values from previous work could distort your results.)

To input the list, 8, 5, 3, 8, 7, 6, 4, 8, 2, 9, 200, type 8 then CHANGE . (Note the word 'DATA' above the 'CHANGE' button.)

Repeat for the remaining ten values.

To find the mean, type ALPHA then 4 then = . (Note the $\bar{x}$ in green over the '4' button.) $\bar{x} = 23 \cdot 64$, correct to two decimal places.

To find the standard deviation, type ALPHA then 6 then = . (Note the σx in green over the '6' button.) $\sigma = 58 \cdot 81$, correct to two decimal places.

Finally type MODE then 0 to exit statistics mode and return to normal.

Example

The weights, in kg, of 125 Junior Certificate students are given in the following frequency table.

Weight in kg	~~40 – 50~~ 45	~~50 – 55~~ 52.5	55 – 60	60 – 70	70 – 75
Number of students	16	22	27	52	8

Note: 40–50 means 40 or more but less than 50, etc.

Using mid-interval values, calculate the mean and standard deviation of the distribution.

Solution

First, rewrite the table, taking mid-interval values, i.e. the mean of each range in the first row.

Weight in kg	45	52·5	57·5	65	72·5
Number of students	16	22	27	52	8

For a *Casio fx-83GT PLUS* calculator, follow these instructions:

Type MODE then 2 then 1 to get into statistics mode for univariate data.

If the frequency column is not displayed, type SHIFT then MODE then the down arrow (on the REPLAY button) then 3 then 1. The calculator returns to the data entry screen with the frequency column displayed.

Type 45 then = to input the first value.

Use the arrows to move the cursor to the frequency column opposite the value of 45. Type 16 then = to input the frequency for this value.

Use the arrows to move the cursor below the 45. Repeat until all the values and their frequencies are inputted.

Press the AC button to exit the data screen.

Type SHIFT then 1 then 4 to access the mean and standard deviation screen.

Type 2 then = to get the mean: $\bar{x} = 59 \cdot 1$ kg.

Again, type SHIFT then 1 then 4 to access the mean and standard deviation screen.

Type 3 then = to get the standard deviation: $\sigma = 7.72$, correct to two decimal places.

Type MODE then 1 to exit statistics mode and return to normal.

For a *Sharp WriteView EL-W531* calculator, follow these instructions:

Type MODE then 1 then 0 to get into statistics mode for univariate data.

Type 2nd F then CA to clear the memory.

To input the first column of the table, type 45 (x,y) 16 CHANGE .
Repeat for the remaining four columns.

To find the mean, type ALPHA then 4 then = . $\bar{x} = 59.1$ kg.

To find the standard deviation, type ALPHA then 6 then = . $\sigma = 7.72$ kg, correct to two decimal places.

Finally, type MODE then 0 to exit statistics mode and return to normal.

Top Tip

You need to know how to calculate the standard deviation of a list of values, or of a frequency table, using your calculator. Use the manual for your model of calculator to learn this properly.

Scatter plots and the correlation coefficient

Bivariate data is made up of pairs of different types of quantity, e.g. a table of height in cm and mass in kg. The relationship between the two different quantities is often illustrated with a scatter plot.

The correlation coefficient measures how close the plot is to a straight line. The symbol for the correlation coefficient is r. It can only take values between −1 and 1.

Here are some examples of scatter plots and their correlation coefficients.

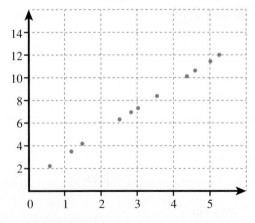

Here, $r = 1$. The points lie on, or extremely close to, a straight line with a positive slope. This is the strongest positive correlation possible.

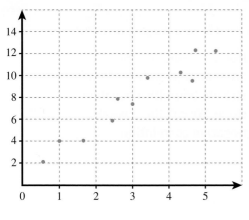

Here, $r = 0.97$. The points do not all lie on the same line, but they're not that far off. We call this a **strong positive correlation**.

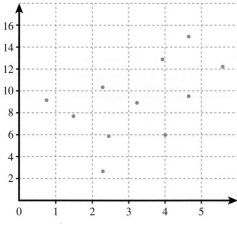

Here, $r = 0.5$. The points are scattered a good deal further from a straight line with a positive slope. We call this a **weak positive correlation**.

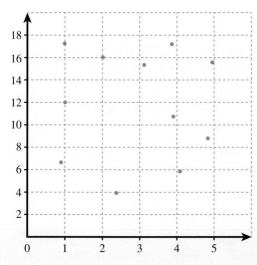

Here, $r = 0$. We say that there is **no correlation**.

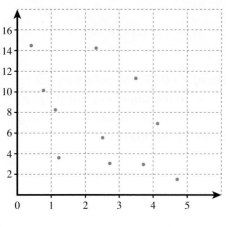

Here, $r = -0.5$. The points are scattered quite far from a straight line with a negative slope. We call this a **weak negative correlation**.

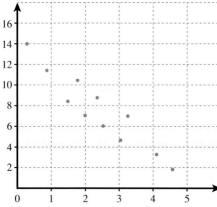

Here, $r = -0.94$. The points are much closer to a straight line with a negative slope. We call this a **strong negative correlation**.

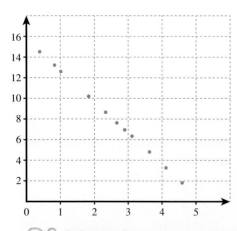

Finally, $r = -1$. The points lie on, or extremely close to, a line with a negative slope. This is the strongest negative correlation possible.

Point to note

Correlation is not causation.

For example, a scatter plot of ice-cream sales versus shark attacks can give a strong positive correlation. However, buying ice-cream does not cause sharks to attack. In this case there is a third variable, temperature. On warm days, people are more likely to go swimming and to buy ice-cream.

The normal distribution and the empirical rule

In around 1900, the heights of 3000 English prisoners were measured. The histogram, as you can see, is symmetric, unimodal and bell-shaped.

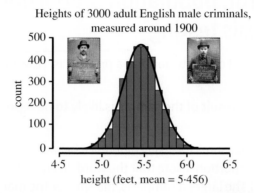

Heights of 3000 adult English male criminals, measured around 1900

The smooth curve, shown in black, is called the **normal distribution curve**. The mean of the curve is at the centre. Many distributions can be described using a normal distribution curve, e.g. the lifetime of a lightbulb, the IQ distribution of a large group of comparable people.

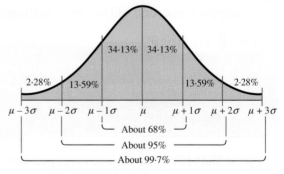

An important property of normal distributions is described by the **empirical rule**. Learn it well.

The empirical rule states that in any normal distribution:

- 68% of the population lie within one standard deviation, σ, of the mean, μ

- 95% of the population lie within two standard deviations of the mean

- 99·7% of the population lie within three standard deviations of the mean.

Note that the rule is said to be empirical as the percentages above are approximations. However, they are very good approximations.

Example

IQ scores are normally distributed with a mean of 100 and a standard deviation of 15. Use the empirical rule to show that 95% of IQ scores in the population are between 70 and 130.

Solution

According to the empirical rule, 95% of the IQ scores are within two standard deviations of the mean.

$100 + 2 \times 15 = 130$.

$100 - 2 \times 15 = 70$.

Margin of error, population proportions and hypothesis testing

Suppose we wish to find out how popular a product is. How big does the sample surveyed have to be?

Big enough so that the result of the sample is likely to be representative of the target population.

The **margin of error** measures the likely difference between the sample proportion and the population proportion. (Note that the word 'likely' in this context refers to a probability of 95%.) The larger a sample is, the smaller the margin of error. That is, the sample proportion will be closer to the population proportion.

> **Point to note**
>
> If n is the size of the sample then the margin of error, at a 5% level of significance, is calculated using the formula
>
> $$\text{margin of error} = \frac{1}{\sqrt{n}}.$$

Suppose that 1000 people are surveyed and 520 say that they are satisfied with the government. As a percentage, this is $\frac{520}{1000} \times 100 = 52\%$. Does that mean that 52% of the entire population of the country are satisfied with the government?

No. Since $n = 1000$, the margin of error is $\frac{1}{\sqrt{1000}} = 0.03162 \approx 0.03$ or 3%.

This means that we can be 95% confident that the actual proportion of the population who are satisfied with the government is between 49% and 55%, since $52\% - 3\% = 49\%$ and $52\% + 3\% = 55\%$. The range 49% to 53% is called a **confidence interval**.

When we say that we are 95% confident this means that if a large number of such surveys were done, then the population proportion would be within the margin of error of the sample proportion in 95% of the surveys.

> ## Remember
>
> The sample proportion is denoted by $\hat{p}$, the population proportion is denoted by p and the sample size is denoted by n.
>
> We can be 95% confident that p is in the interval $\hat{p} \pm \frac{1}{\sqrt{n}}$.
>
> That is, $\hat{p} - \frac{1}{\sqrt{n}} \le p \le \hat{p} + \frac{1}{\sqrt{n}}$ at a confidence level of 95% (also known as a 5% level of significance).

Samples are often used for testing hypotheses about a population. Two hypotheses, or claims, are required for this type of analysis: the **null hypothesis**, H_0, and an **alternative hypothesis**, H_1.

The null hypothesis, denoted by H_0, is a claim or statement about a population. We assume this statement is true until proven otherwise. (The null hypothesis means that nothing is wrong with the claim or statement.)

The alternative hypothesis, denoted by H_1, is a claim or statement which opposes the original statement about a population.

For instance, suppose the government claims that 60% of people are satisfied with them. The null hypothesis, H_0, is that it *is* true to say that 60% of people are satisfied with the government. The alternative hypothesis, H_1, is that it *is not* true to say that 60% of people are satisfied with the government.

Suppose a newspaper surveyed 1000 people as above and found that 520 people were satisfied with the government. Since the figure 60% is outside the confidence interval, 49% to 53%, we *reject* the null hypothesis and *accept* the alternative hypothesis with a 95% probability of having made the right decision.

Example

How big should a sample be in order to have a margin of error of 5%?

Solution

$5\% = \frac{5}{100} = 0.05$ Change the percentage to a decimal.

$\Rightarrow$ Margin of error $= \frac{1}{\sqrt{n}} = 0.05$

$\Rightarrow$ $\frac{1}{n} = (0.05)^2$ Square both sides.

$\Rightarrow$ $n = \frac{1}{(0.05)^2} = 400.$

Thus the minimum sample size for a margin of error of 5% is 400.

Example

A company claims that 30% of people who eat their 'Crispy Bun' product really like it. The confidence level is cited as 95%.

In June an independent survey was carried out on 625 randomly selected people to see if they liked the 'Crispy Bun' product.

(a) Calculate the margin of error.

(b) The result of the survey in June was that 125 people liked the 'Crispy Bun' product. According to the survey, would you say that at a 5% level of significance the company was correct in stating that 30% of people who ate their 'Crispy Bun' product really liked it?

Solution

(a) Margin of error $= \dfrac{1}{\sqrt{n}} = \dfrac{1}{\sqrt{625}} = 0\cdot04 = 4\%$.

(b) The sample proportion, as a percentage, is given by $\dfrac{125}{625} \times 100 = 20\%$.

Thus, at a 5% level of significance, the population proportion should be within 4% of 20%, i.e. between 16% and 24%. The company was incorrect in their claim as 30% is outside this range.

Exercise A

Q1 State what kind of data is produced by the following questions:

(a) How many sisters do you have?

(b) What colour is your car?

(c) What distance have you driven in the last year?

(d) What are your three favourite songs, starting with your top favourite?

Q2 (a) Find the mean of:

(i) 5 and 7   (ii) 8 and 12   (iii) 10 and 20.

(b) What conclusion can you draw from your answers to parts (i), (ii) and (iii)?

(c) Write four different lists of four numbers, each of which has a mean of 5.

(d) A class is asked to calculate the mean of the numbers −3, 4, 7, 11, 2, 9, −4. Jack gets an answer of 13. Jill immediately says that this can't be the right answer. Who is correct? Give a reason for your answer.

Q3 The following is a list of the numbers of goals scored by the top scorer in the English Premiership at the end of each season from 1993 to 2014.

22, 34, 34, 31, 25, 18, 18, 30, 23, 24, 25, 30, 25, 27, 20, 31, 19, 29, 20, 30, 26, 31

(a) Draw a line plot illustrating the data.

(b) Find three measures of central tendency.

(c) Find three measures of variability.

Q4 The table below shows sales of laptops for a month. Note: 200–300 means 200 or more but less than 300.

Cost in €	200 – 300	300 – 400	400 – 500	500 – 600	600 – 700
Number of laptops	51	148	314	193	14

(a) Draw a histogram to illustrate the data.

(b) Draw a pie chart to illustrate the data.

(c) Construct a new table using mean interval values. Use this new table to estimate the mean and standard deviation for the data. Give your answers correct to the nearest euro.

Q5 The number of text messages that a student sent each day over a certain two-week period was as follows. The numbers are in date order, starting on a Monday.

17, 20, 28, 24, 33, 56, 48

12, 19, 32, 2, 37, 50, 42

(a) Construct a stem-and-leaf plot of the data.

(b) Find the median and the range.

(c) There was one day in this two-week period when the student lost her phone in the morning and only found it the following morning. Based on the data, what day of the week do you think that was? Give a reason for your answer.

Q6 Some scientists were studying a certain kind of ant. They selected a sample of 39 of these ants and measured the length of each ant's body, in millimetres. The results are shown in this stem-and-leaf plot:

```
4 | 3
4 | 6  6  8  9
5 | 0  0  1  1  1  2  4
5 | 5  7
6 | 0
6 | 8  9
7 | 0  1  2  4
7 | 5  5  7  8  8  8  9
8 | 0  0  1  1  2  3  4  4
8 | 5  5  8
```

Key: 4|3 means 4·3 mm

(a) What is the length of the longest ant?

(b) What is the median length of the ants in the sample?

(c) Describe the shape of the distribution.

(d) Suggest a reason why the distribution might have this shape.

Q7 Whenever a baby is born, one of the things measured and recorded is the baby's weight. The birth weights of a sample of babies are summarised in the table below.

Weight in kg	2·2 – 2·6	2·6 – 3·0	3·0 – 3·4	3·4 – 3·8	3·8 – 4·2	4·2 – 4·6
Number of babies	12	40	64	56	24	4

(a) How many babies were in the sample?

(b) Draw a histogram of the data.

(c) Complete the following sentence, by using the table and/or the histogram to make an estimate.

'On average, these babies weighed about _____ kg at birth.'

(d) One of the babies weighed 3·675 kg when she was born. How would you describe this baby's weight in comparison to the other babies?

(e) A weight of less than 2·5 kg is called a 'low birth weight'. Estimate the number of low-birth-weight babies in this sample.

Approximately 60 000 babies were born in Ireland in 2005. According to a survey, 20% of the mothers smoked cigarettes during the pregnancy. Suppose that our sample was chosen from among these babies whose mothers smoked.

(f) What is the size of the population from which the sample was drawn?

(g) Using the information from the sample, estimate the number of low-birth-weight babies in that population.

(h) Explain why the sample cannot tell us exactly how many such babies were in the population.

(i) The mean birth weight for all babies born in Ireland that year was 3·51 kg. Do you think that the information from our sample shows that smoking during pregnancy affects the baby's birth weight? Explain your answer.

Q8 Match each of the following correlation coefficients to the correct scatter plot shown below.

(a) $r = 0.99$ (b) $r = 0.63$ (c) $r = 0.50$ (d) $r = 0$ (e) $r = -0.63$

(f) $r = -0.99$

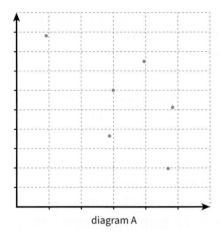

diagram A

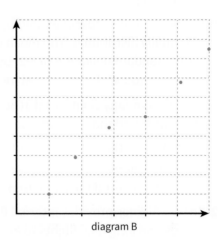

diagram B

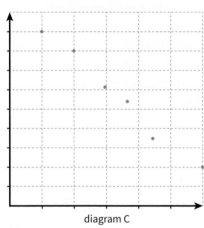

diagram C

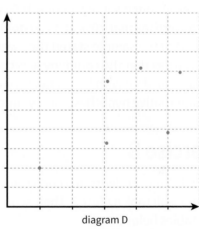

diagram D

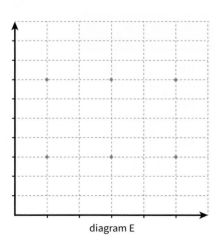

diagram E

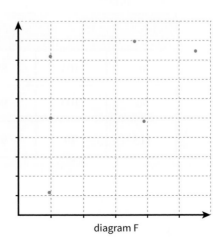

diagram F

Q9 (a) Find the margin of error of a sample of size (i) 10 (ii) 100
      (iii) 10 000. Give your answers correct to two significant figures.

   (b) How big should a sample be to have a margin of error of (i) 10%
       (ii) 20% (iii) 4%? Give your answers correct to the nearest whole
       number.

Q10 The number of sandwiches sold by a shop from 12 noon to 2 p.m. each day
   is normally distributed. The mean of the distribution was 42·6 sandwiches
   with a standard deviation of 8·2. Use the empirical rule to identify the range
   of values around the mean that includes 68% of the sale numbers.

Q11 A sweet company claims that 10% of the sweets it produces are green.
   Students found that in a large sample of 500 sweets, 60 were green.

   (a) Calculate the margin of error, correct to one decimal place.

   (b) State whether 60 greens from 500 is an unusually high proportion of
       green sweets if the claim from the company is assumed to be true.

Q12 Go Fast Airlines provides internal flights in Ireland, short haul flights to
   Europe and long haul flights to America and Asia. Each month the company
   carries out a survey among 1000 passengers. The company repeatedly
   advertises that 70% of its customers are satisfied with its overall service.
   664 of the sample stated they were satisfied with the overall service. Would
   you say that the company was correct in saying that 70% of its customers
   are satisfied with its overall service? State the null hypothesis, the
   alternative hypothesis and your conclusions clearly.

Exercise B

Q1 All of the students in a class took *IQ Test 1* on the same day. A week later
   they all took *IQ Test 2*. Their scores on the two IQ tests are shown in the
   tables below.

IQ Test 1				
86	104	89	105	96
96	103	94	104	119
115	79	97	111	108

IQ Test 2				
83	120	105	111	114
99	111	108	106	97
97	102	94	108	117

(a) Draw a back-to-back stem-and-leaf plot to display the students' scores.

(b) Find the range of scores for each IQ test.

(c) Find the median score for each IQ test.

(d) Find the mean score for each IQ test.

(e) Compare the scores on the two IQ tests. Refer to at least one measure of central tendency and at least one measure of variability (spread) in your answer.

(f) Marshall says that every student in the class must have done better on *IQ Test 2* than on *IQ Test 1*. Is Marshall correct? Explain your answer.

Q2 The data for the line plot is from two classes in a school. The sample size is $n = 59$.

(a) Describe the data in as many ways as you can using numerical and shape descriptions.

(b) One person was absent on the day of the survey. Someone said they would give you €100 if you could guess the number of people in that student's household. What number would you guess? Explain why you chose this number.

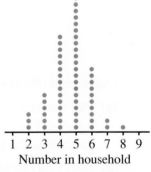

(c) Describe how you might increase your chances of winning the €100?

(d) Calculate the probability of winning with your strategy.

(e) (i) Is it possible that the student who was absent could have 8 people in their household?

(ii) Is it probable that the student who was absent could have 8 people in their household?

Q3 In 1999 a university librarian put a number of measures in place to try to stop students 'stealing' books from the library. To see how effective these measures were she recorded the number of non-returned books over the next nine years. The data is recorded below.

Years	2000	2001	2002	2003	2004	2005	2006	2007	2008
No. of non-returned books	9	10	9	14	6	3	4	5	10

When asked to report to the budget committee on book loss she wrote:

Whilst the drain on resources due to lost books is significant, the histogram below shows that over the last nine years the number of books lost to the library is steadily decreasing, which suggests that the measures implemented to combat this practice are working.

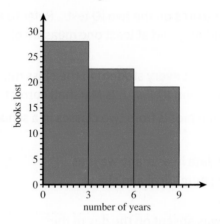

The finance officer was not convinced that the measures were working.

(a) Plot the same data in a histogram but, instead of using three-year intervals like the librarian did, divide the data into nine intervals, one for each of the last nine years.

(b) Does your histogram support the librarian's view that the measures are working, or does it lend more support to the doubts of the finance officer?

(c) Draw a more general conclusion about histograms.

Q4 Below is some recent research about engine sizes. This data shows the engine size and the fuel economy of a range of petrol cars ('kpl' denotes 'kilometres per litre').

Engine size (cc)	1·0	1·1	1·2	1·3	1·4	1·6	1·7	2·0	3·0	3·5	4·0
Fuel economy (kpl)	18	16	14	16	13	12	12·5	12	11	8·8	6·5

(a) Show this information on a scatter diagram.

(b) Describe, in your own words, the relationship between the engine size and fuel economy of these cars.

(c) A car manufacturer produces a new car with a 1·8 litre engine and a fuel efficiency of 17 kilometres per litre. Plot this car's performance on your scatter plot. If you were interested in buying a new car that was fuel efficient with this size engine would you buy this car? Write a short comment.

(d) Which of the following values would you say is closest to the correlation coefficient of the scatter plot?

A 0·9   **B** 0·5   **C** 0   **D** −0·5   **E** −0·9

Q5 The table below shows the prices charged per room of 40 B & B houses in Galway.

Race-Week B&B prices per room (€)									
56	75	60	70	80	70	50	90	80	75
75	50	75	50	70	60	65	60	50	70
84	70	70	60	60	70	70	70	40	60
70	80	60	65	55	50	70	80	50	55

(a) Calculate, correct to one decimal place, the mean and standard deviation of the data.

(b) Show that the empirical rule holds true for one standard deviation around the mean.

(c) Show that the empirical rule holds true for two standard deviations around the mean.

Q6 A survey is being conducted of voters' opinions on several different issues.

(a) What is the overall margin of error of the survey, at 95% confidence, if it is based on a simple random sample of 1111 voters?

(b) A political party has claimed that it has the support of 24% of the electorate. Of the voters in the sample above, 243 stated that they support the party. Is this sufficient evidence to reject the party's claim, at the 5% level of significance?

Q7 RTÉ claim that 60% of all viewers watch *The Late Late Show* every Friday night. An independent survey was carried out on 400 randomly selected TV viewers to see if the claim was true. The result of the survey was that 180 people were watching *The Late Late Show*.

(a) Calculate the margin of error.

(b) State the null and alternative hypotheses.

(c) Would you accept or reject the null hypothesis according to this survey? Give a reason for your conclusion.

Q8 David noticed that his performance time was better than usual on one run. He had drunk a bottle of sports drink before going out. He set about doing an experiment to see whether drinking the sports drink increases performance when running.

He recorded the times of people in his running club to complete a 5 km run without drinking the sports drink and then on another day he recorded the time it took the same people to complete 5 km having taken the sports drink.

He recorded the information in a back-to-back stem-and-leaf plot.

Without taking the sports drink.		Having taken the sports drink.
5	20	3 4
1 1 1	21	3 4 7
8 8 4 3 2	22	
	23	1 2 2
	24	0
	25	8
	26	1
	27	
	28	2 3 6 6 7 7
	29	2 4 4 5 5 5 8 9 9
	30	1 3 4 5 6 7 8 8 9
5	31	
6 4 4 3 0 0	32	1 1 4 9
9 9 6 5 4 4 3 3 2 1	33	3 3 3 2
7 7 5 5 6 6 6 1 0	34	5
8 8 8 3 3	35	0 0
7 3 2	36	1
1	37	2
	38	3 5
2 2	39	
4 4 2 0	40	

Key: On the left, 1│33 means 33·1 minutes. On the right, 32│1 means 32·1 minutes.

(a) Based on the diagram, approximate the median speed without drinking the sports drink and the median speed having taken the sports drink. What does this information tell you?

(b) Compare the distributions of each of the data sets above.

(c) Is there evidence from the diagram to suggest that taking the sports drink improves performance? Justify your conclusions.

(d) Make an argument, based on the two data sets, that taking the sports drink does not improve performance.

(e) After completing the experiment, David wondered how accurate his study was. He realised that he had not specified how much of the sports drink the runners should take. He asked 20 of the runners approximately how many millilitres of sports drink they had taken and recorded this alongside their time. The results are shown on the right.

Display the data in a way that allows you to examine the relationship between the two data sets.

(f) Is there evidence to suggest that there is a relationship between the time taken to complete 5 km and the amount of sports drink taken before the race?

(g) Which of the following is the correct correlation coefficient for data in part (e), based on your graph?

A −0·82　**B** 0·14　**C** 0·95　**D** 0·6

Time (mins)	Sports drink (ml)
20·3	250
21·7	100
21·8	120
24	80
28·6	300
29·4	130
29·5	300
29·9	280
32·1	300
32·1	100
33·2	80
35	220
38·3	180
20·6	100
29·2	200
29·8	250
36·1	80
29·9	120
30·9	240
30·1	280

Exercise C

Q1 Below is a stem-and-leaf plot showing the number of sweets in each of nineteen packets of sweets.

```
2 | 5
2 | 6   6   7
2 | 8   8   8   9   9   9   9   9
3 | 0   0   0   0   1   1
3 | 2
```

Key: 2|5 means 25 sweets.

(a) What is the *median* number of sweets?

(b) What is the *range* of the data?

(c) Find the *interquartile range* of the data.

(d) The sentences below describe the type of data shown in the stem-and-leaf plot above. Delete the incorrect word in each pair of brackets.

'This is a set of [univariate/bivariate] data. The data are [discrete/continuous].' *(2011)*

Q2 One of the items of information gathered in a census is the size of every household. The size of the household is the number of people living in it. The following table shows the number of 'Permanent Private Households' of each size in Ireland, according to the census held in various years from 1926 to 2006. For the purposes of this question, you should ignore the fact that there are also other types of household in Ireland.

	1 person	2 people	3 people	4 people	5 people	6 people	7 people	8 people	9 people	≥10 people	All sizes
1926	51537	98437	102664	96241	82324	65310	48418	33297	21089	23361	622678
1946	68881	118738	116401	103423	84437	62955	44028	28503	17970	17318	662654
1966	88989	139541	114436	97058	79320	61068	42512	27098	16550	20732	687304
1986	176017	195647	143142	155534	127336	83657	44139	23088	8438	7884	964882
2006	326134	413786	264438	243303	136979	54618	15141	5050	1719	1128	1462296

(Source: Central Statistics Office, http://www.cso.ie)

(a) Use the information in the table to answer the following:

(i) In 1966, how many households had exactly 8 people living in them?

(ii) In 1986, how many people lived in households of exactly 7 people?

(iii) Calculate, correct to one decimal place, an estimate of the mean number of people per household in 2006.

(b) Conor, Fiona, and Ray were each asked, separately, to make a presentation about the patterns they could see in the data. They each spoke for one minute and showed one slide. The slides they made are shown below. By considering the slides, state the main point or points that each of them was trying to make.

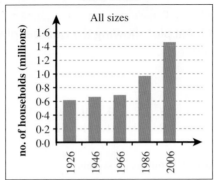

Conor's slide

All sizes

(i) Conor was trying to show ...

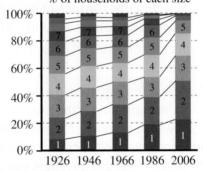

Fiona's slide
% of households of each size

(ii) Fiona was trying to show ...

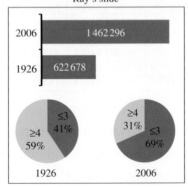

Ray's slide

(iii) Ray was trying to show ...

(c) A household is randomly selected from among all the households in 2006. What is the probability that it has seven or eight people?

(d) 1000 households are to be randomly selected from among all the households in 2006. Let X represent the number of 4-person households selected. Find $E(X)$, the expected value of X.

(e) Mary wonders whether there are differences in size between the households in South Dublin and those in Dublin City. She gets the relevant data for 2006 and makes the following charts.

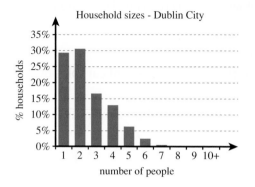

Household sizes - Dublin City

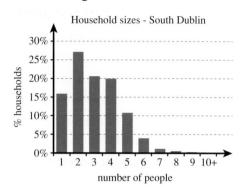

Household sizes - South Dublin

(i) Describe what differences there are, if any, between the two distributions above.

(ii) There are approximately 81 000 households in South Dublin. Approximately how many people live in 4-person households in South Dublin?

(iii) What is the median size for a household in Dublin City?

(iv) A person is selected at random from among all those living in Dublin City. Which is more likely: that the person lives alone, or that the person lives in a 3-person household? Explain your answer.   *(2011)*

Q3 The following table gives data on new private cars sold in Ireland in each quarter of each year from 2006 to 2011.

New private cars sales								
Number of cars sold						Engine type of cars sold		
Year	January to March	April to June	July to September	October to December	Annual Total	Petrol	Diesel	Other
2006	75 769	54 572	32 873	10 059	173 273	128 634	44 010	629
2007	81 750	57 124	32 418	9 462	180 754	128 346	50 560	1 848
2008	77 441	37 128	27 361	4 540	146 470	92 298	50 283	3 889
2009	27 140	15 225	9 049	3 018	54 432	22 802	30 645	985
2010	34 555	26 806	17 011	6 535	84 907	27 124	53 998	3 785
2011	39 484	29 770	13 467	4 211	86 932	23 246	61 730	1 956

(Source: Central Statistics Office, http://www.cso.ie)

(a) **(i)** Show the annual total sales of cars over the six years, using a suitable chart.

(ii) Find the mean number of cars sold per year over the six years.

(iii) Calculate the percentage increase in annual car sales between 2009 and 2011.

(iv) Aoife says that this increase shows car sales are currently going well. Paul says that car sales are currently going badly. He says that sales have fallen by 52% since 2007 and that they are well below average. Complete the sentences below to give a criticism of each argument.

Aoife's argument does not recognise that ...

Paul's argument does not recognise that ...

(v) Give a more balanced description of the pattern of car sales over the six years.

(b) **(i)** Describe how the sales of the cars are distributed over the four quarters of each year.

(ii) Suggest a reason for this pattern of sales.

(iii) The sales for the first quarter of 2012 are 36 081.

Find, with justification, an estimate for the total annual sales for 2012.

(c) **(i)** Two pie charts are being used to show the change from 2006 to 2011 in the popularity of petrol and diesel cars. Copy and complete the second pie chart.

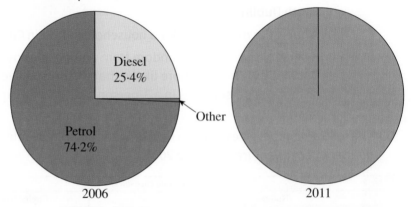

2006   2011

(ii) Which of the following statements best describes the change over time in the popularity of diesel cars as a percentage of the total?

A Diesel cars have suddenly become very popular in the last year or two.

B Diesel cars have increased very steadily in popularity over the last six years.

C Diesel cars have become very popular since car sales started to improve.

D Diesel cars got more popular each year, with an especially big increase in 2009.

E Diesel cars became popular as car sales fell but have been getting less popular as they rise again.

(d) A survey of some of the most popular models of private cars sold in 2011 examined the CO_2 emissions in g/km from diesel engines and petrol engines. The data are shown on the following page.

Diesel engines	Petrol engines
117, 125, 120, 125, 134, 110, 118, 114, 119, 119, 116, 107.	139, 133, 150, 157, 138, 159, 129, 138, 134, 129, 129, 136.

(i) Construct a back-to-back stem-and-leaf plot of the above data.

(ii) Does the information suggest that diesel engines produce lower CO_2 emissions than petrol engines? In your answer you should refer to the stem-and-leaf plot and to an appropriate measure of central tendency.

(iii) Does the information suggest that there is a greater variation in the CO_2 emissions of diesel engines than petrol engines? In your answer you should refer to the stem-and-leaf plot and an appropriate measure of variability. *(2012)*

Q4 The table below shows the rates of births, marriages and deaths in Ireland from 1990 to 2010. The rates are per 10 000 of the estimated population.

Number of Births, Marriages and Deaths in Ireland (per 10 000 of the estimated population)			
Year	Births	Marriages	Deaths
1990	151	51	90
1991	150	49	89
1992	144	47	87
1993	138	47	90
1994	135	46	86
1995	135	43	90
1996	140	45	87
1997	144	43	86
1998	146	45	85
1999	144	50	87
2000	145	51	83
2001	150	50	79
2002	155	52	76
2003	155	51	73
2004	153	52	71
2005	148	52	68
2006	154	52	67
2007	163	52	64
2008	168	50	63
2009	167	48	63
2010	165	46	61

(Source: Central Statistics Office, http://www.cso.ie)

(a) Copy and complete the back-to-back stem-and-leaf plot below to show the marriage rate and death rate in Ireland during the period covered in the table above.

Marriage rate   Death rate

	4	
	5	
	6	
	7	
	8	
	9	

Key:

(b) State one difference that can be observed between the distributions of the marriage rate and the death rate in your plot.

(c) Find the median and interquartile range of the yearly marriage rates in Ireland from 1990 to 2010.

(d) **(i)** Find the mean of the death rate in Ireland from 1990 to 2010. Give your answer correct to one decimal place.

   (ii) The standard deviation of the death rates in the table is 10·3. List all of the death rates that are within one standard deviation of the mean.

(e) In 2010, the number of children born in Ireland was 75 174. Use this number to estimate the total population of Ireland in 2010.

(f) Use your answer to (e) to estimate the number of people who died in Ireland in 2010.

(g) 'More children were born in Ireland in 1990 than in 2000.' Give a reason, based on the data, why this statement is not necessarily true.

(h) Find the ratio, birth rate : death rate, for the two years 1990 and 2010. Based on your answers for the two years, what would you predict about the population of Ireland in future years? Give a reason for your answer.

(i) The birth rate and death rate over the 21 years are plotted against each other in the scatter plot on the following page. The correlation coefficient between the two sets of data is −0·85. Describe the relationship between the two sets of data and suggest a reason why this might be the case.

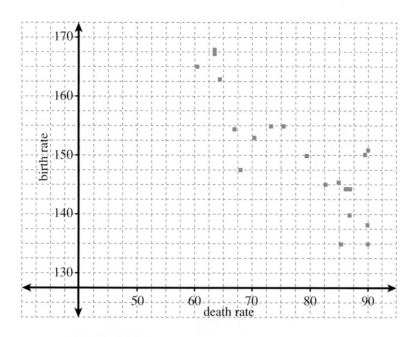

Q5

Lizzie Lee, winner of the King of the Hill triathlon women's event 2010

The King of the Hill triathlon race in Kinsale consists of a 750 metre swim, followed by a 20 kilometre cycle, followed by a 5 kilometre run.

The questions below are based on data from 224 athletes who completed this triathlon in 2010.

Máire is analysing data from the race, using statistical software. She has a data file with each competitor's time for each part of the race, along with various other details of the competitors.

Máire produces histograms of the times for the three events. Here are the three histograms.

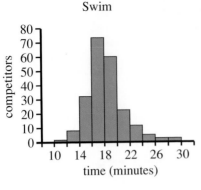

Swim

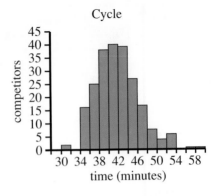

Cycle

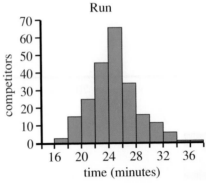

Run

(a) Use the histograms to complete the following sentences:

   (i) The event that, on average, takes longest to complete is the

      _____ .

   (ii) In all three histograms, the times are grouped into intervals
      of _____ minutes.

   (iii) The time of the fastest person in the swim was between
      _____ and _____ minutes.

   (iv) The median time for the run is approximately _____
      minutes.

   (v) The event in which the times are most spread out is the

      _____ .

(b) Máire is interested in the relationship between the athletes' performance
in the run and in the cycle. She produces the following scatter diagram.

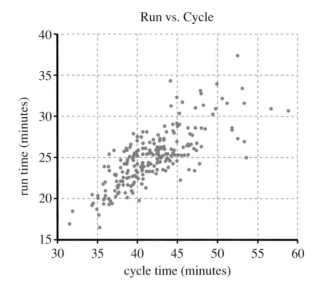

Run vs. Cycle

(i) The correlation coefficient between the times for these two events is one of the numbers below. Which one?

A 0·95

B 0·77

C 0·13

D −0·13

E −0·77

F −0·95

(ii) Frank was the slowest person in the run. How many people took longer to complete the cycle than Frank did?

(iii) Brian did not enter this race. Suppose that he had, and suppose that he completed the cycle in 52 minutes and the run in 18 minutes. Explain why this performance would have been very unusual.

(c) Máire knows already that the male athletes tend to be slightly faster than the female athletes. She also knows that athletes can get slower as they get older. She thinks that male athletes in their forties might be about the same as female athletes in their thirties. She decides to draw a back-to-back stem-and-leaf diagram of the times of these two groups for the swim. There were 28 females in their thirties, and 32 males in their forties. Here is the diagram:

Female, 30–39 years		Male, 40–49 years
4	13	
	14	9
1 0	15	1 3 4 5 6
9 8 8 7 3 2 2	16	3 4 6 7 7 8
6 4 3 2	17	6 7 7
1	18	0 1 3 8 9
9 6 3 1 0 0	19	0 0 1 2 3 4
	20	3 9 9
3 3 2	21	2 2
4	22	
	23	0
8	24	
	25	
5	26	
	27	
	28	
7	29	

Key: For females, 4│13 means 13·4 minutes. For males, 14│9 means 14·9 minutes.

(i) Describe what differences, if any, there are between the two distributions above.

(ii) Máire drew the diagram because she thought that these two groups would be about the same. Do you think that the diagram would cause Máire to confirm her belief or change it? Give reasons for your answer. *(SEC Sample Paper 2014)*

Q6 A newspaper report in October 2013 stated that 90% of homeowners who were liable for property tax had registered for it. The total number of properties liable for the tax was estimated at 1·9 million.

(a) (i) Estimate the number of properties that were registered.

(ii) Suggest one reason why some properties were not registered.

(b) Homeowners who registered were required to value their property in one of a number of given Valuation Bands. The percentage who had valued their properties in each Valuation Band is given in the table below.

Valuation Band	€0–€100 000	€100 001–€150 000	€150 001–€200 000	€200 001–€250 000	€250 001–€300 000	Over €300 000
Percentage of registered homeowners	24·9	28·6	21·9	10·4	4·9	9·3

Represent the data in the table using a pie chart. Label each sector you create and show the angle in each sector clearly.

(c) **(i)** Use the data in the table above and your answer to part (a) (i) above to complete the following table.

Valuation Band	Tax per property	Number of properties	Total tax due (€)
€0–€100 000	€45	425 790	19 160 550
€100 001–€150 000	€112	489 060	
€150 001–€200 000	€157		
€200 001–€250 000	€202		
€250 001–€300 000	€247		
Over €300 000	NA		NA

NA = Not Available

(ii) Find the total tax due on those properties, registered by October 2013, with a valuation up to €300 000.

(iii) The total tax due on all the properties that were registered was estimated at €241 million.

Find the total tax due on those properties with a valuation over €300 000.

(iv) Find the mean estimated tax per property on those properties with a valuation over €300 000.

(v) Some homeowners may under-value their property in order to pay less tax. For example, one estimate stated that 20% of properties in the €100 001–€150 000 band should have been valued in the €150 001–€200 000 band. Based on this estimate, find the amount of extra tax that would be raised if these properties were registered in the correct Valuation Band. *(2014)*

Q7 (a) A widget-manufacturing company repeatedly asserts that 80% of traders recommend their brand of widget. In a survey of 40 traders, 24 said that they would recommend the company's widget. Use a hypothesis test at the 5% level of significance to decide whether there is sufficient evidence to reject the company's claim. State clearly the null hypothesis and your conclusion.

(b) A large group of students has a mean height of 170 cm with a standard deviation of 14 cm. The heights of these students are normally distributed. Use the empirical rule to find a height interval that will contain the heights of approximately 95% of the students.

(SEC Sample Paper 2015)

Solutions to Exercise A

Q1 (a) Numerical, discrete.

(b) Categorical, nominal.

(c) Numerical, continuous.

(d) Categorical, ordinal.

Q2 (a) (i) $\dfrac{5+7}{2} = 6$ **(ii)** $\dfrac{8+12}{2} = 10$ **(iii)** $\dfrac{10+20}{2} = 15$.

(b) The mean of a *pair* of numbers lies halfway between the two numbers. That is, it is the same as their median.

(c) Sample answer: **(i)** 5, 5, 5, 5 **(ii)** 0, 0, 10, 10 **(iii)** 2, 6, 4, 8
(iv) −3, 1, 7, 15

(d) Jill is correct. The mean must lie between the lowest value, −4, and the highest value, 11. Jack's answer, 13, is outside this range.

Q3 First put the list in order.

18, 18, 19, 20, 20, 22, 23, 24, 25, 25, 25, 26, 27, 29, 30, 30, 30, 31, 31, 31, 34, 34.

(a)

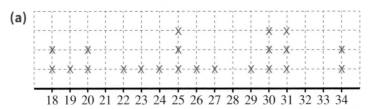

18 19 20 21 22 23 24 25 26 27 28 29 30 31 32 33 34

(b) Three measures of central tendency are the mode, median and mean. There are three modes: 25, 30 and 31 goals.

Since there are twenty two values, the median lies between the 11th and the 12th value. Thus, the median = $\dfrac{25+26}{2}$ = 25·5 goals.

Using a calculator, the mean is 26 goals.

(c) Three measures of variability are the range, the interquartile range (*IQR*) and the standard deviation.

Range = maximum − minimum = 34 − 18 = 16.

To find the *IQR*, proceed as follows.

Divide the ordered values into two equal groups. The first quartile, Q_1, is the median of the lower group. The third quartile, Q_3, is the median of the upper group.

Q_1 Q_3

18, 18, 19, 20, 20, (22), 23, 24, 25, 25, 25,|26, 27, 29, 30, 30, (30), 31, 31, 31, 34, 34

From the diagram, $Q_1 = 22$ and $Q_3 = 30$. Thus, the *IQR* = 30 − 22 = 8 goals.

Note that we could also find the IQR using a more numerical approach.
There are 22 values.

One quarter of the values are less than or equal to the first quartile.
Since $\frac{1}{4} \times 22 = 5\cdot5 \approx 6$, then Q_1 is equal to the 6th value, 22 goals.
(Always round up if the result is not a whole number.)

Three quarters of the values are less than or equal to the third quartile.
Since $\frac{3}{4} \times 22 = 16\cdot5 \approx 17$, then Q_3 is equal to the 17th value, 30 goals.

Thus, as before, the $IQR = 30 - 22 = 8$ goals.

Finally, using a calculator, the standard deviation is 4·96 goals.

Q4 (a)

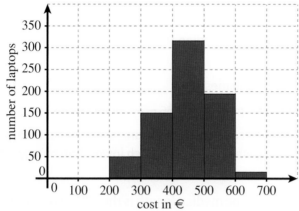

(b) $51 + 148 + 314 + 193 + 14 = 720$

$\frac{51}{720} \times 360° = 25\cdot5°$ $\frac{148}{720} \times 360° = 74°$ $\frac{314}{720} \times 360° = 157°$

$\frac{193}{720} \times 360° = 96\cdot5°$ $\frac{14}{720} \times 360° = 7°$

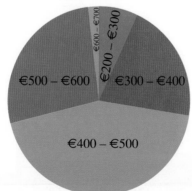

(c)

Cost in €	250	350	450	550	650
Number of laptops	51	148	314	193	14

$\bar{x} = €446$, correct to the nearest euro.

$\sigma = €91$, correct to the nearest euro.

Q5 (a)

0	2
1	2 7 9
2	0 4 (8)
3	(2) 3 7
4	2 8
5	0 6

Key: 2|4 means 24

(b) There are 14 values. The median thus lies between the 7th and 8th values (circled in red).

$$\text{Median} = \frac{28 + 32}{2} = 30 \text{ messages}$$

Range = maximum − minimum = 56 − 2 = 54 messages

(c) Day: Thursday (of second week). Reason: Only two text messages were sent that day, which was very much lower than on any other day.

Q6 (a) 8·8 mm

(b) $\frac{39}{2}$ = 19·5 ≈ 20, thus the median length is the 20th value, i.e. 7·2 mm.

(c) Non-symmetric and bimodal.

(d) There may be two different types of ants, e.g. male and female ants or adult and juvenile ants.

Q7 (a) 12 + 40 + 64 + 56 + 24 + 4 = 200 babies.

(b)

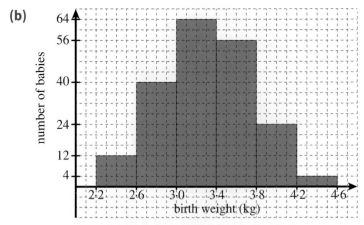

(c) To estimate the average weight, use a measure of central tendency.

To use the table to estimate the mean, redraw it using mid-interval values.

Weight in kg	2·4	2·8	3·2	3·6	4·0	4·4
Number of babies	12	40	64	56	24	4

Using a calculator, $\bar{x}$ = 3·304 ≈ 3·3 kg.

Alternatively, using the graph, we can see that the axis of symmetry is at about 3·3 kg.

(d) 3·675 kg is slightly above average.

(e) Assuming the weights are evenly distributed in each interval, one estimate would be 9 babies. (2·5 kg is three quarters of the way across the first bar and $12 \times \frac{3}{4}$ = 9 babies.)

(f) $60\,000 \times \frac{20}{100} = 12\,000$

(g) $\frac{9}{200} \times 12\,000 = 540$ babies

(h) In a sample of 200, the margin of error is $\frac{1}{\sqrt{n}} = \frac{1}{\sqrt{200}} = 0\cdot0707 \approx 7\%$.

So we can't say for certain that the number in the population would be exactly 540 babies.

(i) You could get full marks whether your answer is yes or no.

For example: Yes. The mean in the sample was 3·3 kg which is quite a bit lower than 3·51 kg.

No. The difference is small enough that it could be due to random variation in the sample.

Q8 (a) r = 0·99 Diagram B (b) r = 0·63 Diagram D (c) r = 0·50 Diagram F
(d) r = 0 Diagram E (e) r = −0·63 Diagram A (f) r = −0·99 Diagram C

Q9 (a) (i) $\frac{1}{\sqrt{n}} = \frac{1}{\sqrt{10}} = 0\cdot316 \approx 32\%$

(ii) $\frac{1}{\sqrt{n}} = \frac{1}{\sqrt{100}} = 0\cdot1 = 10\%$

(iii) $\frac{1}{\sqrt{n}} = \frac{1}{\sqrt{10\,000}} = 0\cdot01 = 1\cdot0\%$

(b) (i) $\frac{1}{\sqrt{n}} = 10\% = 0\cdot1 \Rightarrow \frac{1}{n} = (0\cdot1)^2 = 0\cdot01 \Rightarrow n = \frac{1}{0\cdot01} = 100$

(ii) $\frac{1}{\sqrt{n}} = 20\% = 0\cdot2 \Rightarrow \frac{1}{n} = (0\cdot2)^2 = 0\cdot04 \Rightarrow n = \frac{1}{0\cdot04} = 25$

(iii) $\frac{1}{\sqrt{n}} = 4\% = 0\cdot04 \Rightarrow \frac{1}{n} = (0\cdot04)^2 = 0\cdot0016 \Rightarrow n = \frac{1}{0\cdot0016} = 625$

Q10 68% of values are within one standard deviation from the mean.

42·6 + 8·2 = 50·8

42·6 − 8·2 = 34·4

Thus the range is from 34·4 to 50·8 sandwiches.

Q11 (a) The margin of error is $\frac{1}{\sqrt{n}} = \frac{1}{\sqrt{500}} = 0\cdot0447 \approx 4\cdot5\%$.

(b) The sample proportion is $\hat{p} = \frac{60}{500} = 12\%$.

$$\hat{p} - \frac{1}{\sqrt{n}} = 12\% - 4\cdot5\% = 7\cdot5\% \text{ and } \hat{p} + \frac{1}{\sqrt{n}} = 12\% + 4\cdot5\% = 16\cdot5\%.$$

Since the value of 10% lies within the interval from 7·5% to 16·5% we can conclude that the number 60 is not unusually large. That is, the company's claim can be considered to be true, at the 5% level of significance.

Q12 The null hypothesis, H_0, is that the population proportion is unchanged, i.e. $p = 70\%$.

The alternative hypothesis, H_1, is that the population proportion has changed, i.e. $p \neq 70\%$.

The sample proportion is $\hat{p} = \frac{664}{1000} = 0\cdot664 = 66\cdot4\%$.

The margin of error is $\frac{1}{\sqrt{n}} = \frac{1}{\sqrt{1000}} = 0\cdot0316 = 3\cdot16\%$.

$$\hat{p} - \frac{1}{\sqrt{n}} = 66\cdot4\% - 3\cdot16\% = 63\cdot24\% \text{ and } \hat{p} + \frac{1}{\sqrt{n}} = 66\cdot4\% + 3\cdot16\% = 69\cdot56\%.$$

The value 70% lies outside this range so we reject the null hypothesis. The company is not correct to say that 70% of its customers are satisfied with its overall service, at the 5% level of significance.

Solutions to Exercise B

Q1 (a)

			IQ Test 1				IQ Test 2			
			9	7						
		9	6	8	3					
	7	6 6	4	9	4	7	7	9		
8	5	4 4	3	10	2	5	6	8	8	
		9 5	1	11	1	1	4	7		
				12	0					

Key: For test 1, $9 \,|\, 7$ means a score of 79. For test 2, $8 \,|\, 3$ means a score of 83.

(b) Range of *IQ Test 1*: $119 - 79 = 40$

Range of *IQ Test 2*: $120 - 83 = 37$

(c) There are 15 data points in each set, so the median is the $\frac{15}{2} = 7\cdot5$ $\mapsto 8^{\text{th}}$ data point. Thus the median for *IQ Test 1* is 103 and the median for *IQ Test 2* is 106.

(d) The mean for *IQ Test 1* is $\frac{1506}{15} = 100\cdot4$.

The mean for *IQ Test 2* is $\frac{1572}{15} = 104\cdot8$.

(e) In general, the scores in *IQ Test 2* are slightly higher than in *IQ Test 1*, as both the mean and median are higher for *IQ Test 2*.

The scores are slightly more spread out in *IQ Test 1* than in *IQ Test 2*, as the range is a little bigger for *IQ Test 1*.

Or:

The spread of scores is very similar, as the two ranges are almost the same.

One could also refer to, for example, the standard deviations.

For the first test, $\sigma = 10\cdot55$. For the second test, $\sigma = 9\cdot38$. This would support the view that the scores in *IQ Test 1* are more spread out than those in *IQ Test 2*.

Top Tip

Contradictory interpretations of data may each get full marks as long as they are supported by evidence.

(f) Answer: No. Explanation: The person who got 119 on *IQ Test 1* could have got less, e.g. 94, on *IQ Test 2*.

Q2 (a) The distribution could be described as reasonably symmetric, bell-shaped, unimodal with the data clustered around the middle.

(b) I would guess 5 since it is the mode.

(c) You could increase your chances of winning by choosing a range of numbers, e.g. 4 to 6.

(d) $P = \dfrac{15 + 22 + 10}{59} = \dfrac{47}{59} \approx 80\%.$

(e) (i) Yes, it is possible. (ii) No, it is unlikely.

Q3 (a)

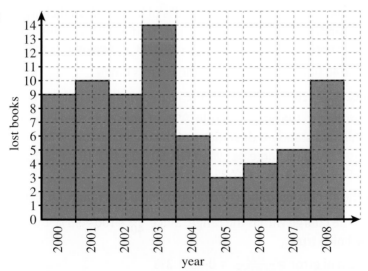

(b) I believe that this histogram supports the finance officer's view that the measures haven't worked. Even though there was a decrease from 2002 to 2004 there has now been a steady increase over 4 years and the number of lost books is back to the same as it was in 2001, which was slightly up from when the measures came in.

(c) The choice of interval lengths in histograms can be used to hide or reveal certain trends.

Q4 (a)

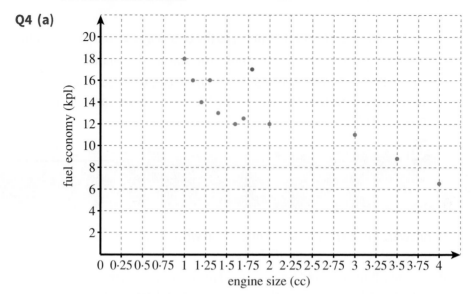

(b) The scatter plot shows that there is a strong negative correlation between engine size and fuel economy.

(c) The point is plotted in red. I would be interested in buying this car since its fuel economy is significantly higher than the others in its engine size.

(d) E: −0·9.

Q5 (a) Using a calculator: mean = €65·50, standard deviation = €11·16.

(b) According to the empirical rule, 68% of houses should charge within one standard deviation of the mean. That is, 68% of houses should charge between €65·50 − €11·16 = €54·34 and €65·50 + €11·16 = €76·66.

Of the 40 houses, 27 charge a price in this range.

Since $\frac{27}{40}$ × 100 = 67·5% ≈ 68%, the empirical rule holds true.

(c) According to the empirical rule, 95% of houses should charge within two standard deviations of the mean. That is, 95% of houses should charge between €65·50 − 2 × €11·16 = €43·18 and €65·50 + 2 × €11·16 = €87·82.

Of the 40 houses, only two charge outside this range, i.e. €40 and €90.

Thus 38 charge within the range. Since $\frac{38}{40}$ × 100 = 95%, the empirical rule holds true.

Q6 (a) Margin of error = $\frac{1}{\sqrt{1111}}$ = 0·03 = 3%

(b) Null hypothesis: 24% of the electorate support the party.

Alternative hypothesis: it is not true that 24% of the electorate support the party.

$\hat{p} = \dfrac{243}{1111} = 0 \cdot 219 \approx 22\%$

$\hat{p} - \dfrac{1}{\sqrt{n}} = 22\% - 3\% = 19\%$

$\hat{p} + \dfrac{1}{\sqrt{n}} = 22\% + 3\% = 25\%$

At the 5% level of significance, there is sufficient evidence to support the party's claim since 24% lies within the range 19% to 25%.

Q7 (a) Margin of error $= \dfrac{1}{\sqrt{400}} = 0 \cdot 05 = 5\%$

(b) Null hypothesis: 60% of viewers watch *The Late Late Show*.

Alternative hypothesis: it is not true that 60% of viewers watch *The Late Late Show*.

(c) $\hat{p} = \dfrac{180}{400} = 0 \cdot 45 = 45\%$

$\hat{p} - \dfrac{1}{\sqrt{n}} = 45\% - 5\% = 40\%$

$\hat{p} + \dfrac{1}{\sqrt{n}} = 45\% + 5\% = 50\%$

I would reject the null hypothesis as 60% is outside the range 40% to 50%.

Q8 (a) Since there are 50 runners, the median time is given by the mean of the times of the 25th and 26th runners.

Median time with no sports drink: $\dfrac{33 \cdot 9 + 33 \cdot 9}{2} = 33 \cdot 9$ minutes.

Median time with sports drink: $\dfrac{29 \cdot 9 + 29 \cdot 9}{2} = 29 \cdot 9$ minutes.

Median speed with no sports drink: $\dfrac{5}{33 \cdot 9} = 0 \cdot 147$ km/min.

Median speed with sports drink: $\dfrac{5}{29 \cdot 9} = 0 \cdot 167$ km/min.

So the median speed increased when they ran 5 km after taking the sports drink.

(b) Range of times without the sports drink: $40 \cdot 4 - 20 \cdot 5 = 19 \cdot 9$ minutes.

Range of times with the sports drink: $38 \cdot 5 - 20 \cdot 3 = 18 \cdot 2$ minutes.

The distribution of times without the sports drink is more skewed than the distribution of times after taking the sports drink, which is more symmetrical.

The data for those who ran without the sports drink is clustered around 32 to 36 minutes.

The data for those who ran with the sports drink is clustered around 28 to 30 minutes.

(c) There is evidence to suggest that performance improves after taking the sports drink. The range of times is smaller after taking the drink. Without the drink only 20% of the runners took less than 32 minutes to run the 5 km. After taking the drink, 70% of the runners completed the 5 km in less than 32 minutes.

(d) 18% of the runners took less than 23 minutes to run the 5 km without taking the sports drink. Only 10% of the runners ran the 5 km in less than 23 minutes after taking the drink.

(e)

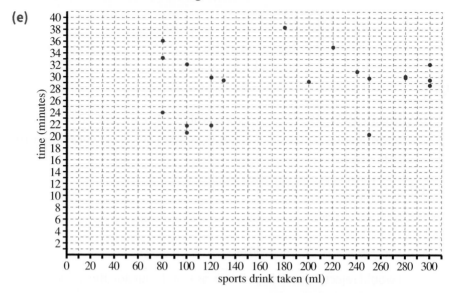

(f) No, the scatter plot does not show a noticeable relationship between the time taken to run the 5 km and the amount of sports drink taken before the run.

(g) B: 0·14

Solutions to Exercise C

Q1 (a) $19 \div 2 = 9\cdot5 \Rightarrow$ the median number is contained in the 10th packet (round 9·5 up to 10).

That is, 29 sweets.

(b) Range = highest − lowest = 32 − 25 = 7 sweets.

(c) $19 \times \frac{1}{4} = 4\cdot75 \Rightarrow$ the first quartile, Q_1, is the number of sweets in the 5th packet, i.e. 28 sweets.

$19 \times \frac{3}{4} = 14\cdot5 \Rightarrow$ the third quartile, Q_3, is the number of sweets in the 15th packet, i.e. 30 sweets.

$IQR = Q_3 - Q_1 = 30 - 28 = 2$ sweets

(d) The words bivariate and continuous should be deleted as the data are univariate and discrete.

Q2 (a) (i) 27 098

(ii) There were 44 139 households with 7 people each. This gives 44 139 × 7 = 308 973 people.

(iii) $326\,134 \times 1 = 326\,134$

$413\,786 \times 2 = 827\,572$

$264\,438 \times 3 = 793\,314$

$243\,303 \times 4 = 973\,212$

$136\,979 \times 5 = 684\,895$

$54\,618 \times 6 = 327\,708$

$15\,141 \times 7 = 105\,987$

$5050 \times 8 = 40\,400$

$1719 \times 9 = 15\,471$

$1128 \times 10 = 11\,280$

$$\text{Total} = 4\,105\,973$$

$$\text{Mean} = \frac{\#\,\text{People}}{\#\,\text{Households}} = \frac{4\,105\,973}{1\,462\,296} = 2{\cdot}8 \text{ people per household.}$$

Top Tip

As you see, you can be asked to find the mean of a large amount of data. This question could also have been solved using the statistics function of your calculator. Download the manual for your calculator and find out how to do this. Don't just write down the final answer given by your calculator. Show some

supporting work, e.g. $\text{Mean} = \dfrac{\#\,\text{People}}{\#\,\text{Households}} = 2{\cdot}8$ people per household.

(b) **(i)** Conor was trying to show that the number of households has more than doubled in the given time period and that there was rapid growth from 1966 to 2006.

(ii) Fiona was trying to show the gradual reduction in the number of people per household.

(iii) Ray was trying to show that the number of households has more than doubled in the time period, and the move has been towards smaller household sizes.

(c) $P(7 \text{ or } 8) = \dfrac{15\,141 + 5050}{1\,462\,296} = \dfrac{20\,191}{1\,462\,296} \approx 0{\cdot}0138$

(d) Find the relative frequency of 4-people households in 2006.

Multiply this by 1000 to get the expected value of 4-people households in the sample.

$$E(x) = \frac{243\,303}{1\,462\,296} \times 1\,000 \approx 166{\cdot}38$$

(e) **(i)** In Dublin City there is a much larger percentage of 1-person households. Dublin City has a heavy concentration of 1- and 2-person households whereas South Dublin is heavily concentrated in 2-, 3- and 4-person households. Dublin City has no households of size 9 or 10+.

2. Statistics   77

(ii) From the chart, we see that 20% of South Dublin households are 4-person. This gives $\dfrac{20}{100} \times 81\,000 = 16\,200$ 4-person households or $16\,200 \times 4 = 64\,800$ people.

(iii) The first two bars on the chart add up to about 29% + 31% = 60%. Since the median is the 50th percentile, it will be in the second bar, i.e. a 2-person household.

(iv) The 1-person households represent about 29% (from the chart). The 3-person households represent about 17%. Those living in a 3-person household will outnumber those living in a 1-person household since there are three times as many of them in each household.

Thus it is more likely that the person is from a 3-person household.

Q3 (a) **(i)** A bar chart or trend graph would be suitable, e.g.

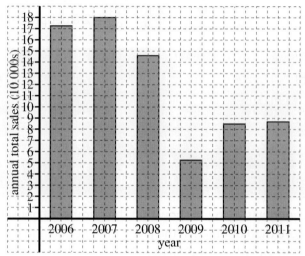

or

Trend graph

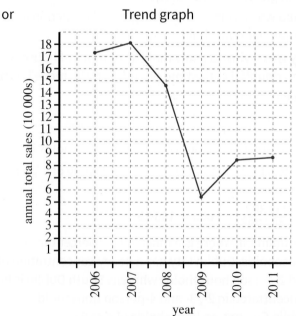

(ii) Mean $= \dfrac{173\,273 + 180\,754 + 146\,470 + 54\,432 + 84\,907 + 86\,932}{6}$

$\quad\quad\quad\quad = \dfrac{726\,768}{6} = 121\,128$ cars.

(iii) Find the increase from 2009 to 2011 then express it as a percentage of the sales in 2009.

Increase $= 86\,932 - 54\,432 = 32\,500$.

Percentage increase $= \dfrac{32\,500}{54\,432} \times 100 = 59\cdot71\%$.

(iv) Aoife's argument does not recognise that while sales are improving compared to 2009, they are still nothing like as high as they were in the three years before that.

Paul's argument does not recognise that while sales are much less than in the years before 2009, the rate of change is positive, i.e. sales are increasing every year.

(v) Sales decreased from 2007, reaching their lowest point in 2009. They have since recovered, but have still not reached the levels of the years before 2009.

(b) **(i)** Highest quarterly sales are in the first quarter and decrease significantly in each subsequent quarter.

(ii) People like to buy new cars early in the year so that they have a new year number plate. (Note that this question was set before plates such as 141 and 142 came in.)

(iii) The first quarter sales in 2012 are higher than those for 2010 but lower than those for 2011. One could estimate the annual sales for 2012 to be between the annual figures for 2010 and 2011, e.g. 85\,900.

This initial estimate could be refined by noticing that the 2012 first quarter figures are less than halfway between those for 2010 and 2011. One could then reduce the estimate to, e.g. 85\,500.

(c) **(i)** Diesel $= \dfrac{61\,730}{86\,932} \times 360° = 256°$, Petrol $= \dfrac{23\,246}{86\,932} \times 360° = 96°$,

Other $= \dfrac{1956}{86\,932} \times 360° = 8°$

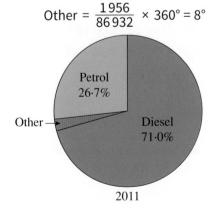

Petrol
26·7%

Other

Diesel
71·0%

2011

Top Tip!
Bring a 360° protractor with you to the exam. It makes drawing reflex angles much easier.

(ii) D

(d) (i)

	Diesel		Petrol
	7	10	
9, 9, 8, 7, 6, 4, 0		11	
5, 5, 0		12	9, 9, 9
4		13	3, 4, 6, 8, 8, 9
		14	
		15	0, 7, 9

Key: For diesel, $7 \mid 10$ means 107. For petrol, $12 \mid 9$ means 129.

(ii) Yes. The diesel engines grouped at the top of the plot have a smaller median value.

(iii) No. The emissions for the petrol engines are more spread out than for the diesel ones. The interquartile range for the petrol engines is greater than that for the diesel engines.

Q4 (a)

Marriage rate		Death rate
9 8 7 7 6 6 5 5 3 3	4	
2 2 2 2 2 1 1 1 0 0 0	5	
	6	1 3 3 4 7 8
	7	1 3 6 9
	8	3 5 6 6 7 7 7 9
	9	0 0 0

Key: For marriage, $3 \mid 4$ means 43. For death, $6 \mid 1$ means 61.

(b) The marriage rates range from 43 to 52 and are grouped at the top of the plot.

The death rates range from 61 to 90 and are grouped at the bottom of the plot.

(c) $21 \div 2 = 10.5 \Rightarrow$ the median of the 21 figures is the 11th value, i.e. 50.

$21 \div 4 = 5.25 \Rightarrow$ the first quartile, Q_1, is the mean of the 5th and 6th values, i.e. 46.

The third quartile, Q_3, is the mean of the 15th and 16th values, i.e. 51.

Thus the interquartile range is $IQR = Q_3 - Q_1 = 51 - 46 = 5$.

(d) (i) Mean $= \dfrac{\text{\# Deaths}}{\text{\# Years}} = \dfrac{1\,645}{21} = 78 \cdot 3$

(ii) $78 \cdot 3 - 10 \cdot 3 = 68$

$78 \cdot 3 + 10 \cdot 3 = 88 \cdot 6$

The following death rates are between the above values:

68, 71, 73, 76, 79, 83, 85, 86, 86, 87, 87, 87.

(e) In 2010 there were 165 births per 10 000 members of the population, so
$$75\,174 = \frac{165}{10\,000} \text{ of the total population.}$$
Population = 75 174 × 10 000 ÷ 165 = 4 556 000.

(f) $\dfrac{61}{10\,000}$ × 4 556 000 = 27 792

(g) The birth rates given are per 10 000 of the population. If the population in 2000 was greater than in 1990, more children could have been born in 2000 than in 1990 even though the birth rate in 2000 was lower.

(h) 1990 ratio = 151 : 90. 2010 ratio = 165 : 61.

Prediction: The population of the country is expected to increase.

Reason: The increase in the ratio from 1990 to 2010 suggests that more children are being born for each person that dies.

Top Tip

To compare ratios like the above it may help to express them as decimals.

Here, $\dfrac{151}{90}$ = 1·68 and $\dfrac{165}{61}$ = 2·70 so the second ratio is clearly the bigger of the two.

(i) Strong negative correlation. With the increasing birth rate, the population is getting younger and the death rate is declining.

Q5 (a) **(i)** The event that, on average, takes longest to complete is the *cycle*.

Note that the longest time for the swim is 30 minutes. This is the shortest time for the cycle. Similarly, the times for the run are much less than those for the cycle.

(ii) In all three histograms, the times are grouped into intervals of *two* minutes.

(iii) The time of the fastest person in the swim was between *ten* and *twelve* minutes.

(iv) The median time for the run is approximately 25 minutes.

Note that the histogram for the run is more or less symmetrical. Thus the median will be around the middle of the graph.

(v) The event in which the times are most spread out is the *cycle*.

Look at the ranges. For the swim the range is 32 − 10 = 22 minutes. For the cycle it is 60 − 30 = 30 minutes. For the run it is 38 − 16 = 22 minutes.

(b) **(i)** The scatter diagram is a moderately positive linear graph. So you can eliminate D, E and F as they are negative. A is too high, it's not *that* linear. C is too low, it's not *that* chaotic. Answer: B.

(ii)

Run vs. Cycle

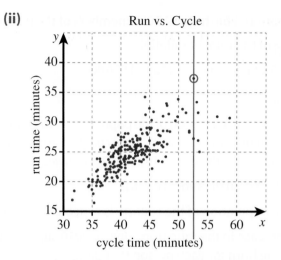

Frank, the slowest runner, is circled in red. Draw a vertical line through Frank's dot. Any dots to the right of this line represent people who took longer than Frank in the cycle. Answer: 6 people.

(iii)

Run vs. Cycle

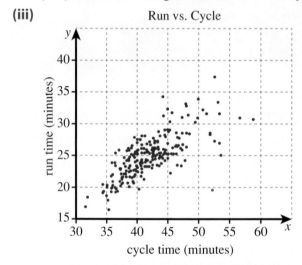

Brian's times are plotted as a red point on the scatter plot. His performance would be unusual as it is an outlier, i.e. far away from the main line of the graph. His cycle time is very slow for such a quick run time.

(c) **(i)** The times for females are more spread out. Their distribution is also less symmetric than the times for males. The times for females are skewed towards the longer times.

(ii) The median for the females is $\dfrac{17{\cdot}6 + 18{\cdot}1}{2} = 17{\cdot}85$ minutes. (There were 28 females so the median is between the 14th and 15th values.) The median for the males is $\dfrac{18{\cdot}0 + 18{\cdot}1}{2} = 18{\cdot}05$ minutes. (There were 32 males so the median is between the 16th and 17th values.)

The two medians are very close, which would cause Máire to confirm her belief. The difference in the two ranges could possibly be reduced with larger samples.

Q6 (a) (i) Find 90% of the estimated number of properties, i.e.

1·9 million × $\frac{90}{100}$ = 1·71 million.

(ii) There are many possible answers here. Any of the following would be accepted: the owner might be abroad, the owner may be unable to do the paperwork, the owner might be unable to pay, the owner may be trying to avoid tax.

(b)

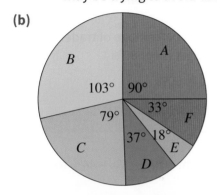

A (€0–€100 000): $\frac{24\cdot9}{100}$ × 360° = 89·64° ≈ 90°

B (€100 001–€150 000): $\frac{28\cdot6}{100}$ × 360° = 102·96° ≈ 103°

C (€150 001–€200 000): $\frac{21\cdot9}{100}$ × 360° = 78·84° ≈ 79°

D (€200 001–€250 000): $\frac{10\cdot4}{100}$ × 360° = 37·44° ≈ 37°

E (€250 001–€300 000): $\frac{4\cdot9}{100}$ × 360° = 17·64° ≈ 18°

F (Over €300 000): $\frac{9\cdot3}{100}$ × 360° = 33·48° ≈ 33°

(c) (i)

Valuation Band	Tax per property	Number of properties	Total tax due (€)
€0–€100 000	€45	425 790	19 160 550
€100 001–€150 000	€112	489 060	54 774 720
€150 001–€200 000	€157	374 490	58 794 930
€200 001–€250 000	€202	177 840	35 923 680
€250 001–€300 000	€247	83 790	20 696 130
Over €300 000	NA	159 030	NA

NA = Not Available

(ii) €19 160 550 + €54 774 720 + €58 794 930 + €35 923 680 +
     €20 696 130 = €189 350 010

(iii) €241 000 000 − €189 350 010 = €51 649 990

(iv) Mean $= \dfrac{\text{tax for that group}}{\text{number of properties}} = \dfrac{51\,649\,990}{159\,030} = €324 \cdot 78$

(v) The number of properties is given by 489 060 × 20% = 97 812.

The difference in tax for each property is 157 − 112 = €45.

Thus, the extra tax would amount to 97 812 × €45 = €4 401 540.

Q7 (a) The null hypothesis is that 80% of traders recommend the company's widget.

(The alternative hypothesis is that the percentage of traders who recommend the company's widget is *not* 80%.)

The sample proportion is $\dfrac{24}{40}$ × 100 = 60%.

The margin of error at the 5% level of significance is

$$\dfrac{1}{\sqrt{n}} = \dfrac{1}{\sqrt{40}} = 0 \cdot 158 \approx 16\%.$$

The confidence interval thus goes from 60% − 16% = 44% to 60% + 16% = 76%.

The figure of 80% lies outside the confidence interval.

We reject the null hypothesis. That is, there is sufficient evidence to reject the company's claim.

(b) 95% of the group are within two standard deviations of the mean.

170 − 2 × 14 = 142 cm and 170 + 2 × 14 = 198 cm.

Thus, by the empirical rule, 95% of the students are between 142 cm and 198 cm in height.

Geometry

3

Learning objectives

In this chapter you will learn to:

- Understand terms such as axiom, theorem, converse and corollary
- Understand terms such as point, line, ray, line segment, and their notation
- Identify different types of angle and polygon
- Identify congruent triangles: SSS, ASA and SAS
- Identify quadrilaterals such as a parallelogram, trapezium, rectangle, rhombus and square
- Understand and use Junior Certificate theorems and constructions (which may be examined for Leaving Certificate)
- Understand and use Leaving Certificate theorems and constructions
- Find images under translation, central symmetry and axial symmetry.

Fundamental concepts

Axioms and theorems

An **axiom** is a statement that is accepted without proof, as a basis for argument. For example, Axiom 1 states that there is exactly one line through any two points.

A **theorem** is a statement that if something (the hypothesis) is true, then something else (the conclusion) is also true. Whenever a hypothesis p is true and the conclusion q is also true, we say p **implies** q. This is denoted $p \Rightarrow q$.

The **converse** of the statement $p \Rightarrow q$ is the statement that $q \Rightarrow p$. The converse of a statement is not always true.

Consider the statement 'if a figure is a square then it has four sides'. The converse, 'if a figure has four sides then it is a square' is false since, for example, a trapezium has four sides but is not a square.

The **proof** of a theorem is a sequence of logical steps that prove that the theorem is true, based on axioms and previously proved theorems.

A **corollary** is a statement which follows immediately from a theorem with little or no additional proof.

Points, lines and triangles

Points are denoted by capital letters, e.g. A, B, C.

Lines are denoted by lower-case letters, e.g. a, b, c. The line through the points A and B may also be denoted by AB.

A **line segment**, $[AB]$, is a subset of the line through, and including, the end-points A and B.

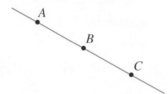

If three, or more, points lie on a single line, we say they are **collinear**.

Let A, B and C be points that are not collinear. **The triangle $\triangle ABC$ is the subset of the plane enclosed by the three line segments $[AB]$, $[BC]$ and $[CA]$. The segments are called its sides and the points are called its vertices.** (Note that the singular of vertices is vertex.)

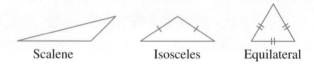

| Scalene | Isosceles | Equilateral |

In a **scalene** triangle, all three sides have different lengths.

In an **isosceles** triangle, two of the sides have the same length.

In an **equilateral** triangle, all three sides have the same length.

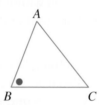

The angle marked in the diagram can be denoted by $\angle CBA$ (or $\angle ABC$), or by $\angle B$.

Angles can also be denoted by numbers, e.g. $\angle 1$, or by Greek letters, e.g. α (alpha), β (beta) or γ (gamma).

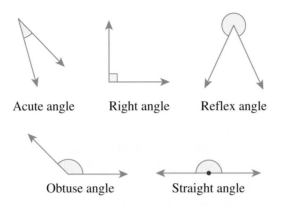

Acute angle   Right angle   Reflex angle

Obtuse angle   Straight angle

A **straight** angle has 180°. **Null** angles have 0°. **Full** angles have 360°. **Reflex** angles have more than 180°. A **right** angle has 90°.

An **ordinary** angle has between 0° and 180°.

An angle is **acute** if it has less than 90°. An angle is **obtuse** if it has more than 90° but less than 180°.

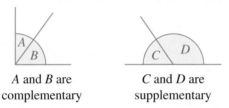

A and B are complementary   C and D are supplementary

If two angles are **complementary**, then their sum has 90°. For example, the two acute angles in a right-angled triangle are complementary.

If two angles are **supplementary**, then their sum has 180°. For example, opposite angles in a cyclic quadrilateral are supplementary.

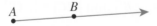

We denote the **distance** between the points A and B or the length of the segment $[AB]$ by $|AB|$.

A ———— B

A **ray** is a half-line, i.e. it has one end-point, but continues without end in the other direction. We denote the ray with end-point A, containing another point B, by $[AB$.

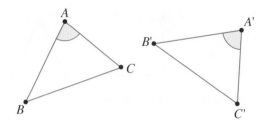

Two triangles are said to be **congruent** if *all* the sides and angles of one are equal to the corresponding sides and angles of the other. In the diagram above, the two triangles are congruent if: $|AB| = |A'B'|$, $|BC| = |B'C'|$, $|AC| = |A'C'|$, $|\angle A| = |\angle A'|$, $|\angle B| = |\angle B'|$ and $|\angle C| = |\angle C'|$.

The following axiom shows when three equalities are sufficient for congruence.

Axiom (SAS, ASA and SSS)

The triangles $\triangle ABC$ and $\triangle A'B'C'$ are congruent:

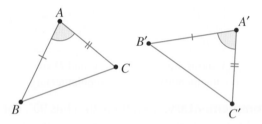

- if $|AB| = |A'B'|$, $|AC| = |A'C'|$ and $|\angle A| = |\angle A'|$ (SAS)

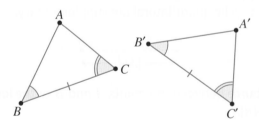

- if $|BC| = |B'C'|$, $|\angle B| = |\angle B'|$ and $|\angle C| = |\angle C'|$ (ASA)

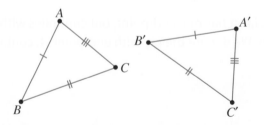

- if $|AB| = |A'B'|$, $|BC| = |B'C'|$ and $|CA| = |C'A'|$ (SSS).

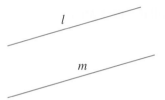

Two lines l and m are **parallel** if they are either identical or have no common point. We write $l \parallel m$ for 'l is parallel to m'.

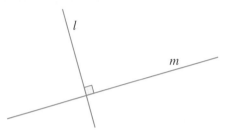

Two lines l and m are **perpendicular** if they meet at an angle of 90°. We write $l \perp m$ for 'l is perpendicular to m'.

Polygons

A **polygon** is a closed shape with any number of sides and vertices.

A **quadrilateral** is a polygon with four vertices.

A **rectangle** is a quadrilateral having right angles at all four vertices.

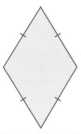

A **rhombus** is a quadrilateral having all four sides equal. A **square** is a rectangular rhombus.

A polygon is **equilateral** if all its sides are equal, and **regular** if all its sides and angles are equal.

A **parallelogram** is a quadrilateral for which both pairs of opposite sides are parallel.

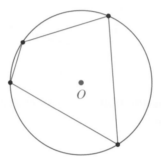

A **cyclic quadrilateral** is one whose vertices lie on a circle.

A **trapezium** is a quadrilateral where two sides are parallel.

Review of Ordinary Level Junior Certificate theorems

Note: Missing numbers in the list below are due to the fact that not all theorems are on the syllabus.

Theorem 1

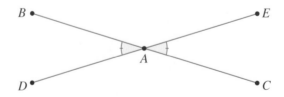

Vertically opposite angles are equal in measure.

$|\angle BAD| = |\angle CAE|$.

Theorem 2

- In an isosceles triangle the angles opposite the equal sides are equal. That is, if $|AB| = |AC|$, then $\angle B = \angle C$.

- The converse is also true: if two angles are equal, then the triangle is isosceles. That is, if $\angle B = \angle C$, then $|AB| = |AC|$.

Theorem 3

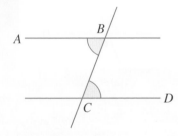

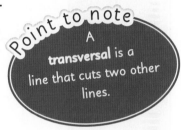

Point to note

A **transversal** is a line that cuts two other lines.

- If $|\angle ABC| = |\angle BCD|$, then $AB \parallel CD$. In other words, if a transversal makes equal alternate angles on two lines, then the lines are parallel.

- The converse is also true: if $AB \parallel CD$, then $|\angle ABC| = |\angle BCD|$. In other words, if two lines are parallel, then any transversal will make equal alternate angles with them.

Students often remember alternate angles as 'angles in a Z'. The Z can be back to front.

Theorem 4

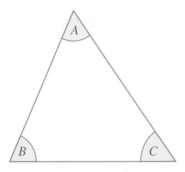

$|\angle A| + |\angle B| + |\angle C| = 180°$. The angles in any triangle add to 180°. That is, the interior angles in a triangle are supplementary.

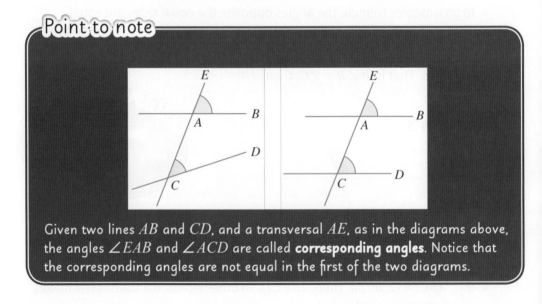
Theorem 5

Two lines are parallel if, and only if, for any transversal, the corresponding angles are equal.

Theorem 6

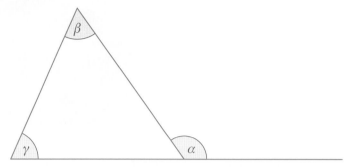

$|\angle\alpha| = |\angle\beta| + |\angle\gamma|$. Each exterior angle of a triangle is equal to the sum of the interior opposite angles.

Theorem 9

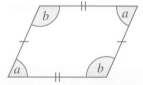

In a parallelogram, opposite sides are equal, and opposite angles are equal.

Theorem 10

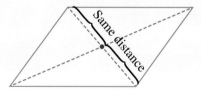

The diagonals of a parallelogram bisect one another.

Theorem 13

This is a required theorem for the Leaving Certificate and is included in the section below.

Theorem 14 (Pythagoras)

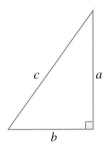

Point to note

In a right-angled triangle, the side opposite the right angle is called the hypotenuse.

$c^2 = a^2 + b^2$. In a right-angled triangle the square of the hypotenuse is the sum of the squares of the other two sides.

Theorem 15 (Converse to Pythagoras)

If the square of one side of a triangle is the sum of the squares of the other two, then the angle opposite the first side is a right angle.

Top Tip

A triangle with sides

(i) 3, 4, 5

(ii) 5, 12, 13

(iii) 8, 15, 17

will be a right-angled triangle.

These numbers are called Pythagorean triples. Learn them well as they frequently appear in examination questions.

Corollary 3

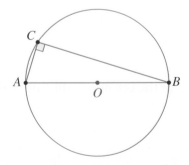

Each angle in a semicircle is a right angle. That is, if AB is a diameter of a circle and C is any other point of the circle, then $|\angle BCA| = 90°$.

Corollary 4

If the angle standing on a chord [BC] at some point of the circle is a right angle, then [BC] is a diameter.

Review of Ordinary Level Junior Certificate constructions

Note: Missing numbers in the list below are due to the fact that not all constructions are on the syllabus.

> **Point to note**
>
> For reasons of space, some of the final diagrams in the following constructions, while in the correct proportions, are smaller than actual size. In the examination, ensure that you draw the lengths in your constructions to the required dimensions.

1 Construct the bisector of a given angle using only compass and straight edge

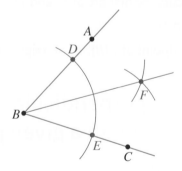

Given: An angle ∠ABC.

Place the pin of the compass on the vertex, B. Draw an arc as shown. The arc cuts the arms of the angle at two points, D and E.

Place the pin of the compass at D. Draw a second arc with the same radius as the first.

Place the pin of the compass at E. Draw a third arc with the same radius as the first.

The second and third arcs intersect at F.

Draw a ray starting at B and going through F. This ray bisects the angle ∠ABC.

2 Construct the perpendicular bisector of a segment, using only compass and straight edge

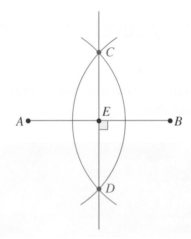

Given: A line segment, [AB].

Place the pin of the compass at A. Set the compass width so that the pencil reaches more than half way along [AB]. Draw an arc.

Place the pin of the compass at B. Do *not* change the compass setting. Draw a second arc which cuts the first arc at C and D.

Draw a line through C and D.

CD passes through the midpoint of [AB], E, at a right angle.

4 Construct a line perpendicular to a given line *l*, passing through a given point, *P*, on *l*

Given: A line, l, and a point, P, on the line.

Set the compass width to whatever you like. Place the pin of the compass on P. Draw an arc either side, intersecting l at C and D.

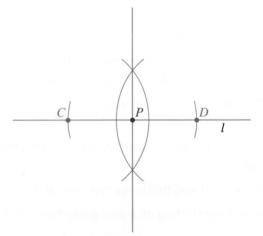

You now have a line segment [CD]. Draw the perpendicular bisector of [CD] as in construction 2.

5 Construct a line parallel to a given line, through a given point

Given: A line, l, and a point, P, not on the line.

Place the edge of the set square on the line, l. Place the ruler along the other side of the set square.

Hold the ruler so it doesn't move. Slide the set square along the ruler to the point, P.

Draw the line parallel to l through P.

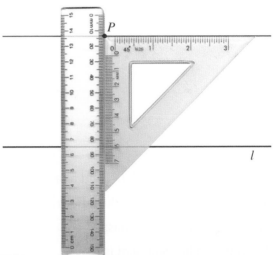

6 Divide a segment into three equal segments, without measuring it

Given: A line segment $[AB]$.

Draw a line, l, through A as shown.

Place the pin of the compass at A. Draw an arc to cut l at C (the radius of the arc doesn't matter).

Place the pin of the compass at C. Draw a second arc, with the same radius as the first, to cut l at D.

Place the pin of the compass at D. Draw a third arc, with the same radius as before, to cut l at E.

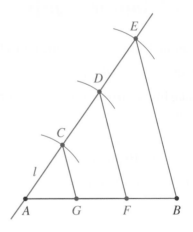

Join E to B.

Use construction 5 to draw a line segment through D, parallel to EB, intersecting AB at F.

Draw a line segment through C, parallel to DF, intersecting AB at G.

The segment is now divided into three equal parts.

If you are asked to divide a line segment into, for example, four equal parts, just draw four arcs instead of three as above.

8 Construct a line segment of a given length on a given ray

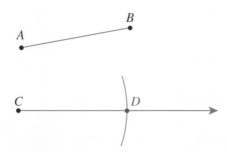

Given: A line segment [AB] and a ray through a point C.

Set the compass width to the length |AB|.

Place the pin of the compass at C. Draw an arc intersecting the ray at D.

The required line segment is [CD].

9 Construct an angle of a given number of degrees with a given ray as one arm

Example: Construct an angle of 110° with [AB as one arm.

Given: A ray [AB.

Place the centre of the protractor on A. Ensure the 0° mark is *on* the ray, as shown.

Since it is the *inner* 0°, in this example, mark C against the line going through the *inner* 110° on the protractor.

Join C and A to finish the construction.

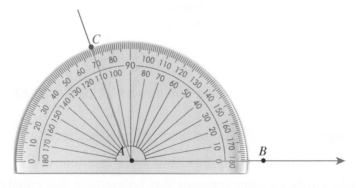

10 Construct a triangle, given lengths of three sides

Example: Construct a
triangle ABC, where
$|AB|$ = 6 cm,
$|AC|$ = 5 cm
and $|BC|$ = 4 cm.

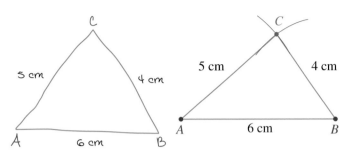

Draw a rough diagram to organise the information.

Use a ruler to draw a base $[AB]$, where $|AB|$ = 6 cm. (It doesn't matter which side you choose as base.)

Since $|AC|$ = 5 cm, C is a distance 5 cm from A. Set the compass width to 5 cm. Place its pin at A and draw an arc.

Since $|BC|$ = 4 cm, C is a distance of 4 cm from B. Set the compass width to 4 cm. Place its pin at B and draw an arc.

The two arcs intersect at C. Join A to C and B to C.

11 Construct a triangle, given SAS data

Example: Construct a triangle ABC, where $|AB|$ = 7·5 cm, $|\angle CAB|$ = 48° and $|AC|$ = 3·5 cm.

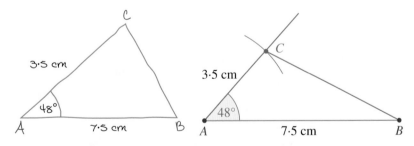

Draw a rough diagram.

Use a ruler to draw a base $[AB]$, where $|AB|$ = 7·5 cm.

Use construction 9 to construct an angle of 48° with $[AB$ as one arm and A as vertex.

Set the compass width to 3·5 cm. Place the pin of the compass on A. Draw an arc on the other arm of the angle. The arc intersects the arm at C.

Join B to C to complete the construction.

12 Construct a triangle, given ASA data

Example: Construct a triangle ABC, where $|AB| = 7$ cm, $|\angle CAB| = 40°$ and $|\angle ABC| = 50°$.

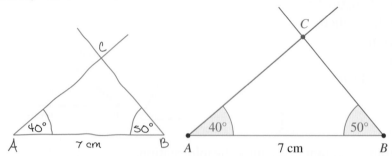

Draw a rough diagram.

Use a ruler to draw a base $[AB]$, where $|AB| = 7$ cm.

Construct an angle of 40° with $[AB$ as one arm and A as vertex.

Construct an angle of 50° with $[AB$ as one arm and B as vertex.

The arms of the two angles intersect at C.

13 Construct a right-angled triangle, given the length of the hypotenuse and one other side

Example: Construct a triangle ABC, where $|AB| = 5$ cm, $|\angle CAB| = 90°$ and $|BC| = 8$ cm.

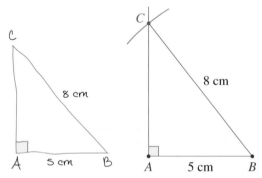

Draw a rough diagram.

Use a ruler to draw a base $[AB]$, where $|AB| = 5$ cm.

Construct an angle of 90° with $[AB$ as one arm and A as vertex.

Set the compass width to 8 cm. Place the pin of the compass at B and draw an arc, cutting the arm of the 90° angle at C.

Complete the construction by joining B to C.

14 Construct a right-angled triangle, given one side and one of the acute angles

Example: Construct a triangle ABC, where $|AB| = 5$ cm, $|\angle ABC| = 90°$ and $|\angle ACB| = 40°$.

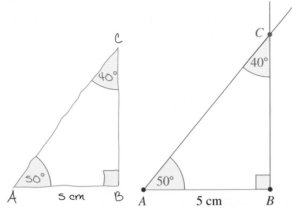

Draw a rough diagram.

Write in all the angles. Note that $|\angle CAB| = 50°$ since the three angles must add to 180°.

Use a ruler to draw a base $[AB]$ where $|AB| = 5$ cm.

Construct an angle of 50° with $[AB$ as one arm and A as vertex.

Construct an angle of 90° with $[AB$ as one arm and B as vertex.

The arms intersect at C.

15 Construct a rectangle, given side lengths

Example: Construct a rectangle $ABCD$, where $|AB| = 8$ cm and $|BC| = 6$ cm.

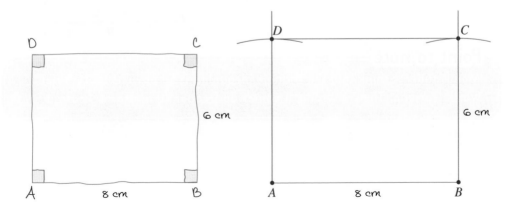

Draw a rough diagram.

Use a ruler to construct [AB], where |AB| = 8 cm.

Draw a perpendicular to [AB] through B.   (Use a set square or construction 4.)

Set the compass width to 6 cm. Draw an arc with centre B intersecting the perpendicular at C.

Draw a perpendicular to [AB] through A. Draw an arc with centre A and radius 6 cm intersecting the perpendicular at D.

Join C to D.

Required theorems for Leaving Certificate

Theorem 7

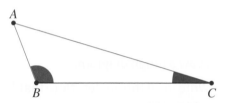

- In △ABC, suppose that |AC| > |AB|. Then |∠ABC| > |∠ACB|. In other words, the bigger angle is the one opposite the bigger side.

- The converse is also true: if |∠ABC| > |∠ACB|, then |AC| > |AB|. In other words, the bigger side is opposite the bigger angle.

Theorem 8 (THE TRIANGLE INEQUALITY)

Two sides of a triangle are together greater than the third.

If a, b and c are the lengths of the sides of a triangle, then $a + b > c$, $b + c > a$ and $c + a > b$.

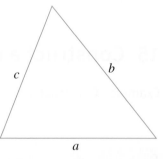

Point to note

Many students think that the triangle inequality is so obvious that it's not worth learning. They're wrong. It comes up frequently in exams. Learn it.

Theorem 11

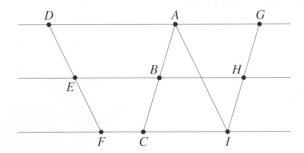

If three parallel lines cut off equal segments on some transversal line, then they will cut off equal segments on any other transversal. That is, if $|AB| = |BC|$ then $|DE| = |EF|$ and $|GH| = |HI|$.

Recall that a transversal is a line that cuts two other lines.

Theorem 12

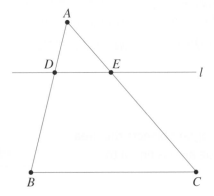

Let $\triangle ABC$ be a triangle.

If a line l is parallel to BC and cuts $[AB]$ in the ratio $s : t$, then it also cuts $[AC]$ in the same ratio. For example, if $|AD| : |DB| = 1:3$ then $|AE| : |EC| = 1:3$.

Theorem 13

If two triangles $\triangle ABC$ and $\triangle A'B'C'$ are similar, then their sides are proportional, in order:

$$\frac{|AB|}{|A'B'|} = \frac{|BC|}{|B'C'|} = \frac{|CA|}{|C'A'|}.$$

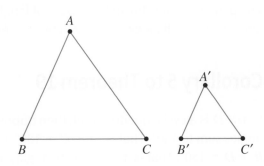

Note that two triangles are similar if each angle in one has a corresponding angle in the other which is equal to it in measure, e.g. $|\angle A| = |\angle A'|$, $|\angle B| = |\angle B'|$ and $|\angle C| = |\angle C'|$.

Quantities are proportional if their ratios are constant.

Theorem 16

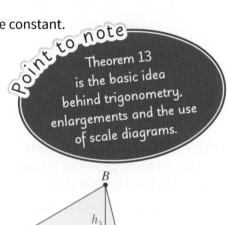

Point to note

Theorem 13 is the basic idea behind trigonometry. enlargements and the use of scale diagrams.

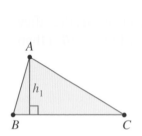 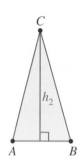

For a triangle, base times height does not depend on the choice of base. The above diagrams show the same triangle in three different orientations.

Theorem 16 states that $|BC| \times h_1 = |AB| \times h_2 = |CA| \times h_3$.

Theorem 17

A diagonal of a parallelogram bisects the area. (In the diagram, the blue area is equal to the pink area.)

Theorem 18

The area of a parallelogram is the base multiplied by the height.

The parallelogram shown has a base of length b and a height h. Its area, A, is given by $A = bh$.

Corollary 5 to Theorem 19

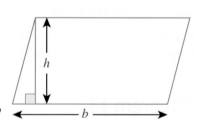

If $ABCD$ is a cyclic quadrilateral, then opposite angles sum to 180°. That is, $A + C = 180°$ and $B + D = 180°$. That is, the opposite angles are supplementary.

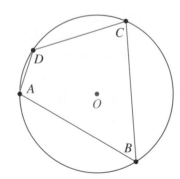

Theorem 20

- Each tangent is perpendicular to the radius that goes to the point of contact.

- If P lies on the circle s, and a line l through P is perpendicular to the radius of s through P, then l is tangent to s.

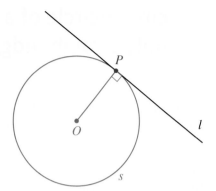

Theorem 21

- The perpendicular from the centre of a circle to a chord bisects the chord. That is, if $OC \perp AB$ then $|AC| = |CB|$.

- The perpendicular bisector of a chord passes through the centre.

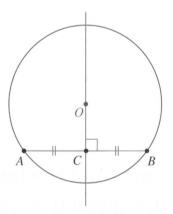

Point to note

Suppose you are given a drawing of a circle and you have to find the centre. Theorem 21 gives one possible method.

Draw a chord. Construct its perpendicular bisector. Repeat for a second chord. The two bisectors will intersect at the centre of the circle.

Required constructions for Leaving Certificate

The **circumcircle** of a triangle is a circle passing through the vertices of that triangle. The **circumcentre** is the centre of the circumcircle.

The **incircle** of a triangle is a circle having each side of the triangle as a tangent. The **incentre** is the centre of the incircle.

16 Construct the circumcentre and circumcircle of a given triangle, using only straight edge and compass

Given: $\triangle ABC$.

Construct e, the perpendicular bisector of $[AB]$, using a compass. (See construction 2 above.)

Construct f, the perpendicular bisector of $[AC]$, using a compass.

The perpendicular bisectors, e and f, intersect at the circumcentre, O.

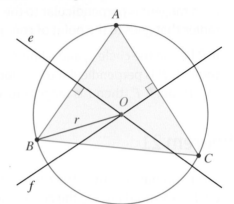

Draw a line segment from the circumcentre, O, to the vertex B.
$r = |OB|$ is the radius of the circumcircle.

Using a compass, draw the circumcircle with centre O and radius r.

17 Construct the incentre and incircle of a given triangle, using only straight edge and compass

Given: $\triangle ABC$.

Construct d, the bisector of the angle B, using a compass. (See construction 1 above.)

Construct e, the bisector of the angle C, using a compass.

These bisectors intersect at the incentre, O.

Draw a line segment, $[OD]$, perpendicular to BC, using a set square. $|OD| = r$, the radius of the incircle.

Using a compass, draw the incircle with centre O and radius r.

18 Construct an angle of 60°, without using a protractor or set square

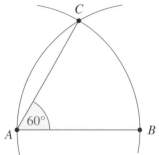

Draw a line segment $[AB]$, size doesn't matter.

Use a compass to draw an arc of radius $|AB|$ with centre A.

Draw a second arc of radius $|AB|$ with centre B.

The two arcs intersect at C. Join A to C.

$|\angle CAB| = 60°$ since $\triangle CAB$ is equilateral.

19 Construct a tangent to a given circle at a given point on it

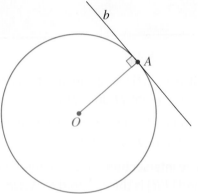

Given: A circle with centre O and a point on the circle, A.

Draw the radius $[OA]$.

Draw the line, b, perpendicular to the radius $[OA]$ at the point A.

The line, b, is the tangent to the circle at the point A.

20 Construct a parallelogram, given the length of the sides and the measure of the angles

Example: Construct a parallelogram $ABCD$, where $|AB| = 6$ cm, $|BC| = 4$ cm and $|\angle ABC| = 70°$.

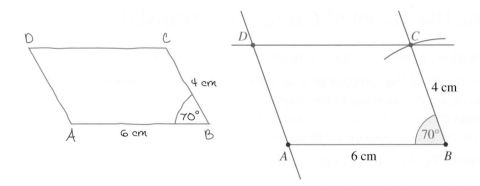

Draw a rough diagram.

Use a ruler to draw a base [AB], where |AB| = 6 cm.

Construct an angle of 70° with B as vertex.

Draw an arc with centre B and radius 4 cm to intersect the arm of the angle at C.

Construct a line parallel to [AB] through C.

Construct a line parallel to [BC] through A.

The two parallel lines intersect at D.

21 Construct the centroid of a triangle

Given: △ABC.

Bisect [AB] using construction 2 to find its midpoint D. Join D to C.

Bisect [AC] using construction 2 to find its midpoint E. Join E to B.

The intersection, G, of the medians [DC] and [EB] is the centroid of △ABC.

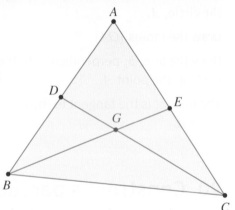

Transformations: translation, axial symmetry, central symmetry

Find the image of C under the translation $\overrightarrow{AB}$

Draw a line, l, through C parallel to AB.

Place the pin of the compass on A and pencil on B, i.e. set the compass to the length |AB|. Without changing the compass setting, place the pin on C and draw an arc through l.

The point D, where the arc cuts l, is the image of C under the translation $\overrightarrow{AB}$.

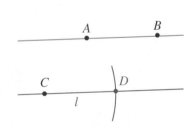

Find the image of A under an axial symmetry in l

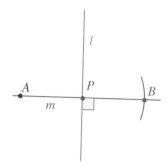

Draw a line, m, through A perpendicular to l. Let m intersect l at P.

Set the compass to the length $|AP|$.

Place the pin of the compass at P and draw an arc which cuts m at B.

The point B is the image of A under an axial symmetry in l.

Find the image of A under a central symmetry in B

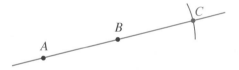

Draw a line, l, through A and B.

Set the compass to the length $|AB|$. Place the pin of the compass at B and draw an arc which cuts l at C.

The point C is the image of the point A under a central symmetry in the point B.

> **Remember**
>
> Suppose you wish to find the image of $\triangle ABC$ under one of the above transformations.
>
> Find the image of A, A', the image of B, B', then the image of C, C'. Then $\triangle A'B'C'$ is the image of $\triangle ABC$ under the transformation.
>
> You will need to do this in co-ordinate geometry when finding the area of a triangle when the origin is not a vertex.

Exercise A

Q1 Here are four groups of three lengths.

 A 5 cm, 5 cm, 7 cm

 B 6 cm, 5 cm, 12 cm

 C 3 cm, 4 cm, 5 cm

 D 8 cm, 8 cm, 8 cm

Which group, or groups:

(a) could form a scalene triangle

(b) could form an isosceles triangle

(c) could form an equilateral triangle

(d) could form a right-angled triangle

(e) could not form a triangle?

Justify your answers.

Q2

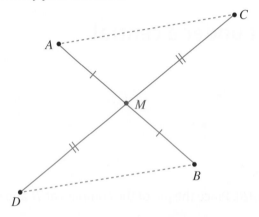

In the diagram, M is the midpoint of $[AB]$ and is also the midpoint of $[CD]$. Show that $|AC|$ must be equal to $|BD|$.

Q3 (a) The diagram below shows a triangle with one side extended.

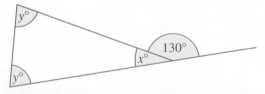

(i) Find the value of x.

(ii) The other two angles in the triangle are equal. Each is $y°$. Find the value of y.

(b) The diagram below shows another triangle with one side extended. Find the value of s and the value of t.

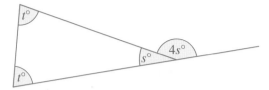

Q4 (a) Construct a parallelogram $PQRS$ in which $|PQ| = 7$ cm, $|QR| = 5$ cm and $|\angle PQR| = 120°$. Show all the construction lines clearly.

(b) Use your protractor to measure the angle RSP.

(c) Explain how you could use the measurement in part (b) to check the accuracy of your construction.

Q5

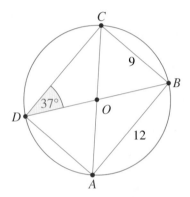

$ABCD$ is a parallelogram. A circle of centre O passes through the four vertices of the parallelogram. The diagonals of the parallelogram intersect at O.

$|AB| = 12$, $|BC| = 9$ and $|\angle CDB| = 37°$.

(a) Write down $|\angle BCD|$.

(b) Calculate $|DB|$.

(c) Name two isosceles triangles in the diagram.

(d) Find $|\angle BOC|$.

(e) Find the area of the triangle ABD.

Q6 (a) Construct a triangle PQR in which $|PQ| = 7$ cm, $|QR| = 5$ cm and $|\angle PQR| = 80°$.

(b) On the diagram in part (a), construct the image of the triangle PQR under a central symmetry in the point P.

(c) Use your protractor to measure the angle RPQ.

Q7

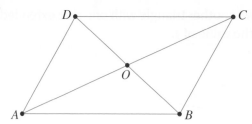

ABCD is a parallelogram. The diagonals of ABCD intersect at O.
$|AB| = 9$ cm, $|BC| = 6$ cm and $|\angle DAB| = 60°$.

(a) Find $|DC|$.

(b) Find $|\angle ABC|$.

(c) Name one pair of parallel lines in the diagram.

(d) Is the statement $|DO| = |OB|$ and $|AO| = |OC|$ true or false? Give a reason for your answer.

Q8

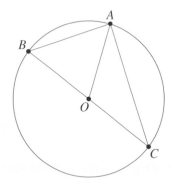

A circle of centre O passes through the points A, B and C, as shown.
$|AB| = 6$ cm and $|AC| = 8$ cm. $[BC]$ is a diameter of the circle.

(a) Find $|BC|$.

(b) What is the length of $[OA]$?

(c) Identify two isosceles triangles from the diagram.

(d) Given that $|\angle AOC| = 106°$ to the nearest degree, find

    (i) $|\angle AOB|$ **(ii)** $|\angle OBA|$.

Q9 (a) How long does it take   **(i)** the hour hand **(ii)** the minute hand of a clock to rotate through an angle of 360°?

(b) Find the angle between the hour and the minute hand for each of the following clocks.

(i)   **(ii)**

(iii) 　　**(iv)**

(c) There is no formal definition for the concept of angle on our course. It is an undefined concept. How would you define 'angle'?

Exercise B

Q1 Alex has a large collection of sticks. They come in lengths of 1 unit, 2 units, 3 units and so on. The picture shows two of the sticks of length 1 unit.

(a) Alex picks a third stick. What is the smallest length that Alex could pick so that the three sticks, including the two shown, *cannot* form a triangle? Justify your answer.

(b) Alex picks a fourth stick. What is the smallest length that Alex could pick so that no three of the four sticks can form a triangle?

(c) Alex picks a fifth stick. What is the smallest length that Alex could pick so that no three of the five sticks can form a triangle?

(d) Alex picks eight sticks in total. No three sticks selected from the eight can form a triangle.

  (i) List the sequence of lengths, starting with the smallest.

  (ii) What is the name of this sequence?

Q2 ABC is a triangle with $|AB|$ = 6 cm, $|AC|$ = 4·5 cm and $|BC|$ = 7·5 cm.

(a) Construct $\triangle ABC$ with $[BC]$ as base.

(b) (i) Name the largest angle in $\triangle ABC$.

  (ii) How many degrees has the angle in part (i)? Justify your answer.

(c) Construct the circumcircle of $\triangle ABC$.

Q3 (a) Prove that any rectangle is a cyclic quadrilateral.

(b) Describe how you would find the centre of the circle which goes through the vertices of a rectangle.

Q4

A circle is shown. Construct its centre using two different methods.

Q5 (a) Draw a shape which has exactly three axes of symmetry. Show the axes on the diagram.

(b) Draw a shape which has exactly four axes of symmetry. Show the axes on the diagram.

Q6 (a)

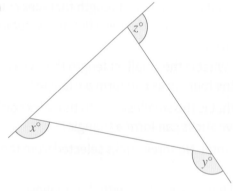

Prove that $x + y + z = 360°$.

(b)

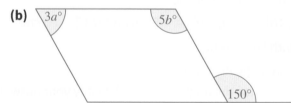

The diagram shows a parallelogram and one exterior angle. Find the value of a and the value of b.

Q7

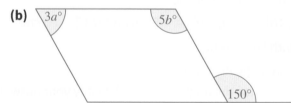

40°

l_1

α

l_2

β

115° γ

l_3

If l_1, l_2 and l_3 are parallel lines, find the measure of the angles $α$, $β$ and $γ$.

Q8 In the diagram below, $|\angle MNP| = |\angle PRQ|$.

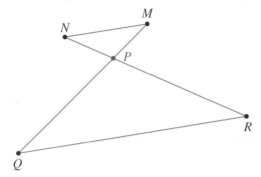

(a) Prove that $\triangle MNP$ and $\triangle QRP$ are similar.

(b) Is NM parallel to QR? Give a reason for your answer.

(c) Given $|MN| = 6, |NP| = 4, |QP| = 9$ and $|PR| = 10$, find:

    (i) $|QR|$ (ii) $|QM|$.

Q9

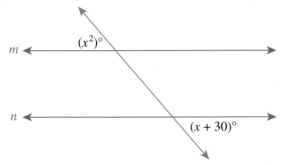

The lines m and n above are parallel. Find two possible values for the angles marked.

Q10

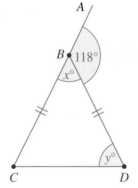

In the diagram, $|BC| = |BD|$ and $|\angle ABD| = 118°$.

(a) Find x.

(b) Find y.

Q11

The diagram shows an arc of circle. Find the centre of the circle of which the arc is a part.

Exercise C

Q1 (a) Show clearly how to construct the centroid of the triangle below.

(Note: all instruments are permitted. If you are using measurements, show your measurements and calculations.)

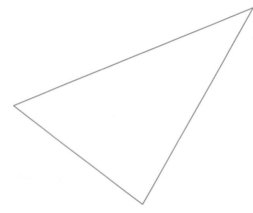

(b) State what is meant by the word axiom, and explain why axioms are needed in order to prove theorems.   *(2011)*

Q2 In the diagram, $ABCD$ is a cyclic quadrilateral and $ABCF$ is a parallelogram.

Show that $DEFG$ is a cyclic quadrilateral.

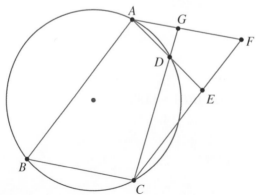

(2011)

Q3 (a) **(i)** Write down a geometrical result that can be used to construct a tangent to a circle at a point.

(ii) On the diagram shown, construct the tangent to the circle at A.

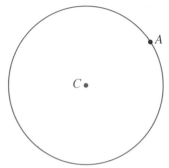

(b) Construct the circumcentre and circumcircle of the triangle below, using only a straight edge and compass. Show all construction marks clearly.

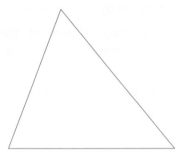

(2012)

Q4 $ABCD$ is a parallelogram.

The points A, B and C lie on the circle which cuts $[AD]$ at P.

The line CP meets the line BA at Q.

Prove that $|CD| = |CP|$.

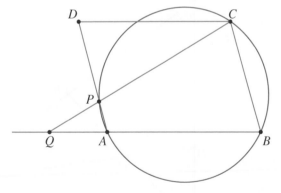

(2012)

Q5 (a) Construct the triangle ABC such that $|AB| = 8$ cm, $|BC| = |AC| = 5$ cm.

(b) On the same diagram, construct the image of the triangle ABC under axial symmetry in AB.

(c) Justify the statement '$AC'BC$ is a parallelogram' where C' is the image of C under axial symmetry in AB.

(2013)

Q6 In the acute-angled triangle ABC: $AP \perp BC$, $BQ \perp AC$ and $CR \perp AB$.

Prove that $|\angle ABQ| + |\angle BCR| + |\angle CAP| = 90°$.

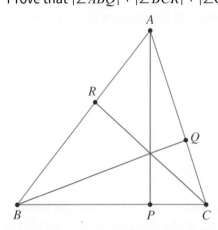

(2013)

Q7 (a) Explain what is meant by the converse of a theorem.

(b) There are some geometric statements that are true, but have converses that are false. Give one such geometric statement, and state also the (false) converse. *(SEC Sample Paper 2014)*

Q8 $ABCD$ is a cyclic quadrilateral. The opposite sides, when extended, meet at P and Q, as shown.

The angles α, β, and γ are as shown.

Prove that $\beta + \gamma = 180° - 2\alpha$.

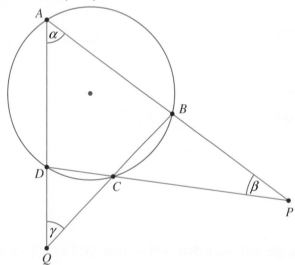

(SEC Sample Paper 2014)

Q9 (a) (i) Construct the incircle of the triangle ABC below. Show all your construction lines clearly.

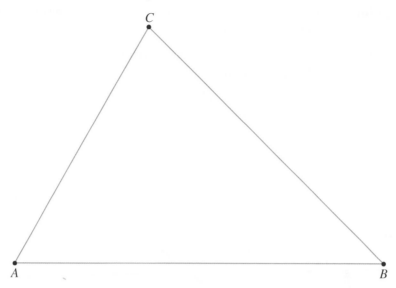

(ii) Measure and write down the length of the radius of the circle constructed in part (i).

(b) The point P is on the circle c with centre O and diameter $[MN]$.

The length of the radius of c is $2\sqrt{5}$ cm. $|MP| = x$ cm and $|PN| = 2x$ cm.

Find the value of x.

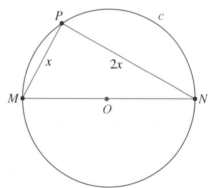

(2014)

Q10 Two circles, c_1 and c_2, intersect at the points B and X as shown.

The circle c_1 has diameter $[AB]$.

The circle c_2 has diameter $[BC]$.

The line CB is a tangent to c_1.

Prove that X is on the line AC.

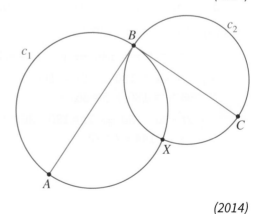

(2014)

Solutions to Exercise A

Q1 (a) C: 3 cm, 4 cm, 5 cm could form a scalene triangle since all three sides have different lengths.

(b) A: 5 cm, 5 cm, 7 cm could form an isosceles triangle since two sides have the same length.

(c) D: 8 cm, 8 cm, 8 cm could form an equilateral triangle since all three sides have the same length.

(d) C: 3 cm, 4 cm, 5 cm could form a right-angled triangle since $3^2 + 4^2 = 25 = 5^2$.

(e) B: 6 cm, 5 cm, 12 cm cannot form a triangle since $6 + 5 < 12$ and in any triangle the sum of any two lengths must be greater than the third.

Q2

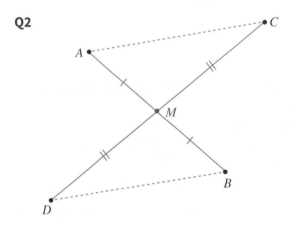

$|AM| = |MB|$ since M is the midpoint of $[AB]$.

$|CM| = |MD|$ since M is the midpoint of $[CD]$.

$|\angle CMA| = |\angle BMD|$ since they are vertically opposite angles.

Thus $\triangle AMC$ and $\triangle MDB$ are congruent, as two sides and the included angle are equal (SAS). Thus $|AC| = |BD|$.

Q3 (a) (i) $x = 180 - 130 = 50$ (a straight angle has 180°)

(ii) $y + y = 130 \Rightarrow y = 130 \div 2 = 65$ (exterior angle theorem)

(b) $s + 4s = 180 \Rightarrow 5s = 180$

$\Rightarrow s = 180 \div 5 = 36$ (straight angle)

$2t + 36 = 180 \Rightarrow 2t = 180 - 36 = 144$

$\Rightarrow t = 144 \div 2 = 72$ (angles in a triangle add to 180°)

Q4 (a)

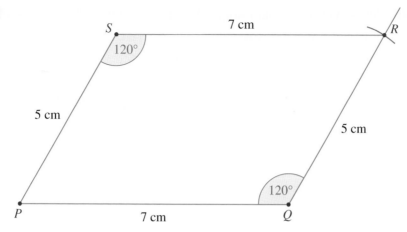

(b) $|\angle RSP| = 120°$

(c) Opposite angles in a parallelogram are equal in measure.
If $|\angle RSP| = 120° = |\angle PQR|$, then the construction is accurate.

Q5

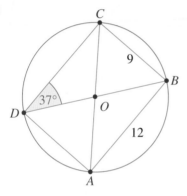

(a) $|\angle BCD| = 90°$ (each angle in a semicircle is a right angle)

(b) $|DB|^2 = |BC|^2 + |CD|^2 = 9^2 + 12^2 = 225$ (Pythagoras)
Thus, $|DB| = \sqrt{225} = 15$.

Top Tip

You were previously asked to learn that a triangle with sides 3, 4, 5 will form a right-angled triangle.

Similarly, multiples of these numbers, e.g. 6, 8, 10 or 9, 12, 15 will form a right-angled triangle.

Knowing the basic Pythagorean triples, e.g. 3, 4, 5; 5, 12, 13 and 8, 15, 17, will help you spot their multiples. This can help you to see the answer before you calculate it, which allows you to check your calculation.

(c) Any of the four triangles which have two radii as sides will be isosceles, e.g. $\triangle OCB$ or $\triangle OAB$.

(d) Since $\triangle DCB$ is a right-angled triangle, $|\angle OBC| = 90° - 37° = 53°$.

But, since $\triangle OCB$ is isosceles, $|\angle OCB| = |\angle OBC| = 53°$.

Thus, as the angles in a triangle add to 180°,
$|\angle BOC| = 180° - 53° - 53° = 74°$.

(e) The area of $\triangle ABD = \frac{1}{2} \times |AD| \times |AB| = \frac{1}{2} \times 9 \times 12 = 54$ square units.

Q6 (a) and **(b)**

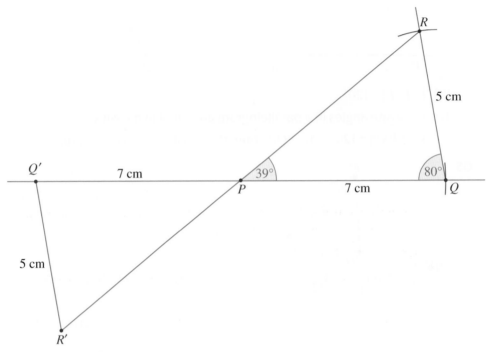

(c) $|\angle RPQ| = 39°$.

Q7 (a) $|DC| = |AB| = 9$ cm (opposite sides in a parallelogram are equal in length)

(b) $|\angle ABC| = 180° - |\angle DAB| = 180° - 60° = 120°$ (adjacent angles in a parallelogram add to 180°)

(c) AB is parallel to DC or AD is parallel to BC.

(d) Yes, since the diagonals of a parallelogram bisect each other.

Q8 (a) Each angle in a semicircle is a right angle, so we can use Pythagoras' theorem.

$|BC|^2 = |AB|^2 + |AC|^2 = 6^2 + 8^2 = 100$

Thus, $|BC| = \sqrt{100} = 10$ cm.

Note that this triple, 6, 8, 10, is a multiple of the Pythagorean triple 3, 4, 5.

(b) $[BC]$ is a diameter, so the radius $[OA]$ is half its length, i.e. 5 cm.

(c) $\triangle OBA$ and $\triangle OCA$ are isosceles since both triangles have two radii as sides.

(d) **(i)** $\angle AOC$ and $\angle AOB$ form a straight angle, thus $|\angle AOB| = 180° - 106° = 74°$.

 (ii) $|\angle OBA| = 53°$ since $|\angle AOC| = 106°$ is an exterior angle and $|\angle OBA| = |\angle OAB|$.

Q9 (a) **(i)** 12 hours **(ii)** 1 hour or 60 minutes

(b) **(i)** 180°

 (ii) 90°

 (iii) $\frac{5}{12} \times 360° = 150°$

 (iv) Every hour, the hour hand travels $\frac{1}{12} \times 360° = 30°$. Thus, in half an hour it travels 15°. Thus, the angle between the hands is $180° - 15° = 165°$.

(c) Although the question asks 'How would you define "angle"?', it's not a free-for-all. Answers which use keywords and geometric ideas will get more marks than answers which don't.

Here are two sample answers:

- An angle is the amount of turn between two rays that have a common end-point.

- The angle between two rays is the rotation required to map one of the rays onto the other.

Solutions to Exercise B

Q1 (a) The third stick must have length 2 units. According to the triangle inequality, the lengths 1, 1 and 2 cannot form a triangle since the sum of any two sides must be greater than the third side and $1 + 1 = 2$.

(b) The fourth stick must have length 3 units. No three sticks chosen from those of length 1, 1, 2, 3 can form a triangle since they will not satisfy the triangle inequality. For example, given 1, 1, 3 or 1, 2, 3, Alex will have to pick two lengths which do not exceed the third length.

(c) The fifth stick must be 5 units in length. Of the sequence 1, 1, 2, 3, 5, it is impossible to pick three where the sum of any two is greater than the third length.

(d) **(i)** 1, 1, 2, 3, 5, 8, 13, 21, …

 (ii) This is a Fibonacci sequence.

Q2

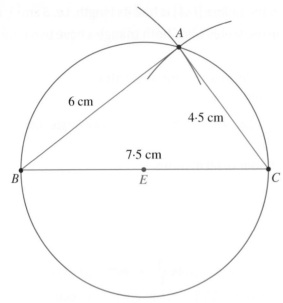

(a) Draw a base $|BC| = 7\cdot5$ cm using a ruler. Set the compass to 6 cm and draw an arc centred at B.

Now set the compass to 4·5 cm and draw an arc centred at C. The two arcs intersect at A.

Join B to A and C to A.

(b) (i) The largest angle in $\triangle ABC$ is $\angle BAC$ since it is opposite the largest side, $[BC]$.

(ii) $|\angle BAC| = 90°$ since $6^2 + 4\cdot5^2 = 7\cdot5^2$ (Pythagoras)

(c) $|\angle BAC| = 90°$ so $[BC]$ is a diameter of the circumcircle, since the angle in a semicircle is a right angle. Bisect $[BC]$ to find the circumcentre, E, and draw the circumcircle with radius $[EC]$, as shown.

Q3 (a) All the internal angles in a rectangle are right angles. Thus opposite angles sum to 180°, i.e. every rectangle is a cyclic quadrilateral.

(b)

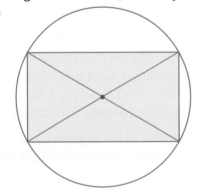

Each diagonal is a diameter since the opposite angle is a right angle. Thus the intersection of the two diameters is the centre of the circle passing through the four vertices.

Q4 Method 1

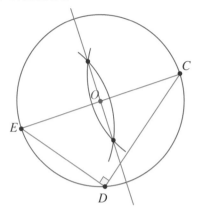

Draw a chord [CD].

Draw a perpendicular at D which intersects the circle at E.

Join E to C. Since $|\angle EDC| = 90°$, [EC] is a diameter.

Construct the midpoint, O, of [EC] by finding the perpendicular bisector. O is the centre of the circle.

Method 2

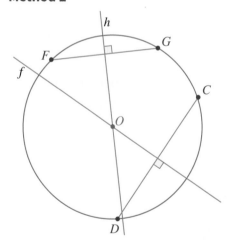

Draw a chord [CD].

Construct its perpendicular bisector, f. (Recall that the perpendicular bisector of a chord goes through the centre of the circle.)

Draw a second chord [FG].

Construct its perpendicular bisector, h.

f and h intersect at the centre O.

Q5 (a)

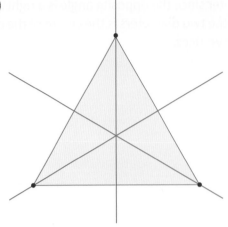

An equilateral triangle has exactly three axes of symmetry, the perpendicular bisector of each of the sides.

(b)

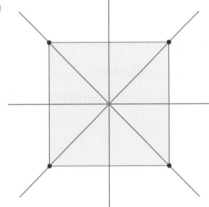

A square has exactly four axes of symmetry, the perpendicular bisectors of the sides and the lines through the diagonals.

Q6 (a)

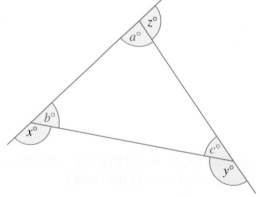

$x = a + c$ (exterior angle theorem)
$y = a + b$ (exterior angle theorem)
$z = b + c$ (exterior angle theorem)

Thus

$$x + y + z = a + c + a + b + b + c$$
$$= 2(a + b + c) = 2(180°) = 360°,$$

since the sum of the interior angles in a triangle is 180°.

(b)

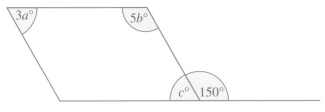

$5b = 150 \Rightarrow b = 30$ (alternate angles)

$c + 150 = 180 \Rightarrow c = 30$ (straight angle)

$3a = c = 30 \Rightarrow a = 10$ (opposite angles in a parallelogram)

Q7

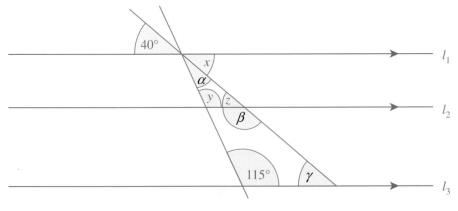

$x = 40°$ (opposite angles)

$z = x = 40°$ (alternate angles)

$y = 115°$ (corresponding angles)

Thus, $\alpha = 180° - 40° - 115° = 25°$ (interior angles in a triangle sum to 180°)

and $\beta = \alpha + y = 25° + 115° = 140°$ (exterior angle theorem).

Finally, $\gamma = 40°$ (corresponding angles)

Q8 $|\angle MNP| = |\angle PRQ|$.

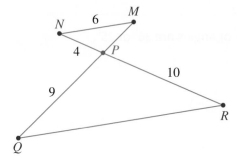

$|\angle MNP| = |\angle PRQ|$ (given)

$|\angle MPN| = |\angle RPQ|$ (opposite angles)

$|\angle NMP| = 180° - |\angle MPN| - |\angle MNP|$

$\qquad\qquad = 180° - |\angle RPQ| - |\angle PRQ|$

$\qquad\qquad = |\angle RQP|$

Thus the two triangles are similar.

(b) NM is parallel to QR since alternate angles are equal.

(c) By similar triangles $\triangle MNP$ and $\triangle QRP$:

(i) $\dfrac{|QR|}{6} = \dfrac{10}{4} \Rightarrow |QR| = \dfrac{10}{4} \times 6 = 15$

(ii) $\dfrac{|PM|}{9} = \dfrac{6}{15} \Rightarrow |PM| = \dfrac{6}{15} \times 9 = 3{\cdot}6$

$\qquad |QM| = 9 + 3{\cdot}6 = 12{\cdot}6$

Q9

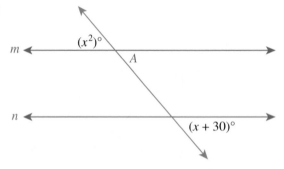

$A = x + 30$ (corresponding angles)

$x^2 = A$ (vertically opposite angles)

Thus $x^2 = x + 30 \Rightarrow x^2 - x - 30 = 0$.

Factorising and solving the quadratic, we get:

$x^2 - x - 30 = 0 \Rightarrow (x - 6)(x + 5) = 0$

$\Rightarrow x = 6 \text{ or } x = -5$

Substituting, we get:

$x = 6 \Rightarrow x + 30 = 36 = x^2$

and $x = -5 \Rightarrow x + 30 = 25 = x^2$.

Thus, two values for the pair of angles are 36° or 25°.

Q10

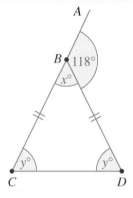

(a) $x + 118 = 180$ (straight angle).

Thus, $x = 180 - 118 = 62$.

(b) $|\angle C| = |\angle D| = y°$ (angles opposite the equal sides of an isosceles
                                triangle are equal)

$x + y + y = 180$ (the interior angles of a triangle add to 180°)

$\Rightarrow 62 + 2y = 180 \Rightarrow 2y = 180 - 62 = 118 \Rightarrow y = 118 \div 2 = 59$

Or:

$y + y = 118$ (the exterior angle is equal to the sum of the two opposite
                  interior angles)

$\Rightarrow y = 118 \div 2 = 59$

Q11

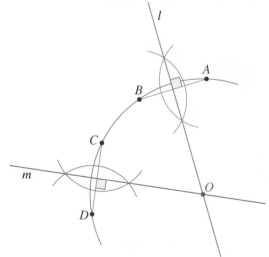

Choose two points, A and B, on the arc. Join them.

Use a compass to construct l, the perpendicular bisector of the chord $[AB]$.

Choose two other points, C and D on the arc. Join them.

Use a compass to construct m, the perpendicular bisector of the chord $[CD]$.

Since the diameter of a circle bisects a chord at right angles, l and m intersect at O, the centre of the circle.

Solutions to Exercise C

Q1 (a) Find the midpoint of one side. This can be done by constructing its perpendicular bisector or by measuring its length and dividing it by two. Join the midpoint to the opposite vertex. The join is called a median. Repeat this for another side. The intersection of the two medians is the centroid.

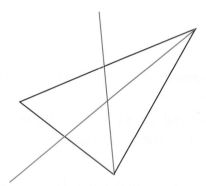

(b) An axiom is a statement which is accepted without proof. Theorems are proved by making a logical argument based on some starting points. Without axioms we would have no starting points.

Q2

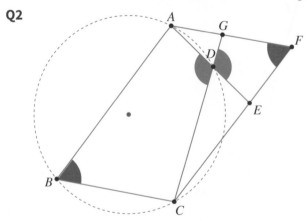

$ABCD$ is a cyclic quadrilateral $\Rightarrow |\angle ABC| + |\angle ADC| = 180°$.

But $|\angle ABC| = |\angle AFC|$ (opposite angles in a parallelogram are equal)

and $|\angle ADC| = |\angle GDE|$ (vertically opposite angles are equal)

and $|\angle AFC|$ and $|\angle GFE|$ are two names for the same angle

$\Rightarrow |\angle GFE| + |\angle GDE| = 180°$, thus $DEFG$ is a cyclic quadrilateral.

Q3 (a) **(i)** A tangent is perpendicular to the radius at the point of contact.

(ii) Draw a radius by joining the centre C to the point on the circle A.

Construct a tangent by drawing a line through A perpendicular to the radius. You may use a set square to do this.

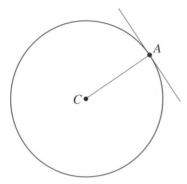

(b) Use a compass and straight edge to construct the perpendicular bisector of one side of the triangle.

Repeat for a second side. The intersection of the two bisectors is the circumcentre.

Join the circumcentre to any vertex of the triangle to find a radius, r.

Construct the circumcircle with this radius and with the circumcentre as its centre.

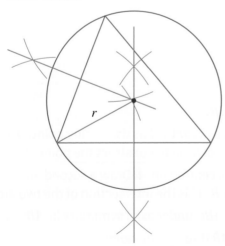

Q4

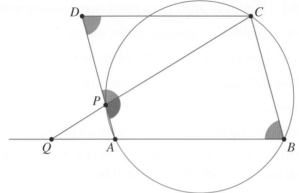

$|\angle ABC| = |\angle CDP|$ (opposite angles in a parallelogram are equal)

$|\angle ABC| + |\angle CPA| = 180°$ (opposite angles in a cyclic quadrilateral sum to 180°)

$|\angle DPC| + |\angle CPA| = 180°$ (a straight angle)

$\Rightarrow |\angle ABC| = |\angle DPC|$

Hence, PCD is an isosceles triangle $\Rightarrow |CD| = |CP|$

Q5

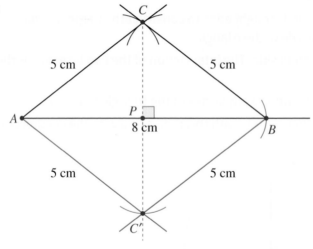

(a) To construct the triangle ABC:

Draw a point A. Construct a ray with A as its starting point. Using a compass, mark off a length of 8 cm to construct the point B.

Draw an arc of radius 5 cm, centred on A. Draw a second arc of radius 5 cm, centred on B. C is the intersection of the two arcs.

(b) To construct the image of ABC under axial symmetry in AB:

Draw a perpendicular to AB through the point C.

Suppose that the perpendicular cuts AB at P.

Draw an arc of radius $|CP|$ centred on P.

The intersection of this arc and the perpendicular is C'.

Join C' to A and to B.

(c) The diagonals AB and CC' bisect each other. Thus $AC'BC$ is a parallelogram.

Q6

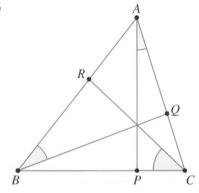

We are required to show that the marked angles add up to 90°.

Top Tip

In a complex diagram, mark in the important angles or sides. Use highlighters if more than one colour seems useful.

In a right-angled triangle, the two acute angles add up to 90°.

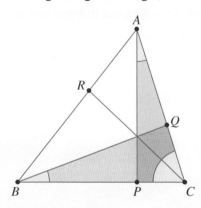

In the right-angled triangle APC, $|\angle CAP| + |\angle PCA| = 90°$.

In the right-angled triangle QBC, $|\angle QBC| + |\angle BCQ| = 90°$.

Hence, $|\angle CAP| = |\angle QBC|$ (since $|\angle PCA|$ and $|\angle BCQ|$ are the same angle).

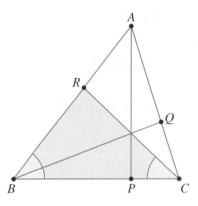

In the right-angled triangle RBC, $|\angle RBC| + |\angle BCR| = 90°$.

But $|\angle RBC| = |\angle RBQ| + |\angle QBC| = |\angle RBQ| + |\angle CAP|$.

Thus $|\angle RBQ| + |\angle CAP| + |\angle BCR| = 90°$.

Q7 **(a)** A theorem states that if a condition holds then a conclusion is true. The converse states that if that conclusion is true, then the condition holds.

(b) Statement: If a figure is a rectangle, the sum of its interior angles is 360°.   (True).

Converse: If the sum of the interior angles of a figure is 360°, then it is a rectangle.   (False).

Note that, here, 'False' means that it not true in all cases.

Q8 In $\triangle ADP$, $\alpha + \beta + \angle D = 180°$.   (interior angles in a triangle sum to 180°)

In $\triangle AQB$, $\alpha + \gamma + \angle B = 180°$.   (interior angles in a triangle sum to 180°)

Adding these: $2\alpha + \beta + \gamma + \angle D + \angle B = 360°$.

But, $\angle D + \angle B = 180°$.   (opposite angles in a cyclic quadrilateral sum to 180°)

Thus, $2\alpha + \beta + \gamma = 180° \Rightarrow \beta + \gamma = 180° - 2\alpha$.

If you can't make progress in a geometry question like Q8, try to write something.

Look for keywords, in this case 'cyclic quadrilateral'.

If you write a relevant fact, e.g. '$\angle A + \angle C = 180°$ since opposite angles in a cyclic quadrilateral sum to 180°' you'd be surprised at how many marks you would get. *Don't* leave a blank.

Q9 (a) (i)

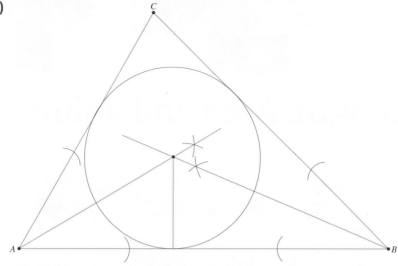

(ii) $r \approx 2 \cdot 5$ cm.

(b) Since the radius is $2\sqrt{5}$ cm, the diameter is $4\sqrt{5}$ cm. Note that the diameter here is the hypotenuse of a right-angled triangle since the angle in a semicircle is 90°.

By Pythagoras' theorem: $x^2 + (2x)^2 = \left(4\sqrt{5}\right)^2 \Rightarrow x^2 + 4x^2 = 80 \Rightarrow 5x^2 = 80$ $\Rightarrow x^2 = 16 \Rightarrow x = 4$ or $x = -4$. Since x is a distance, we take the positive solution only, $x = 4$ cm.

Q10

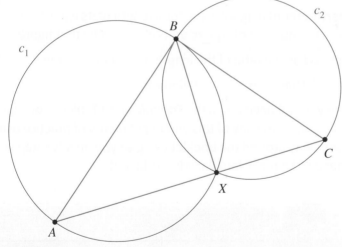

Join B to X and A to C.

In triangle ABX, $|\angle AXB| = 90°$, since it is an angle in a semicircle of c_1.

In triangle BXC, $|\angle BXC| = 90°$, since it is an angle in a semicircle of c_2.

$|\angle AXC| = |\angle AXB| + |\angle BXC| = 90° + 90° = 180°$.

Thus, since $\angle AXC$ is a straight angle, X is on the line AC.

4 Length, Area and Volume

Learning objectives

In this chapter you will learn to:

- Calculate the perimeter and area of plane figures, e.g. rectangles, squares, parallelograms, trapezia, discs, sectors of discs and figures made from combinations of these

- Draw nets and identify them with their corresponding solids

- Find the surface area and volume of cylinders, cones, spheres and combinations of these

- Use the trapezoidal rule.

Plane figures

The length of the **perimeter** of a figure is the total length of its exterior sides. The **area** of a figure is the number of square units enclosed by that figure.

The number π is defined as the ratio of the length of the circumference, l, of a circle to its diameter, d. That is, $\pi = \dfrac{l}{d}$ by definition.

Most of the formulae you will need are in the *Formulae and Tables* booklet. It's a very good idea to buy your own copy of this and to get plenty of practice using it. Being able to find your way around the booklet will give you an advantage in the examination. You need to be really familiar with its layout.

> **Top Tip**
>
> Every time you use a formula, write it out. This way you will learn it without trying. You will also get a very good sense of the context in which to use each formula. Follow these steps:
>
> - Identify the shape or shapes in a question. Highlight the quantity required, e.g. length, area or volume.
>
> - Write down the correct formula.

Point to note

The formulae for rectangles and squares are *not* included in the *Formulae and Tables* booklet. Make sure you know them well.

Area formulae

Note that P stands for the length of the perimeter and A stands for area.

Rectangle

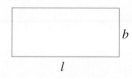

$P = 2(l + b)$, $A = lb$

Square

$P = 4l$, $A = l^2$

Triangle

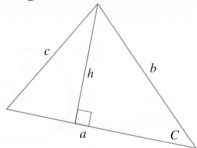

$P = a + b + c$,
$A = \dfrac{1}{2}ah$ or $A = \dfrac{1}{2}ab \sin C$

Parallelogram

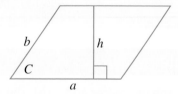

$P = 2(a + b)$, $A = ah$ or $A = ab \sin C$

Trapezium

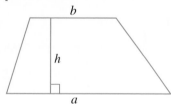

$A = \left(\dfrac{a + b}{2}\right)h$

Circle/disc

$d = 2r$, where d is the diameter and r is the radius of the circle

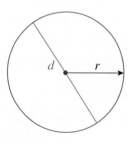

$l = 2\pi r$, where l is the length of the circumference

$A = \pi r^2$

Arc/sector

$l = 2\pi r\left(\dfrac{\theta}{360°}\right)$, where l is the length of the arc,

and θ is the angle subtended by the arc

$A = \pi r^2\left(\dfrac{\theta}{360°}\right)$, where A is the area of the sector

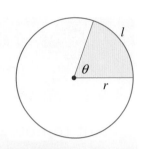

Point to note

θ is the Greek letter *theta*. Many words in English, e.g. thesaurus, theology, theory, theorem, are descended from a Greek word starting with *theta*. It is used to represent quantities that can be measured in degrees, e.g. angles or temperatures.

Note that $\dfrac{\theta}{360°}$ is simply the fraction of the circumference taken up by the arc, or the fraction of the total area taken up by the sector. For example, if $\theta = 90°$, then the fraction is $\dfrac{90°}{360°} = \dfrac{1}{4}$.

Example

Find **(a)** the perimeter and **(b)** the area of a piece of card in the shape of a rectangle and semicircle as in the diagram. Give your answers correct to one decimal place.

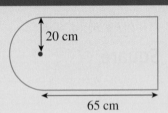

20 cm

65 cm

Solution

(a) $P = \pi r + 2l + b = \pi(20) + 2(65) + 40 = 232\cdot8$ cm.

(b) $A = \dfrac{1}{2}\pi r^2 + lb = \dfrac{1}{2}\pi(20)^2 + (65)(40) = 3228\cdot3$ cm^2.

Example

A student cut a sector of angle 55° from a circle of radius 4 cm when constructing a Pacman.
Calculate, correct to two decimal places:

(a) the area of the finished Pacman **(b)** its perimeter.

Solution

(a) $360° - 55° = 305°$

$A = \pi r^2\left(\dfrac{\theta}{360°}\right) = \pi(4)^2\left(\dfrac{305°}{360°}\right) = 42\cdot59$ cm^2.

(b) $P = 2\pi r\dfrac{\theta}{360°} + 2r = 2\pi(4)\left(\dfrac{305°}{360°}\right) + 2(4) = 29\cdot29$ cm.

Give a reason why each of the following statements is true.

(a) The area of a rectangle is given by $A = lb$.

(b) The area of a parallelogram is given by $A = ah$, where a is the length of the base and h is the perpendicular height.

(c) The area of a trapezium is given by $A = \left(\dfrac{a+b}{2}\right)h$, where a and b are the lengths of the two parallel sides and h is the perpendicular distance between them.

Solutions

(a) Consider a rectangle where $l = 3$ cm and $b = 2$ cm.

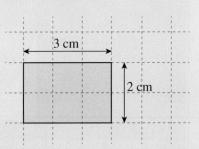

Its area is the number of square centimetres it encloses. There are two rows of three such squares enclosed in the diagram.

Its area is $A = 2 \times 3 = 6$ cm^2.

Thus multiplying length by breadth is just a way of counting the unit squares enclosed by the rectangle.

(b)

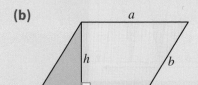 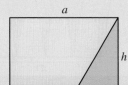

The above diagram of a parallelogram can be rearranged as a rectangle by moving the blue region.

From the rectangle formula, $A = lb = ah$.

(c) Consider the trapezium below.

When put together with a second, identical trapezium, a parallelogram is formed.

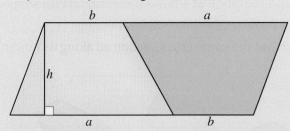

From the parallelogram formula, $A = \text{base} \times \text{height} = (a + b)h$.

This gives the area for two trapezia. Thus, divide by two to find the area of one trapezium: $A = \left(\dfrac{a+b}{2}\right)h$.

Two identical triangles can also be put together to form a parallelogram. Thus, the area of a triangle is given by $A = \frac{1}{2}ah$.

A circle can also be rearranged into something like a parallelogram.

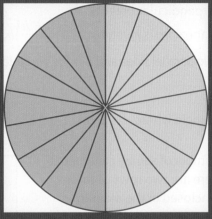

The above circle has been divided into 18 sectors.

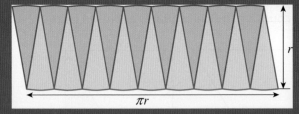

This approximates to a parallelogram of base πr (half the circumference) and height r.

Thus, A = base × height = πr^2.

Nets

A net is a two-dimensional representation of a three-dimensional (3D) shape. You need to know the nets for prisms, cylinders and cones.

A prism is a solid object which has the same cross-section all along its length. Here are some examples.

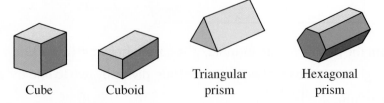

Cube   Cuboid   Triangular   Hexagonal
                              prism   prism

Another name for a cuboid is a rectangular prism.

Example

Draw an accurate net for the rectangular prism to the right.

7 cm

2 cm

3 cm

Solution

Draw (i) the base
  (ii) the sides
(iii) the front and back and
 (iv) don't forget the top!

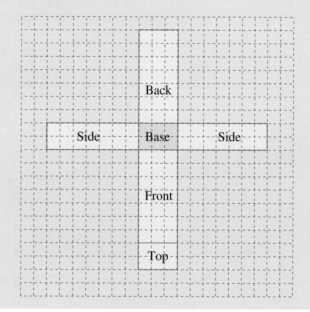

Back

Side   Base   Side

Front

Top

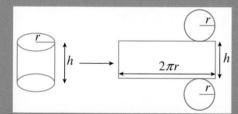
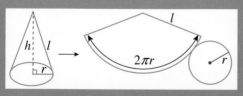

Surface area and volume formulae

Note that in these formulae A stands for surface area and V stands for volume.

Cube

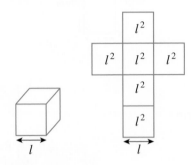

$V = l^3$ and, from the net of the cube, $A = 6l^2$

Cuboid

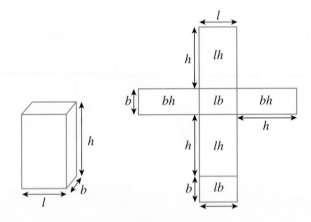

$V = lbh$ and, from the net of the cuboid, $A = 2(lb + lh + bh)$.

Cylinder

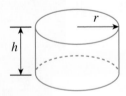

Curved surface area: $CSA = 2\pi rh$

Total surface area: $A = 2\pi r^2 + 2\pi rh = 2\pi r(r + h)$

$V = \pi r^2 h$

Note that the volume is given by the area of the circular cross-section multiplied by the height.

Cone

Curved surface area: $CSA = \pi r l$

Total surface area: $A = \pi r l + \pi r^2 = \pi r (l + r)$

$V = \dfrac{1}{3}\pi r^2 h$

The relation $r^2 + h^2 = l^2$ is frequently required to find one of the three variables given the other two.

Sphere

$A = 4\pi r^2$

$V = \dfrac{4}{3}\pi r^3$

Example

A sphere has a radius of length 5 cm.

(a) Calculate its volume, correct to one decimal place.

(b) Calculate the volume of the smallest rectangular box that contains the sphere.

(c) Jonas says that the box is half empty. Is he correct? Justify your answer.

(d) What is the minimum amount of wrapping paper required to wrap the box?

Solution

(a) $V = \dfrac{4}{3}\pi r^3 = \dfrac{4}{3}\pi(5)^3 = 523.6 \text{ cm}^3$

(b) The smallest box will be a cube with a length equal to the diameter of the sphere, $l = d = 2r = 10$ cm.

$V = (10)^3 = 1000 \text{ cm}^3$

(c) Volume not occupied $= 1000 - 523.6 = 476.4 \text{ cm}^3$

To express this as a percentage, make a fraction then multiply it by 100.

$\dfrac{476.4}{1000} \times 100 = 48\% < 50\%$, correct to the nearest integer. Jonas is not correct,

but he's not far off.

(d) $A = 6l^2 = 6(10)^2 = 600 \text{ cm}^2$

The trapezoidal rule

The lengths y_1, y_2, etc. are called **offsets** or **ordinates**. The length h is the horizontal gap between the offsets.

The trapezoidal rule gives an estimate for the area of the irregular shape shown. It is an estimate as it is the sum of the areas of the trapezia formed by joining consecutive ordinates.

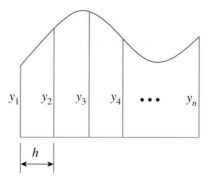

The formula for this sum can be rearranged as:

$$A \approx \frac{h}{2}\left[y_1 + y_n + 2(y_2 + y_3 + y_4 + \ldots + y_{n-1})\right]$$

or

$$A \approx \frac{h}{2}[\text{first + last + twice the rest}].$$

Example

The graph shows the instantaneous speed of a car over a time of 6 seconds.

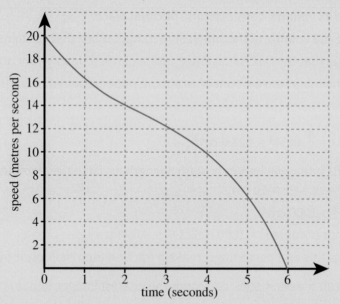

(a) The speed at x seconds is given by the function $f(x) = -\dfrac{x^3}{6} + \dfrac{5x^2}{4} - \dfrac{29x}{6} + 20.$

Copy and complete the table, giving your values for $f(x)$ correct to two decimal places.

x	0	1	2	3	4	5	6
Speed $= f(x)$							

(b) Using the trapezoidal rule, estimate the distance travelled over the 6 seconds.

(c) The actual distance travelled was 69 m. Calculate the percentage error in your estimate in part (b). Give your answer correct to one significant figure.

(d) Calculate the average speed of the car over the 6 seconds. Give your answer in km/h.

Solution

(a) $x = 0 \Rightarrow f(0) = -\dfrac{(0)^3}{6} + \dfrac{5(0)^2}{4} - \dfrac{29(0)}{6} + 20 = 20$ m/s

$x = 1 \Rightarrow f(1) = -\dfrac{(1)^3}{6} + \dfrac{5(1)^2}{4} - \dfrac{29(1)}{6} + 20 = 16 \cdot 25$ m/s

$x = 2 \Rightarrow f(2) = -\dfrac{(2)^3}{6} + \dfrac{5(2)^2}{4} - \dfrac{29(2)}{6} + 20 = 14$ m/s

$x = 3 \Rightarrow f(3) = -\dfrac{(3)^3}{6} + \dfrac{5(3)^2}{4} - \dfrac{29(3)}{6} + 20 = 12 \cdot 25$ m/s

$x = 4 \Rightarrow f(4) = -\dfrac{(4)^3}{6} + \dfrac{5(4)^2}{4} - \dfrac{29(4)}{6} + 20 = 10$ m/s

$x = 5 \Rightarrow f(5) = -\dfrac{(5)^3}{6} + \dfrac{5(5)^2}{4} - \dfrac{29(5)}{6} + 20 = 6 \cdot 25$ m/s

$x = 6 \Rightarrow f(6) = -\dfrac{(6)^3}{6} + \dfrac{5(6)^2}{4} - \dfrac{29(6)}{6} + 20 = 0$ m/s

x	0	1	2	3	4	5	6
Speed $= f(x)$	20	16.25	14	12.25	10	6.25	0

(b) The distance travelled is given by the area under a speed-time graph. The gap between x-values is $h = 1$.

$d = A \approx \dfrac{h}{2}[\text{first + last + twice the rest}]$

$= \dfrac{1}{2}[20 + 0 + 2(16 \cdot 25 + 14 + 12 \cdot 25 + 10 + 6 \cdot 25)] = 68 \cdot 75$ m

(c) Percentage error $= \dfrac{\text{error}}{\text{true value}} \times 100 = \dfrac{(69 - 68 \cdot 75)}{69} \times 100 = 0 \cdot 4\%.$

(d) Average speed $= \dfrac{\text{distance}}{\text{time}} = \dfrac{69}{6} = 11 \cdot 5$ m/s.

11·5 metres every second $\Rightarrow 11 \cdot 5 \times 60 \times 60$ metres every hour

$\Rightarrow \dfrac{11 \cdot 5 \times 60 \times 60}{1000} = 41 \cdot 4$ km/h.

Exercise A

Q1 Find **(i)** the perimeter **(ii)** the area of each of the following plane figures.

Each square on the grid can be taken to be 1 cm in length.

(a)

(d)

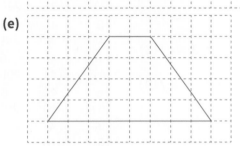

(b)

(e)

(c)

Q2 Find **(i)** the perimeter **(ii)** the area of each of the following plane figures.

O is the centre of each figure.

Each square on the grid can be taken to be 1 cm in length.

Give your answers correct to one decimal place.

(a)

O

(b)

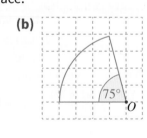

75°

O

Q3 The diagram shows a field.
(Not drawn accurately to scale.)

(a) Work out the area of the field.

(b) 1 acre = 4047 square metres.

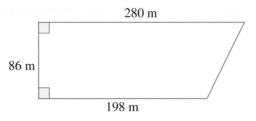

280 m

86 m

198 m

A farmer keeps cows in the field. He is allowed 7 cows per acre. Work out the maximum number of cows he is allowed to put in the field.

Q4 This shape is made from identical quarter circles.
Work out the perimeter of the shape. Give your answer correct to four significant figures.

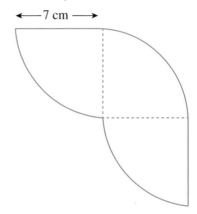

←—7 cm —→

Q5 The cylindrical tank is one-quarter full of oil.

The radius of the base of the cylinder is 90 cm.
The height of the cylinder is 200 cm.

(a) Work out the number of litres of oil in the tank.
Give your answer correct to four significant figures.

(b) If the price of oil is €0·73 per litre, calculate the cost of filling the tank from its current level.

Q6 In the trapezium, a = 8·3 m, b = 6·5 m and h = 3·2 m.

The trapezium is the cross-section of a tunnel.
The tunnel is 200 metres long.

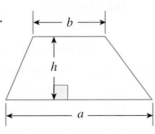

←— b —→

h

a

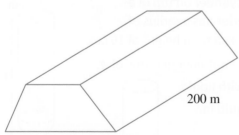

200 m

Work out the volume of the tunnel.

Q7 This shape is made by cutting out an equilateral triangle from a square.

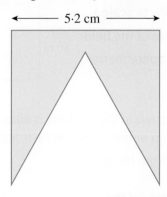

← 5·2 cm →

Two of these shapes are then put together to make a new shape as shown below.

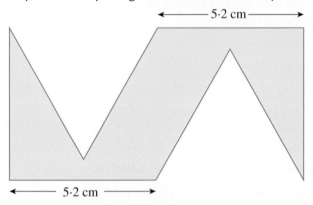

← 5·2 cm →

← 5·2 cm →

Work out the perimeter of this new shape.

Q8 The diameter of a cylindrical can is 8·6 cm.

(a) Calculate the circumference of the circular base. Give your answer correct to the nearest centimetre.

(b) The label for the can is just long enough to go around the can. The ends of the label do not overlap. The height of the label is 4 cm.

Use your answer to part (a) to find the area of the label.

Q9 A container is in the shape of a cylinder on top of a hemisphere as shown. The cylinder has a radius of length 3 cm and the container has a total height of 15 cm.

(a) Calculate the volume of the container in terms of π.

(b) The container is half filled with liquid.

Calculate x, the height of liquid in the container.

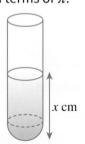

x cm

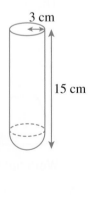

3 cm

15 cm

Q10

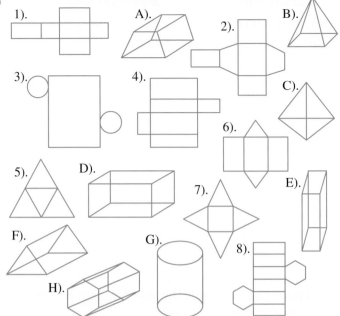

Copy and complete the table below to match each 3D shape with its net.

3D Shape	A	B	C	D	E	F	G	H
Net								

Q11 A toy consists of a cone which fits exactly on top of a hemisphere. The common radius is 5 cm and the slant height of the cone is 13 cm.

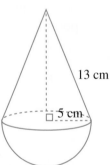

13 cm

5 cm

(a) Find the height of the cone.

(b) Find the total surface area of the toy. Give your answer correct to three significant figures.

(c) Calculate the volume of the toy in terms of π.

Q12 The sketch shows a lake bounded on one side by a straight dam.

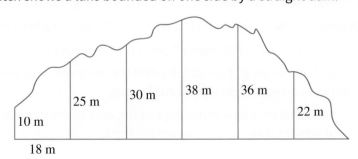

25 m   30 m   38 m   36 m

22 m

10 m

18 m

At equal intervals of 18 m along the dam, perpendicular measurements are made to the opposite bank, as shown on the sketch.

(a) Use the trapezoidal rule to estimate the area of the lake.

(b) If the lake contains 15 000 m³ of water, calculate the average depth of water in the lake, correct to the nearest metre.

Q13

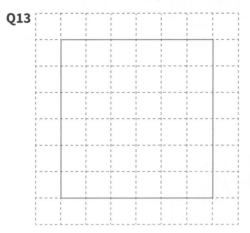

How many different ways can you divide the above square into two parts of equal area? Use diagrams to show your work.

Exercise B

Q1 A 13 m wire connects two poles of different length. The height of the taller pole is equal to the perpendicular distance between the centres of the two poles.

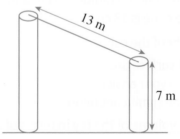

13 m

7 m

If the height of the shorter pole is 7 m, find the height of the taller pole.

Q2 A rectangular sheet of metal has a length of 21 cm and a breadth of 14 cm.

(a) How many discs of diameter 7 cm can be cut from this sheet?

(b) Calculate the area of metal left when the discs are removed. Give your answer correct to two significant figures.

(c) Express this area as a percentage of the area of the original sheet. Give your answer correct to the nearest integer.

Q3 Which of the following are nets of a cube?

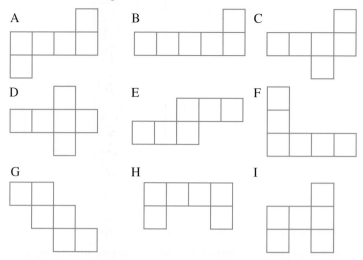

A B C

D E F

G H I

Q4 The box for an individual mobile phone is 13 cm long, 8 cm wide, and 6 cm high, as shown.

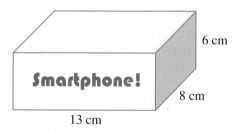

6 cm

Smartphone!

8 cm

13 cm

(a) Find the volume of an individual mobile phone box.

These individual mobile phone boxes will be shipped in a large rectangular box. Below are diagrams of the nets of two large boxes that could be used, Box **A** and Box **B**.

Box A

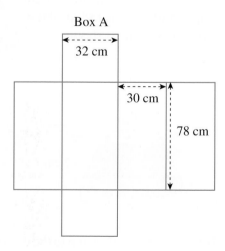

32 cm

30 cm

78 cm

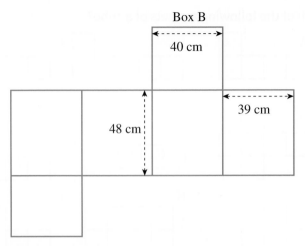

Box B

40 cm

39 cm

48 cm

(b) Show that Box **A** and Box **B** have the same volume.

(c) What is the largest number of individual mobile phone boxes that will fit in each large box?

(d) Find the surface area of each large box.

(e) The large boxes are made from cardboard. The cardboard costs €0·67 per m². The cardboard just covers the net of a box. Find the cost of the box that uses the least amount of cardboard.

(f) On average, 140 large boxes are produced each month. Find the saving, per annum, if you choose to make the box that uses the least amount of cardboard.

Q5 A solid cone has a radius of 6 cm and a height of 14 cm, as shown.

(a) Find the volume of the cone. Give your answer in terms of π.

The shape shown below is a *frustum*. This is made by cutting the cone horizontally at a height of 7 cm, and removing the upper portion. The radius of the circular top of the frustum is 3 cm, as shown in the diagram.

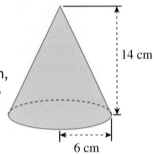

14 cm

6 cm

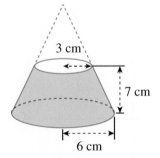

3 cm

7 cm

6 cm

(b) Find the ratio of the volume of the frustum to the volume of the original cone.

Q6 (a) Give two examples of a rectangle where the values for its perimeter and area are equal.

(b) Joelle and Cian have enough money to buy either 3 twelve inch pizzas or 2 eighteen inch pizzas.

Cian says that it doesn't matter. Joelle disagrees, saying that it is better to buy the two eighteen inch pizzas. Who is right? Give a reason for your answer.

(c) π is an irrational number. Anna says that the circumference of any circle must also be irrational since it is equal to $2\pi r$. Jakub disagrees, saying that he can think of a circle whose circumference is a natural number. Who is right? Give a reason for your answer.

(d) Megan has to calculate the area of a rectangle. She is worried that if she mixes up the length and the breadth she will get the answer wrong. Should she worry? Justify your answer.

Q7 The diagram shows a cuboid. The length is $(5x + 1)$ cm. The width is $(2x + 3)$ cm. The height is x cm.

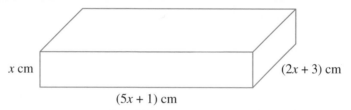

The length is 7 cm longer than the width.

(a) Calculate the volume of the cuboid.

(b) Calculate the total surface area of the cuboid.

Q8 A steelworks buys steel in the form of solid cylindrical rods of radius 10 centimetres and length 3 metres. The steel rods are melted to produce solid spherical ball-bearings. No steel is wasted in the process.

(a) Find the volume of steel in one cylindrical rod, in terms of π.

(b) The radius of a ball-bearing is 2 cm. How many such ball-bearings are made from one steel rod?

(c) The steelworks gets an order for a new, smaller ball-bearing. One steel rod makes 225 000 of these new ball-bearings. Find the radius of the new ball-bearings. Give your answer correct to three significant figures.

Q9 The diagram below shows a pencil. It is made up of a cylinder and a cone.

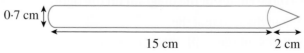

The cylinder has a diameter of 0·7 cm and a height of 15 cm. The cone has a diameter of 0·7 cm and a height of 2 cm.

(a) Calculate the volume of the pencil, giving your answer correct to three significant figures.

The diagram shows 12 of these pencils, which just fit into a box.

(b) Calculate the volume of the box.

(c) Calculate the percentage of the volume of the box which is not occupied by the pencils, correct to one decimal place.

Q10 The sketch shows a piece of land.

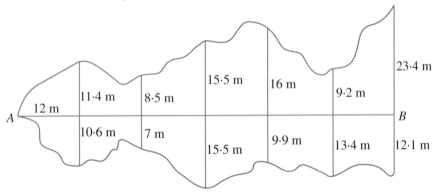

At equal intervals of 12 m along [AB], perpendicular measurements are made to the boundary, as shown on the sketch.

(a) Use the trapezoidal rule to estimate the area of the piece of land.

(b) The land is valued at €280 000 per hectare. Find the value of the piece of land. Note: 1 hectare = 10 000 m².

Q11 (a) In 225 BC, the Greek mathematician Archimedes published *On the Sphere and the Cylinder*. In it, he derived the surface area and volume formulae for the sphere and cylinder.

He was especially pleased with one result.

Take a sphere. Then take the smallest cylinder into which the sphere will fit. Archimedes proved that the volume of the sphere is exactly $\frac{2}{3}$ of the volume of the containing cylinder.

Verify his discovery, using your choice of dimensions for the cylinder and the sphere.

(b) Make three copies of the diagram on the right.

Complete them so that the trapezoidal rule gives **(i)** the exact area **(ii)** an underestimate of the area and **(iii)** an overestimate of the area for the finished diagram.

Q12 Investigate whether the following statements are true or not:

    (a) Two rectangles that have the same perimeter always have the same area.

    (b) If the area of a rectangle is enlarged its perimeter will also always get longer.

    (c) For each rectangle there is another rectangle that has the same area but a longer perimeter.

Exercise C

Q1

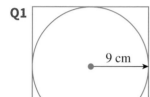

    (a) A circle is inscribed in a square as shown. The radius of the circle is 9 cm.

        (i) Find the perimeter of the square.

        (ii) Calculate the area of the square.

    (b) The diagram shows a sketch of a field $ABCD$ that has one uneven edge. At equal intervals of 5 m along $[BC]$, perpendicular measurements are made to the uneven edge, as shown on the sketch.

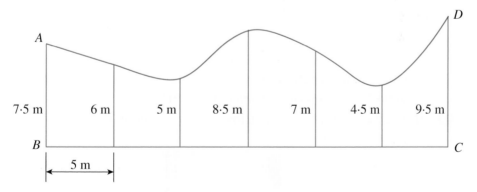

        (i) Use the trapezoidal rule to estimate the area of the field.

        (ii) The actual area of the field is 200 m². Find the percentage error in the estimate.

(c) The diameter of a solid metal sphere is 9 cm.

    (i) Find the volume of the sphere in terms of π.

The sphere is melted down. All of the metal is used to make a solid shape which consists of a cone on top of a cylinder, as shown in the diagram.

The cone and the cylinder both have height 8 cm.

The cylinder and the base of the cone both have radius r cm.

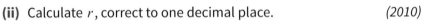

8 cm

r cm

8 cm

    (ii) Calculate r, correct to one decimal place.   *(2010)*

Q2 (a) Find the volume of a cylinder of radius 6 mm and height 20 mm. Give your answer in two forms, as follows: **(i)** in terms of π, and   **(ii)** correct to two decimal places.

    (b) A solid rectangular block measures 60 mm × 35 mm × 20 mm.

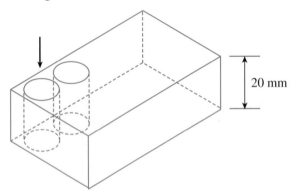

20 mm

Cylindrical holes of radius 6 mm are drilled, one at a time, through the block, in the direction shown. After how many holes will more than half of the original block have been removed?   *(2011)*

Q3 (a) The diagram shows a circle inscribed in a square. The area of the square is 16 cm².

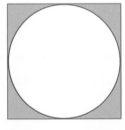

    (i) Find the radius length of the circle.

    (ii) Find the area of the shaded region, in cm², correct to one decimal place.

(b) A solid wax candle is in the shape of a cylinder with a cone on top, as shown in the diagram.

The diameter of the base of the cylinder is 3 cm and the height of the cylinder is 8 cm.

The volume of the wax in the candle is 21π cm^3.

    (i) Find the height of the candle.

    (ii) Nine of these candles fit into a rectangular box. The base of the box is a square. Find the volume of the smallest rectangular box that the candles will fit into.

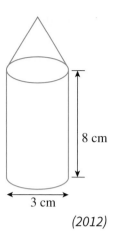

8 cm

3 cm

(2012)

Q4 In order to estimate the area of the irregular shape shown below, a horizontal line was drawn across the widest part of the shape and five offsets (perpendicular lines) were drawn at equal intervals along this line.

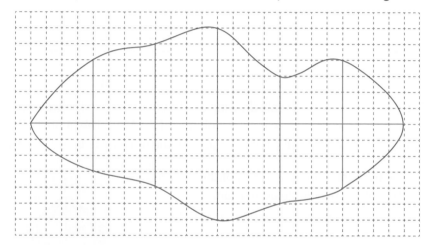

    (a) Find the lengths of the horizontal line and the offsets, taking each grid unit as 5 mm, and record the lengths on the diagram.

    (b) Use the trapezoidal rule to estimate the area of the shape.   *(2012)*

Q5 A solid cylinder has a radius of 10 mm and a height of 45 mm.

    (a) Draw a sketch of the net of the surface of the cylinder and write its dimensions on the sketch.

    (b) Calculate the volume of the cylinder. Give your answer in terms of π.

    (c) A sphere has the same volume as the cylinder. Find the surface area of the sphere. Give your answer in terms of π.   *(2013)*

Q6 The diagram below shows a shape with two straight edges and one irregular edge. By dividing the edge [AB] into five equal intervals, use the trapezoidal rule to estimate the area of the shape.

Record your constructions and measurements on the diagram. Give your answer correct to the nearest cm².

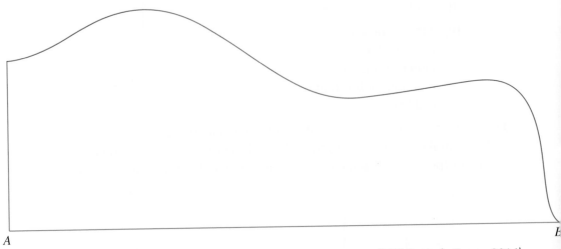

A

B

(SEC Sample Paper 2014)

Q7 The diagram below is a scale drawing of a hopper tank used to store grain. An estimate is needed of the capacity (volume) of the tank. The figure of the man standing beside the tank allows the scale of the drawing to be estimated.

(a) Give an estimate, in metres, of the height of an average adult man.

(b) Using your answer to part (a), estimate the dimensions of the hopper tank.

(c) Taking the tank to be a cylinder with a cone above and below, find an estimate for the capacity of the tank, in cubic metres.

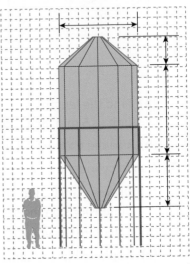

(SEC Sample Paper 2014)

Q8 (a)

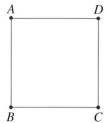

The square $ABCD$ has an area of 81 cm^2. Find $|AD|$.

(b) A sector of a circle, centre B and radius $|BC|$, is drawn inside $ABCD$ as shown by the shaded region.

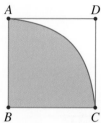

(i) Find the area of the sector, correct to one decimal place.

A second sector of a circle, centre D and radius $|DA|$, is drawn.

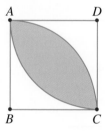

(ii) Find the area of the shaded region (the overlap of the two sectors), correct to one decimal place.

(c) The point P is on the arc of the sector DAC, as shown.

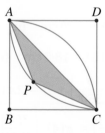

The triangle APC is isosceles. Find the area of the triangle APC, correct to one decimal place. *(2014)*

Solutions to Exercise A

Q1 (a) (i) $P = 4l = 4(3) = 12$ cm   **(ii)** $A = l^2 = (3)^2 = 9$ cm^2

(b) (i) $P = 2(l + b) = 2(5 + 4) = 18$ cm   **(ii)** $A = lb = (5)(4) = 20$ cm^2

(c) (i) $P = a + b + c = 4 + 3 + 5 = 12$ cm

Note that from Pythagoras' theorem the longest side is given by $\sqrt{3^2 + 4^2} = 5$ cm.

(ii) $A = \dfrac{1}{2}ah = \dfrac{1}{2}(4)(3) = 6$ cm^2

Do yourself a favour and learn these Pythagorean triples:

- 3, 4 and 5
- 5, 12 and 13
- 8, 15 and 17.

They frequently appear in examination questions.

(d)

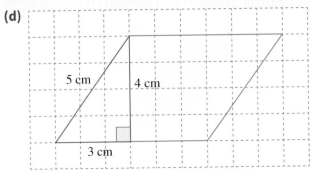

5 cm   4 cm

3 cm

(i) $P = 2(a + b) = 2(5 + 6) = 22$ cm (Those 3-4-5 triangles get everywhere!)   **(ii)** $A = ah = (6)(4) = 24$ cm^2

(e) (i) $P = 8 + 5 + 2 + 5 = 20$ cm   **(ii)** $A = \left(\dfrac{a + b}{2}\right)h = \left(\dfrac{8 + 2}{2}\right)(4) = 20$ cm^2

Q2 (a) (i) $l = 2\pi r = 2\pi(3) = 18.8$ cm   **(ii)** $A = \pi r^2 = \pi(3)^2 = 28.3$ cm^2

(b) (i) $P = l = 2\pi r\left(\dfrac{\theta}{360°}\right) + 2r = 2\pi(4)\left(\dfrac{75°}{360°}\right) + 2(4) = 13.2$ cm

(ii) $A = \pi r^2\left(\dfrac{\theta}{360°}\right) = \pi(4)^2\left(\dfrac{75°}{360°}\right) = 10.5$ cm^2

Q3 (a) $A = \left(\dfrac{a + b}{2}\right)h = \left(\dfrac{198 + 280}{2}\right)(86) = 20\,544$ m^2

(b) First find the number of acres: $20\,544 \div 4047 = 5.08$ acres.

At 7 cows on each complete acre, this gives $5 \times 7 = 35$ cows.

Q4 $P = \frac{3}{4}(2\pi r) + 2r = \frac{3}{4}(2\pi(7)) + 2(7) = 46{\cdot}99$ cm

Q5 (a) The volume of the oil is $V = \frac{1}{4}\pi r^2 h$

$$= \frac{1}{4}\pi(90)^2(200) = 1272345 \approx 1272000 \text{ cm}^3.$$

Given $1000 \text{ cm}^3 = 1$ litre $\Rightarrow 1272000 \div 1000 = 1272$ litres.

(b) One quarter of a tank of oil is 1272 litres. The tank requires three times this amount to be added to fill it.

This will cost $3 \times 1272 \times 0{\cdot}73 = €2785{\cdot}68$.

Q6 First get the area of the trapezium: $A = \left(\frac{a+b}{2}\right)h = \left(\frac{8{\cdot}3+6{\cdot}5}{2}\right)(3{\cdot}2) = 23{\cdot}68 \text{ m}^2$.

The volume, V, of a prism of uniform cross-section is given by the product of the area of cross-section by the length of the prism.

$V = 23{\cdot}68 \times 200 = 4736 \text{ m}^3$

Q7 All the sides are equal in length and there are 8 sides.

Thus $P = 8l = 8(5{\cdot}2) = 41{\cdot}6$ cm.

Q8 (a) $\frac{C}{d} = \pi$ is the definition of π. Thus $C = \pi d = \pi(8{\cdot}6) = 27$ cm.

(b) $A = lb = (27)(4) = 108 \text{ cm}^2$.

Q9 (a) Note that the height of the cylinder is $15 - 3 = 12$ cm.

$V = V_{\text{cylinder}} + V_{\text{hemisphere}} = \pi r^2 h + \frac{2}{3}\pi r^3 = \pi(3)^2(12) + \frac{2}{3}\pi(3)^3 = 126\pi \text{ cm}^3.$

(b) Let h be the height of the cylindrical part of the liquid. Don't forget that the total height will be $h + 3$ cm.

$\pi r^2 h + \frac{2}{3}\pi r^3 = \pi(3)^2 h + \frac{2}{3}\pi(3)^3 = \frac{126\pi}{2} = 63\pi$

$\Rightarrow 9\not{\pi}h + 18\not{\pi} = 63\not{\pi} \Rightarrow 9h = 63 - 18 = 45 \Rightarrow h = 45 \div 9 = 5$ cm.

Thus, the height of the liquid is $h + 3 = 5 + 3 = 8$ cm.

Point to note

Whenever you see 'in terms of π' in a question, leave π as a letter.

As you see in question 9, this allows you to divide both sides of the equation by π, which makes for easier calculations.

Q10

3D Shape	A	B	C	D	E	F	G	H
Net	2	7	5	1	4	6	3	8

Q11 (a) If you've learned the Pythagorean triples suggested above, you may have spotted that $h = 12$ cm. It's still a good idea to show the working out.

$$h^2 + 5^2 = 13^2 \Rightarrow h = \sqrt{13^2 - 5^2} = 12 \text{ cm}$$

(b) A = curved surface area of cone and hemisphere

$$\Rightarrow A = \pi rl + 2\pi r^2 = \pi(5)(13) + 2\pi(5)^2 = 361 \text{ cm}^2$$

(c) $V = \dfrac{1}{3}\pi r^2 h + \dfrac{2}{3}\pi r^3 = \dfrac{1}{3}\pi(5)^2(12) + \dfrac{2}{3}\pi(5)^3 = 183\dfrac{1}{3}\pi \text{ cm}^3$

Q12 (a) $A \approx \dfrac{h}{2}[\text{first} + \text{last} + \text{twice the rest}] = \dfrac{18}{2}[10 + 0 + 2(25 + 30 + 38 + 36 + 22)]$

$$= 2808 \text{ m}^2$$

(b) The volume is equal to the surface area multiplied by the average depth.

$$Ad = V \Rightarrow d = V \div A = 15\,000 \div 2808 = 5 \text{ m to the nearest metre.}$$

Q13

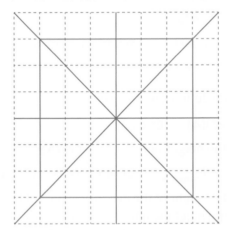

Any of the four axes of symmetry will divide the square into two regions of equal area.

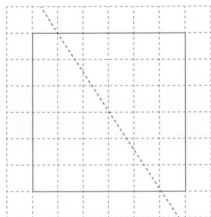

A non-diagonal line such as the one above gives another solution to the problem.

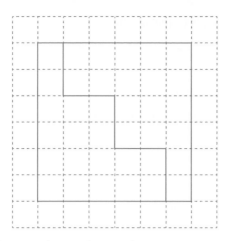

A zig-zag such as the one above also works.

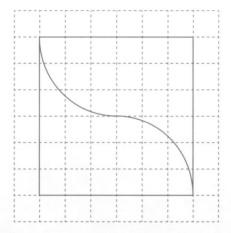

In fact, even curves will work. There are an infinite number of solutions.

Solutions to Exercise B

Q1

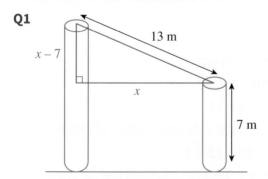

If you have learned your Pythagorean triples, you might see that the
5-12-13 triangle is worth checking. It works. $x = 12$ m.

Another approach is to use algebra.

$(x - 7)^2 + x^2 = 13^2 \Rightarrow x^2 - 14x + 49 + x^2 = 169 \Rightarrow 2x^2 - 14x - 120 = 0$

$\Rightarrow x^2 - 7x - 60 = 0 \Rightarrow (x + 5)(x - 12) = 0 \Rightarrow x = -5$ or $x = 12$. Since x must be positive, we choose the solution $x = 12$ m.

Q2 (a) Drawing a diagram may help here.

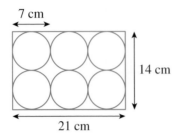

7 cm

14 cm

21 cm

Two rows of three discs, i.e. 6 discs, can be cut from the sheet.

(b) A = area left = area of sheet − area of six discs

$\Rightarrow A = lb - 6\pi r^2 = (21)(14) - 6\pi(3 \cdot 5^2) = 63$ cm²

(c) $\dfrac{63}{(14)(21)} \times 100 = 21\%$

> ## Top Tip
>
> Always check you substitute the radius and *not* the diameter into a formula. In Q2 (b) such a mistake would give a negative answer for the area left.
>
> Figuring out why this has happened could be stressful while taking up valuable time.

Q3 Only nets A, C, D, E and G are nets of a cube.

If you can't see why, draw the nets on squared paper, cut them out and see which ones can be folded into cubes.

Q4 (a) $V = 13 \times 8 \times 6 = 624$ cm³

(b) Box **A**: $V = lbh = (32)(30)(78) = 74\,880$ cm³

Box **B**: $V = lbh = (48)(40)(39) = 74\,880$ cm³

(c) Box **A**: $32 \div 8 = 4, 30 \div 6 = 5, 78 \div 13 = 6$

Thus Box **A** can hold $4 \times 5 \times 6 = 120$ individual mobile phone boxes.

Box **B**: $48 \div 6 = 8, 40 \div 8 = 5, 39 \div 13 = 3$

Thus Box **B** can also hold $8 \times 5 \times 3 = 120$ individual mobile phone boxes.

(d) Box **A**: $A = 2(32 \times 30 + 32 \times 78 + 30 \times 78) = 11\,592$ cm²

Box **B**: $A = 2(48 \times 40 + 48 \times 39 + 40 \times 39) = 10\,704$ cm²

(e) Box **B** uses less cardboard.

Note the mixture of units: cm² and m².

$100 \text{ cm} = 1 \text{ m} \Rightarrow 100^2 \text{ cm}^2 = 1 \text{ m}^2$.

The cost of box **B** is: $\dfrac{10\,704}{100^2} \times 0{\cdot}67 = €0{\cdot}72$ (correct to the nearest cent)

(f) First work out the cost of box **A**: $\dfrac{11\,592}{100^2} \times 0{\cdot}67 = €0{\cdot}78$

This gives a saving of €0·78 − €0·72 = €0·06 per box, of €0·06 × 140 per month and €0·06 × 140 × 12 = €100·80 per annum.

Q5 (a) $V = \dfrac{1}{3}\pi r^2 h = \dfrac{1}{3}\pi(6)^2(14) = 168\pi \text{ cm}^3$

(b) The volume of the cone removed is $\dfrac{1}{3}\pi(3)^2(7) = 21\pi$.

Thus the volume of the frustum is $168\pi - 21\pi = 147\pi$.

$\dfrac{V_{\text{frustum}}}{V_{\text{cone}}} = \dfrac{147\pi}{168\pi} = \dfrac{7}{8}$ which is a ratio of 7 : 8.

Q6 (a) **(i)** A rectangle of length 6 cm and breadth 3 cm.

$P = 2(l + b) = 2(6 + 3) = 18 \text{ cm}$ and $A = lb = (6)(3) = 18 \text{ cm}^2$

(ii) A rectangle of length 4 cm and breadth 4 cm.

$P = 2(l + b) = 2(4 + 4) = 16 \text{ cm}$ and $A = lb = (4)(4) = 16 \text{ cm}^2$

Point to note

A rectangle is defined (on this syllabus) as a quadrilateral where each interior angle is a right angle. Under this definition, every square is also a rectangle.

(b) Assuming the pizzas are all the same thickness, then the amount of pizza will be proportional to the total area. 3 twelve inch pizzas have a total area of $3\pi r^2 = 3\pi(6)^2 = 108\pi$ square inches. 2 eighteen inch pizzas have a total area of $2\pi r^2 = 2\pi(9)^2 = 162\pi$ square inches. So Joelle is right. Perhaps Cian was thinking that they would be the same since 3 × 12 = 2 × 18 = 36, but that's not relevant here. He's just plain wrong.

(c) Jakub is right. For example, a circle of radius $\dfrac{1}{2\pi}$ cm has a circumference of $C = 2\pi r = 2\pi\left(\dfrac{1}{2\pi}\right) = 1$ cm.

(d) Megan should not worry. Calculating the area of a rectangle involves multiplying two numbers. Since multiplication is commutative the answer will be the same no matter which of the two she calls the length.

People often call the longest side of a rectangle the length, but the observation of this custom does not affect the calculation of area.

Q7 (a) If the length is 7 cm longer than the width, then

$(5x + 1) = (2x + 3) + 7 \Rightarrow 5x + 1 = 2x + 10 \Rightarrow 3x = 9 \Rightarrow x = 3$ cm.

Thus, the length is $5(3) + 1 = 16$ cm, the width is $2(3) + 3 = 9$ cm and the height is $x = 3$ cm.

Thus the volume is $V = lbh = (16)(9)(3) = 432$ cm³.

(b) $A = 2(lb + lh + bh) = 2((16)(9) + (16)(3) + (9)(3)) = 438$ cm²

Q8 Notice the mixture of units, 10 cm and 3 m. Change the 3 m to $3 \times 100 = 300$ cm.

(a) $V = \pi r^2 h = \pi(10)^2(300) = 30\,000\pi$ cm³

(b) The volume of one ball-bearing is $V = \dfrac{4}{3}\pi r^3 = \dfrac{4}{3}\pi(2)^3 = \dfrac{32\pi}{3}$ cm³.

The number of ball-bearings each rod can make is

$30\,000\,\pi \div \dfrac{32\pi}{3} = 2812{\cdot}5 \approx 2812$.

(c) $\dfrac{4}{3}\cancel{\pi}r^3 = \dfrac{30\,000\,\cancel{\pi}}{225\,000} \Rightarrow r^3 = \dfrac{30\,000}{225\,000} \times \dfrac{3}{4} \Rightarrow r = \sqrt[3]{\dfrac{30\,000}{225\,000} \times \dfrac{3}{4}} = 0{\cdot}464$ cm

Q9 (a) $r = \dfrac{d}{2} = \dfrac{0{\cdot}7}{2} = 0{\cdot}35$ cm

$V = V_{cylinder} + V_{cone} = \pi r^2 h + \dfrac{1}{3}\pi r^2 h$

$\Rightarrow V = \pi(0{\cdot}35)^2(15) + \dfrac{1}{3}\pi(0{\cdot}35)^2(2) = 6{\cdot}03$ cm³

(b) $V = lbh = (6 \times 0{\cdot}7)(2 \times 0{\cdot}7)(15 + 2) = 99{\cdot}96$ cm³

(c) $\dfrac{(99{\cdot}96 - 12 \times 6{\cdot}03)}{99{\cdot}96} \times 100 = 27{\cdot}6\%$.

Q10 (a) $A \approx \dfrac{h}{2}[\text{first} + \text{last} + \text{twice the rest}]$

$= \dfrac{12}{2}[0 + 35{\cdot}5 + 2(22 + 15{\cdot}5 + 31 + 25{\cdot}9 + 22{\cdot}6)] = 1617$ m².

(b) Value $= \dfrac{1617}{10\,000} \times €280\,000 = €45\,276$

Q11 (a) Since you can take any dimensions, you might as well choose a sphere of radius 3 cm. That way, you will avoid fractions.

The cylinder has the same radius, but the height will have to be the same as the diameter, 6 cm.

$\dfrac{V_{sphere}}{V_{cylinder}} = \dfrac{\dfrac{4}{3}\pi r^3}{\pi r^2 h} = \dfrac{\dfrac{4}{3}\pi(3)^3}{\pi(3)^2(6)} = \dfrac{36\cancel{\pi}}{54\cancel{\pi}} = \dfrac{2}{3}$

(b) (i)

By joining the offsets with straight lines you make six trapezia. The trapezoidal rule calculates the sum of their areas exactly.

(ii)

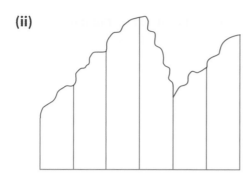

Drawing outside the lines shown in part (i) gives a figure with a greater area than diagram (i). Thus, the trapezoidal rule will give an underestimate for this figure.

(iii)

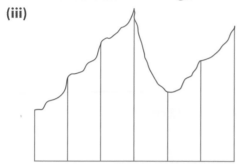

Drawing inside the lines in part (i) gives a figure with a smaller area than diagram (i). Thus, the trapezoidal rule will give an overestimate for this figure.

Q12 (a) This is not true. A rectangle of length 8 cm and breadth 4 cm has a perimeter of 24 cm and an area of 32 cm². A rectangle of length 10 cm and breadth 2 cm also has a perimeter of 24 cm but its area is 20 cm².

(b) This is true. Enlarging the area by a factor of k^2 enlarges the perimeter by a factor of k, $k > 1$. (See Chapter 7 for more on enlargements.)

(c) This is true. Consider the rectangle below.

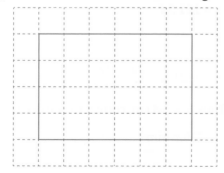

It has an area of 24 cm² and a perimeter of 20 cm. Cut it in half as shown and reassemble the two parts as a new rectangle.

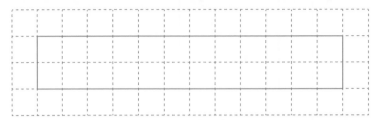

The new rectangle has an area of 24 cm², as before, but its perimeter is now 28 cm.

This process can be repeated indefinitely. Thus, for each rectangle there is another rectangle that has the same area but a longer perimeter.

Solutions to Exercise C

Q1 (a) (i) $l = 2r = 2 \times 9 = 18$ cm. $P = 4l = 72$ cm.

(ii) $A = l^2 = 18^2 = 324$ cm²

(b) (i) $A = \dfrac{h}{2}\{\text{first} + \text{last} + \text{twice the rest}\}$

$$= \frac{5}{2}\{7 \cdot 5 + 9 \cdot 5 + 2(6 + 5 + 8 \cdot 5 + 7 + 4 \cdot 5)\}$$

$$= 197 \cdot 5 \text{ m}^2$$

(ii) % Error $= \dfrac{\text{error}}{\text{true value}} \times 100 = \dfrac{(200 - 197 \cdot 5)}{200} \times 100 = 1 \cdot 25\%$

(c) (i) $r = \dfrac{d}{2} = \dfrac{9}{2} = 4 \cdot 5$ cm $\Rightarrow V = \dfrac{4}{3}\pi r^3 = \dfrac{4}{3}\pi (4 \cdot 5)^3 = 121 \cdot 5\pi$ cm³

(ii) $V_{\text{cone}} + V_{\text{cylinder}} = V_{\text{sphere}}$

$$\Rightarrow \frac{1}{3}\cancel{\pi} r^2(8) + \cancel{\pi} r^2(8) = 121 \cdot 5\cancel{\pi}$$

$$\Rightarrow \frac{8}{3}r^2 + 8r^2 = 121 \cdot 5$$

$$\Rightarrow \frac{32}{3}r^2 = 121 \cdot 5 \Rightarrow r^2 = 121 \cdot 5 \div \frac{32}{3} = \frac{729}{64}$$

$$\Rightarrow r = \sqrt{\frac{729}{64}} = 3 \cdot 375. \text{ Thus, } r = 3 \cdot 4 \text{ cm, correct to one decimal place.}$$

Q2 (a) (i) $V = \pi r^2 h = \pi (6)^2 (20) = 720\pi$ mm³

(ii) $V = 720\pi = 2\,261 \cdot 95$ mm³.

(b) Volume of block $= 60 \times 35 \times 20 = 42\,000$ mm³. Half of this is $21\,000$ mm³. Each hole has a volume of $2\,261 \cdot 95$ mm³, from (a) part (ii).

The number of holes that would remove half the volume of the block

is $= \dfrac{21\,000}{2\,261 \cdot 95} = 9 \cdot 28$.

Thus, after 10 holes have been drilled, more than half of the original block will have been removed.

Q3 (a) **(i)** $A = l^2 = 16 \Rightarrow l = 4 \Rightarrow r = 2\,\text{cm}$

(ii) $A = 16 - \pi(2)^2 = 3 \cdot 4\,\text{cm}^2$

(b) **(i)** Volume of cylinder $= \pi(1 \cdot 5)^2 8 = 18\pi$

Volume of cone $= 21\pi - 18\pi = 3\pi$

$\dfrac{1}{3}\cancel{\pi}(1 \cdot 5)^2 h = 3\cancel{\pi} \Rightarrow \dfrac{3}{4}h = 3 \Rightarrow h = 4\,\text{cm} =$ height of cone.

Thus, the height of candle $= 8 + 4 = 12\,\text{cm}$.

(ii) Since the base is a square, the candles can be arranged upright in three rows of three.

Thus, each side of the square is 9 cm long, i.e. three times the diameter, 3 cm, of each candle.

Thus, the box has volume $9 \times 9 \times 12 = 972\,\text{cm}^3$.

Q4 (a)

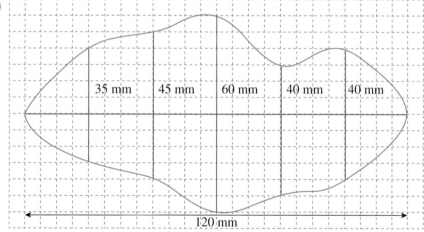

(b) $A = \dfrac{h}{2}\{\text{first} + \text{last} + \text{twice the rest}\}$

$= \dfrac{20}{2}\{0 + 0 + 2(35 + 45 + 60 + 40 + 40)\}$

$= 4400\,\text{mm}^2$

Q5 (a)

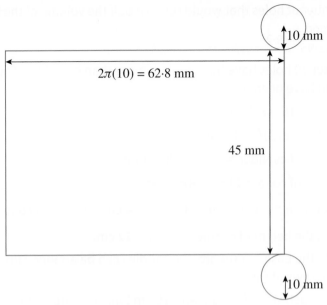

$2\pi(10) = 62 \cdot 8$ mm

10 mm

45 mm

10 mm

(b) $V = \pi r^2 h = \pi(10)^2(45) = 4500\pi$ mm^3

(c) $\frac{4}{3}\pi r^3 = 4500\pi \Rightarrow r^3 = 4500 \div \frac{4}{3} = 3375 \Rightarrow r = \sqrt[3]{3375} = 15$ mm

$A = 4\pi r^2 = 4\pi(15)^2 = 900\pi$ mm^2

Q6

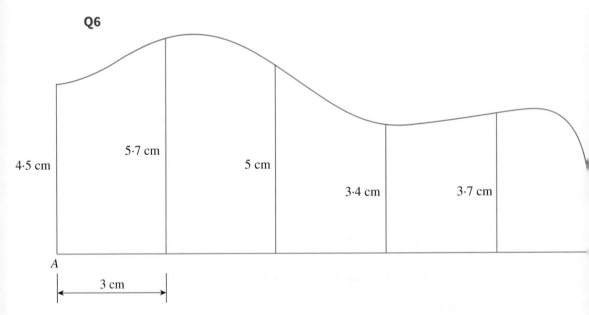

4·5 cm

5·7 cm

5 cm

3·4 cm

3·7 cm

A

3 cm

Since $|AB| = 15$ cm, the edge can be divided into five by marking it off in 3 cm intervals.

$A = \frac{h}{2}\{\text{first} + \text{last} + \text{twice the rest}\} = \frac{3}{2}\{4 \cdot 5 + 0 + 2(5 \cdot 7 + 5 + 3 \cdot 4 + 3 \cdot 7)\}$

$= 60$ cm^2

Q7 (a) An average man is less than 2 m tall, estimate it at 1·8 m.

(b)

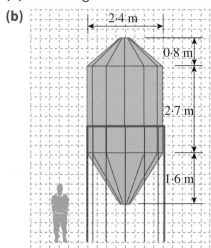

The man is 6 squares tall, thus, each square represents about 1·8 ÷ 6 = 0·3 m.

Multiply the number of squares taken up by each dimension by 0·3 to find its length in metres.

8 × 0·3 = 2·4 m

2·75 × 0·3 = 0·8 m

9 × 0·3 = 2·7 m

5·25 × 0·3 = 1·6 m (Note: all figures are correct to one decimal place.)

(c) $V = \left(\frac{1}{3}\pi r^2 h\right)_{\text{upper cone}} + \left(\pi r^2 h\right)_{\text{cylinder}} + \left(\frac{1}{3}\pi r^2 h\right)_{\text{lower cone}}$

$= \frac{1}{3}\pi (1·2)^2(0·8) + \pi (1·2)^2(2·7) + \frac{1}{3}\pi (1·2)^2(1·6)$

$= 15·83 \approx 16 \text{ m}^3$

Q8 (a) $|AD| = \sqrt{81} = 9$ cm

(b) (i) $A = \frac{1}{4}\pi r^2 = \frac{1}{4}\pi (9)^2 = 63·6 \text{ cm}^2$

(ii) The unshaded area in the second diagram is given by
81 − 63·6 = 17·4 cm².

Subtract two of these areas from the total to get the shaded area in the third diagram.

That is, $A = 81 - 2 \times 17·4 = 46·2$ cm².

(c) The base, b, of the triangle is $|AC| = \sqrt{9^2 + 9^2} = 9\sqrt{2}$ cm (Pythagoras).

Its height is equal to the radius, $|PD|$, minus half a diagonal length.

That is, $h = 9 - \dfrac{9\sqrt{2}}{2}$.

$A = \frac{1}{2}bh = \frac{1}{2}\left(9\sqrt{2}\right)\left(9 - \dfrac{9\sqrt{2}}{2}\right) = 16·8 \text{ cm}^2$

5 The Line

The co-ordinate axes, translations, central symmetry and midpoints

The diagram shows the co-ordinate plane. It is also called the Cartesian plane or the x-y plane. **The x-axis is horizontal and the y-axis is vertical.** The co-ordinates of A, B, C and D are $(2, 3)$, $(-4, 2)$, $(-2, -2)$ and $(2{\cdot}5, -3)$ respectively.

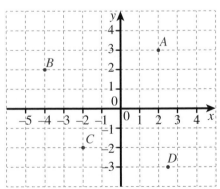

The **origin**, O, is the point where the x-axis and the y-axis intersect. It has co-ordinates $(0, 0)$.

The axes divide the plane into four **quadrants**. A is in the first quadrant, B is in the second quadrant, C is in the third quadrant and D is in the fourth quadrant.

A **translation** is a transformation which maps a point P with co-ordinates (x, y) to a point P' with co-ordinates $(x + h, y + k)$ where $h, k \in \mathbb{R}$. It is often convenient to use a line segment to identify the values for h and k.

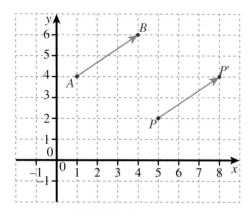

In the diagram the segment $[AB]$ defines the translation $x \rightarrow x + 3$ and $y \rightarrow y + 2$. That is $h = 3$ and $k = 2$. The image of $P(5, 2)$ under this translation is $P'(8, 4)$ since $5 \rightarrow 5 + 3 = 8$ and $2 \rightarrow 2 + 2 = 4$. Notice that $AP P'B$ is a parallelogram.

A **central symmetry** is a reflection in a point.

In the diagram, A' is the image of A under a central symmetry in the point B. Note that A' is also the image of B under the translation $A \rightarrow B$. This is often written as $A \rightarrow B \rightarrow A'$.

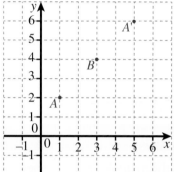

The **midpoint** of a line segment $[AB]$ is a point C on the line segment lying halfway between A and B. That is, $|AC| = |CB|$ and $C \in [AB]$.

In the diagram, $C(3, 1)$ is the midpoint of $[AB]$, where $A(1, 1)$ and $B(5, 1)$. $F(3, 5)$ is the midpoint of $[DE]$, where $D(2, 3)$ and $E(4, 7)$. The midpoint of $[AF]$ is D.

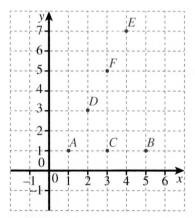

On page 18 of the *Formulae and Tables* booklet, the midpoint of $[PQ]$ is given as

$$\left(\frac{x_1 + x_2}{2}, \frac{y_1 + y_2}{2} \right) \text{ for } P(x_1, y_1) \text{ and } Q(x_2, y_2).$$

Point to note

$\dfrac{x_1 + x_2}{2}$ is the mean of x_1 and x_2 and $\dfrac{y_1 + y_2}{2}$ is the mean of y_1 and y_2.

The formula $\left(\dfrac{x_1 + x_2}{2}, \dfrac{y_1 + y_2}{2} \right)$ agrees with the above diagram.

For example, take $D(2, 3)$ and $E(4, 7)$. The mean of the x co-ordinates, 2 and 4, is 3. The mean of the y co-ordinates, 3 and 7, is 5. Thus the midpoint of $[DE]$ is $F(3, 5)$.

Length of a line segment

On page 18 of the *Formulae and Tables* booklet, the formula $|PQ| = \sqrt{(x_2 - x_1)^2 + (y_2 - y_1)^2}$ is given. This gives the distance between $P(x_1, y_1)$ and $Q(x_2, y_2)$.

The diagram shows P and Q plotted in the first quadrant. A right-angled triangle is drawn, with $[PQ]$ as hypotenuse.

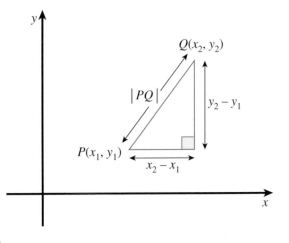

From Pythagoras' theorem we see that $|PQ|^2 = (x_2 - x_1)^2 + (y_2 - y_1)^2$
$\Rightarrow |PQ| = \sqrt{(x_2 - x_1)^2 + (y_2 - y_1)^2}$.

You will be expected to be aware that the distance formula is based on Pythagoras' theorem.

Example

C is the midpoint of $[AB]$ where A has co-ordinates $(-1, 2)$ and C has co-ordinates $(2, 4)$.

(a) Find the co-ordinates of B.

(b) Verify that C is the midpoint of $[AB]$ by showing that $|AC| = |CB|$.

Solution

Method 1   Graphical approach

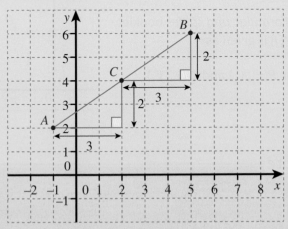

(a) From the diagram, the co-ordinates of B are $(5, 6)$.

(b) Pythagoras' theorem $\Rightarrow |AC|^2 = 3^2 + 2^2 = 13 \Rightarrow |AC| = \sqrt{13}$.

Similarly, $|CB|^2 = 3^2 + 2^2 = 13 \Rightarrow |AC| = \sqrt{13}$.

Thus, $|AC| = |CB|$.

Method 2 Algebraic approach

(a) Use central symmetry: $A \to C \to B$.

$A(-1, 2) \to C(2, 4) \Rightarrow x \to x+3$ and $y \to y+2 \Rightarrow C(2, 4) \to B(5, 6)$

(b) $A(-1, 2) \qquad\qquad C(2, 4)$

$\quad (x_1, y_1) \qquad\qquad (x_2, y_2)$

$|AC| = \sqrt{(x_2 - x_1)^2 + (y_2 - y_1)^2} = \sqrt{(2 - (-1))^2 + (4 - 2)^2} = \sqrt{(3)^2 + (2)^2} = \sqrt{13}$

$\quad C(2, 4) \qquad\qquad B(5, 6)$

$\quad (x_1, y_1) \qquad\qquad (x_2, y_2)$

$|CB| = \sqrt{(x_2 - x_1)^2 + (y_2 - y_1)^2} = \sqrt{(5 - 2)^2 + (6 - 4)^2} = \sqrt{3^2 + 2^2} = \sqrt{13}$

Thus, $|AC| = |CB|$.

Top Tip

Write a formula out in full whenever you use it. This makes you quicker at spotting which formula is needed in the examination. It also makes you more accurate.

Follow the steps:

- Label the points
- Write out the formula
- Substitute the values
- Calculate.

Use a DAL (direct algebraic logic) calculator and you'll be able to type exactly what you've written.

Point to note

You need to know both the graphical and the algebraic approaches, as in the example above.

The graphical one is often quicker if the numbers are simple. For more complicated values the algebraic method may be essential.

Notice that both approaches give the same answer.

Slopes

The **slope** of a line, or a line segment, tells you the rate at which it is rising or falling. The symbol for slope is m.

You can calculate slope using the formula: slope $= \dfrac{\text{rise}}{\text{run}}$. (This formula is *not* in the *Formulae and Tables* booklet. Make sure to learn it.)

In the diagram, the slope of AB is

$$m = \frac{\text{rise}}{\text{run}} = \frac{4}{2} = 2.$$

The slope of CD is

$$m = \frac{\text{rise}}{\text{run}} = \frac{(-3)}{1} = -3.$$

(A line which is falling as you go from left to right is said to have a negative rise.)

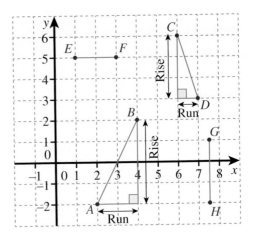

The slope of EF is zero, as it is not rising at all.

The slope of GH is undefined. This is because its run is zero, and you can't divide by zero.

Page 18 of the *Formulae and Tables* booklet gives the slope of a line PQ as

$$m = \frac{y_2 - y_1}{x_2 - x_1}.$$

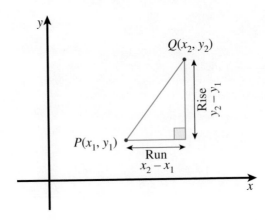

This is just another version of the previous definition. From the diagram,

$$m = \frac{y_2 - y_1}{x_2 - x_1} = \frac{\text{rise}}{\text{run}}.$$

Point to note

You will be expected to make the connection between slopes and rates of change. Two important examples of this are:

- the slope of a distance-time graph gives the instantaneous speed
- the slope of a speed-time graph gives the acceleration.

Recall that speed is the rate of change of distance with time, and acceleration is the rate of change of speed with time.

Parallel and perpendicular lines

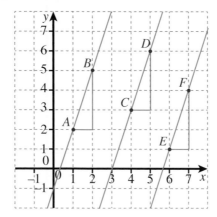

The lines AB, CD and EF in the diagram above all have the same slope, $m = \dfrac{\text{rise}}{\text{run}} = \dfrac{3}{1} = 3$.

The three lines are parallel to each other.

The line AB in the second diagram has slope $m_1 = \dfrac{\text{rise}}{\text{run}} = \dfrac{2}{1} = 2$.

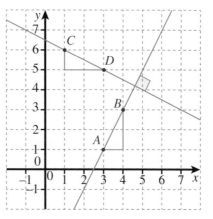

The line CD has slope $m_2 = \dfrac{\text{rise}}{\text{run}} = -\dfrac{1}{2}$.

Notice that the rise of AB is equal to the run of CD. The run of AB is equal to but opposite in sign to the rise of CD.

Thus $m_1 m_2 = (2)\left(-\dfrac{1}{2}\right) = -1$.

Remember

Suppose two lines have slopes m_1 and m_2 respectively.

If $m_1 = m_2$, then the lines are parallel.

If $m_1 m_2 = -1$, then the lines are perpendicular.

Top Tip

Suppose you know the slope of a line. To get the slope of a line perpendicular to it:

- flip the fraction
- change the sign.

Slope	$\dfrac{2}{3}$	$-1\dfrac{1}{4} = -\dfrac{5}{4}$	$3 = \dfrac{3}{1}$	1
Slope of perpendicular	$-\dfrac{3}{2}$	$\dfrac{4}{5}$	$-\dfrac{1}{3}$	-1

Note that this will not work for a horizontal line since its slope is zero. Flipping the fraction would demand division by zero, which is undefined.

The equation of a line

Suppose you have a line. Any pair of points on that line will have the same slope.

Consider the diagram on the right.

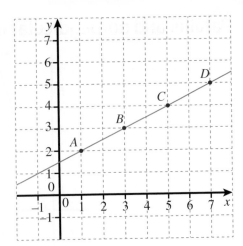

$$m_{AB} = \frac{\text{rise}}{\text{run}} = \frac{1}{2} = m_{BC} = m_{CD}$$

Similarly, $m_{AC} = \dfrac{\text{rise}}{\text{run}} = \dfrac{2}{4} = \dfrac{1}{2}$ and

$$m_{AD} = \frac{\text{rise}}{\text{run}} = \frac{3}{6} = \frac{1}{2}.$$

This is the basic idea behind the first form of the equation of a line on page 18 of the *Formulae and Tables* booklet.

Suppose you have a line, l, with slope m, and (x_1, y_1) is a particular point on that line. Pick any other point, (x, y). If it is on the line l, then $m = \dfrac{y - y_1}{x - x_1}$, since any pair of points on a particular line must have the same slope.

Rearranging this we get: $y - y_1 = m(x - x_1)$. This is the point–slope form of the equation of a line.

The second form of the equation of a line in the *Formulae and Tables* booklet is based on an equally simple idea.

Say you have a point, e.g. $(-2, -2)$ and a slope, e.g. $m = \dfrac{\text{rise}}{\text{run}} = \dfrac{3}{2}$.

Start at $(-2, -2)$. Go across 2 steps and up 3 steps. Repeat this process several times. The points produced will all be collinear. Look at the diagram below.

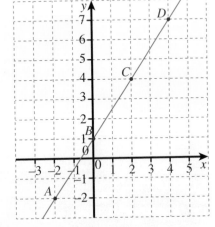

Let's work out the line's equation using

$(x_1, y_1) = (-2, -2)$ and $m = \dfrac{3}{2}$.

$y - y_1 = m(x - x_1) \Rightarrow y - (-2) = \dfrac{3}{2}(x - (-2))$

$\Rightarrow y + 2 = \dfrac{3}{2}x + 3 \Rightarrow y = \dfrac{3}{2}x + 1.$

This form, $y = \dfrac{3}{2}x + 1$, is known as the slope–intercept form, since the coefficient of x, $\dfrac{3}{2}$, is the slope and the constant term, 1, is the y-intercept.

Note that the y-intercept of a line is the y co-ordinate of the point where the line crosses the y-axis. In this case the line crosses the y-axis at $B(0, 1)$ so the y-intercept is 1.

Finally, rearranging this gives a third form of the equation of a line.

$y = \dfrac{3}{2}x + 1 \Rightarrow 2y = 3x + 2 \Rightarrow 3x - 2y + 2 = 0$. This is called the standard form of the equation of a line.

Top-Tip

A line in standard form, $ax + by + c = 0$, has slope $m = -\dfrac{a}{b}$. Learn this well, as it is not in the *Formulae and Tables* booklet.

Rearranging, we get: $ax + by + c = 0 \Rightarrow by = -ax - c \Rightarrow y = -\dfrac{a}{b}x - \dfrac{c}{b}$ $\Rightarrow m = -\dfrac{a}{b}$.

Horizontal and vertical lines have particularly simple equations.

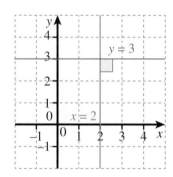

For example, the horizontal line $y = 3$ and the vertical line $x = 2$ are shown above.

Point to note

There are two ways to find the point of intersection of a pair of lines.

- Graph both lines. The point of intersection is where they cross and its co-ordinates can be read from the graph.

- Solve the equations of the lines algebraically as simultaneous equations. The solution to the simultaneous equations gives the co-ordinates of the point of intersection.

Example

The line, l, has equation $3x + 4y - 24 = 0$.

(a) Find the co-ordinates of the points A and B where l crosses the x-axis and the y-axis respectively.

(b) Show the graph of l on the co-ordinate axes.

(c) Find the area of the triangle bounded by l, the x-axis and the y-axis.

(d) Prove that the point $(4, 3)$ is on the line l.

(e) Find the equation of the line k which contains the point $(4, 3)$ and is perpendicular to l. Give your answer in standard form.

Solution

(a) l crosses the x-axis when its y co-ordinate is zero.

$3x + 4(0) - 24 = 0 \Rightarrow 3x = 24 \Rightarrow x = 8$, i.e. A has co-ordinates $(8, 0)$.

l crosses the y-axis when its x co-ordinate is zero.

$3(0) + 4y - 24 = 0 \Rightarrow 4y = 24 \Rightarrow y = 6$, i.e. B has co-ordinates $(0, 6)$.

(b)

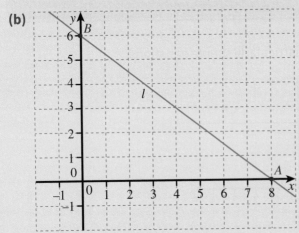

(c) $A = \dfrac{1}{2}ah = \dfrac{1}{2}(8)(6) = 24$ square units

(d) To see if $(4, 3)$ is on the line l, substitute $x = 4$ and $y = 3$ into the equation for l. If the resulting number equation is true, then the point is on the line.

$3(4) + 4(3) - 24 = 12 + 12 - 24 = 0$, which is true, thus $(4, 3)$ is on the line l.

(e) $3x + 4y - 24 = 0$ has slope $m = -\dfrac{x - \text{coefficient}}{y - \text{coefficient}} = -\dfrac{3}{4}$.

The perpendicular, k, thus has slope $\dfrac{4}{3}$ (flip the fraction and change the sign).
The point $(x_1, y_1) = (4, 3)$ is on k.

Thus, $y - y_1 = m(x - x_1) \Rightarrow y - 3 = \dfrac{4}{3}(x - 4) \Rightarrow 3y - 9 = 4x - 16 \Rightarrow 4x - 3y - 7 = 0$.

The area of a triangle

It is very important to check if the triangle is right-angled. Then one can simply use the formula $A = \frac{1}{2}ah$ as in the previous example. This could save you a lot of time. If the triangle is not right-angled, do the following.

- If the vertices are $(0, 0)$, (x_1, y_1) and (x_2, y_2), use the formula $A = \frac{1}{2}|x_1 y_2 - x_2 y_1|$ which is on page 18 of the *Formulae and Tables* booklet.

- If $(0, 0)$ is *not* a vertex, translate one vertex to the origin. Then find the images of the other two vertices under the same translation. Then use the formula $A = \frac{1}{2}|x_1 y_2 - x_2 y_1|$ as above, taking care to substitute the co-ordinates of the images of the two vertices.

You do *not* have to prove that this formula works. However, you may be interested in the following geometric justification.

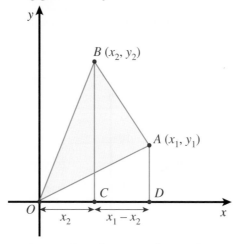

The area of triangle OAB is equal to the area of triangle OCB plus the area of trapezium $CDAB$ less the area of triangle OAD,

i.e. $|\triangle OAB| = |\triangle OCB| + |CDAB| - |\triangle OAD|$

$$\Rightarrow |\triangle OAB| = \left|\frac{1}{2}x_2 y_2\right| + \left|\left(\frac{y_1 + y_2}{2}\right)(x_1 - x_2)\right| - \left|\frac{1}{2}x_1 y_1\right|$$

$$\Rightarrow |\triangle OAB| = \frac{1}{2}x_2 y_2 + \frac{1}{2}y_1 x_1 - \frac{1}{2}y_1 x_2 + \frac{1}{2}y_2 x_1 - \frac{1}{2}y_2 x_2 - \frac{1}{2}x_1 y_1 = \frac{1}{2}|x_1 y_2 - x_2 y_1|.$$

Examples

(a) Find the area of the triangle with vertices $(0, 0)$, $(8, 6)$ and $(2, -4)$.

(b) $A(-4, 3)$, $B(6, -1)$ and $C(2, 7)$ are three points.

    (i) Find the area of the triangle ABC.

    (ii) $ABCD$ is a parallelogram in which $[AC]$ is a diagonal. Find the co-ordinates of the point D.

Solutions

(a) Since $(0, 0)$ is a vertex, we don't have to translate points.

$(x_1, y_1) = (8, 6)$, $(x_2, y_2) = (2, -4)$

$A = \frac{1}{2}\left|x_1 y_2 - x_2 y_1\right| = \frac{1}{2}\left|(8)(-4) - (2)(6)\right| = \frac{1}{2}\left|-44\right| = 22$ square units

Recall that the symbol $|\ |$ in the formula represents the modulus sign. In other words, if the calculation gives a negative result, simply make it positive as above.

(b) (i) Here, since none of the vertices are equal to $(0, 0)$, we need to translate one of them. It doesn't matter which one, you'll still get the same answer.

$A(-4, 3) \rightarrow (0, 0) \Rightarrow x \rightarrow x + 4$ and $y \rightarrow y - 3$,

$\Rightarrow B(6, -1) \rightarrow (10, -4)$ and $C(2, 7) \rightarrow (6, 4)$.

$(x_1, y_1) = (10, -4)$, $(x_2, y_2) = (6, 4)$

$A = \frac{1}{2}\left|x_1 y_2 - x_2 y_1\right| = \frac{1}{2}\left|(10)(4) - (6)(-4)\right| = \frac{1}{2}\left|64\right| = 32$ square units.

(ii) Graphically, this can be solved by plotting A, B and C and completing the parallelogram so that $[AC]$ is a diagonal.

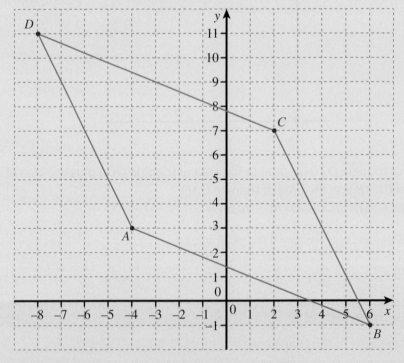

From the diagram we see that D has co-ordinates $(-8, 11)$.

Algebraically, we can use translations to find D.

$B(6, -1) \rightarrow C(2, 7) \Rightarrow x \rightarrow x - 4$ and $y \rightarrow y + 8 \Rightarrow A(-4, 3) \rightarrow D(-8, 11)$

Exercise A

Q1 (a) Plot the point $A(1, 3)$ on a co-ordinate plane.

(b) Plot three more points, B, C and D, where the second co-ordinate is twice the first co-ordinate, plus one.

(c) What kind of graph do the points A, B, C and D lie on?

Q2 (a) Plot the point $P(2, 4)$ on a co-ordinate plane.

(b) Plot two more points, Q and R, where the second co-ordinate is equal to the square of the first co-ordinate.

(c) What kind of graph do the points P, Q and R lie on?

Q3 $A(-1, 2)$ and $B(4, 3)$ are points.

(a) Find P', the image of $P(2, 5)$ under the translation $\overrightarrow{AB}$.

(b) Plot the points A, B, P and P' on a co-ordinate plane.

(c) Find the midpoint of **(i)** $[AP']$ **(ii)** $[PB]$.

(d) What does your answer to part (c) tell you about the quadrilateral $ABP'P$?

Q4 $A(1, 3)$ and $B(9, 7)$ are points.

(a) Find the co-ordinates of a point C which is halfway between A and B.

(b) Find the co-ordinates of a point D which is a quarter of the way between A and B.

(c) Find the co-ordinates of a point E so that B is halfway between A and E.

Q5 $A(4, 1)$, $B(6, 5)$ and $C(8, 4)$ are points.

(a) Calculate m_1, the slope of AB.

(b) Calculate m_2, the slope of BC.

(c) Evaluate $m_1 m_2$. What does your answer tell you about the lines AB and BC.

(d) Graph the lines AB and BC on a co-ordinate plane.

Q6 The line l_1 passes through the points $P(1, 6)$ and $Q(4, 2)$. The line l_2 has equation $3x - 4y - 12 = 0$.

(a) Plot P and Q on the co-ordinate plane and show the line l_1.

(b) Find the slope of the line l_1.

(c) On the same diagram as part (a), draw the graph of l_2.

(d) State whether or not the two lines l_1 and l_2 are perpendicular to each other. Give a reason for your answer.

Q7 (a) A line has a rise of zero.

(i) What kind of line is it?

(ii) Give an example of an equation of such a line.

(b) A line has a run of zero.

   (i) What kind of line is it?

   (ii) Give an example of an equation of such a line.

(c) Alana states, correctly, that if the slopes of two lines are the same then they are parallel. Is the converse of this statement true? Justify your answer.

(d) Bernard says 'Suppose you have four points and no matter which two you pick you always get the same answer for the slope. This doesn't mean that the four points are collinear. Two of them could be on one line and the other two on a parallel line.' Is he right? Justify your answer.

Q8 (a) Graph the lines   **(i)** $x + y = 6$ **(ii)** $x = 1$ and   **(iii)** $y = 2$.

(b) Find the area of the triangle enclosed by the three lines in part (a).

Q9 The line l_1 has equation $x - 3y = -3$. The line l_2 has equation $2x + y = 8$.

(a) Find A, the point of intersection of l_1 and l_2,

   (i) graphically   **(ii)** algebraically.

(b) Find the equation of the line l_3 which is parallel to l_2 and contains the point $(5, 4)$.

Q10 (a) $A(3, -1)$ and $B(9, 7)$ are points. O is the origin $(0, 0)$. Find the area of the triangle OAB.

(b) $P(-1, -3)$, $Q(4, 1)$ and $R(2, 3)$ are points. Find the area of the triangle PQR.

Exercise B

Q1 The table below gives the equations of six lines.

Line 1	$y = 3x - 6$
Line 2	$y = 3x + 12$
Line 3	$y = 5x + 20$
Line 4	$y = x - 7$
Line 5	$y = -2x + 4$
Line 6	$y = 4x - 16$

(a) Which line has the greatest slope? Give a reason for your answer.

(b) Which lines are parallel? Give a reason for your answer.

(c) Draw a sketch of Line 1, using suitable co-ordinate axes.

(d) The diagram below represents one of the given lines. Which line does it represent?

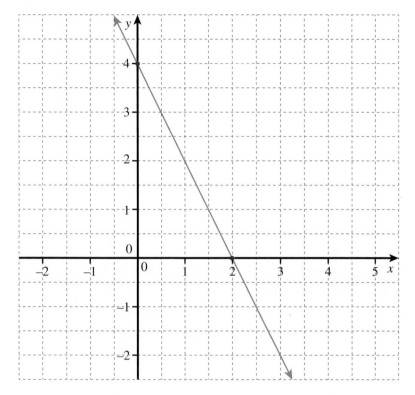

(e) The table shows some values of x and y for the equation of one of the lines.

Which equation do they satisfy?

(f) There is one value of x which will give the same value of y for Line 4 as it will for Line 6. Find, using algebra, this value of x and the corresponding value of y.

(g) Verify your answer to (f) above.

x	y
7	12
9	20
10	24

Q2 (a) **(i)** Plot the points $A(1, 2)$, $B(6, 1)$ and $C(5, 6)$ on a co-ordinate plane.

    (ii) Draw $\triangle ABC$ on the same diagram.

(b) **(i)** Plot D, the midpoint of $[BC]$ and E, the midpoint of $[AC]$.

    (ii) On the same diagram as in part (a), draw the lines AD and BE.

    (iii) What geometrical term describes the lines AD and BE?

(c) Find the equation of **(i)** AD **(ii)** BE.

(d) Find the co-ordinates of $F = AD \cap BE$ **(i)** graphically **(ii)** algebraically.

(e) **(i)** What geometric term is used to describe the point F?

(ii) Calculate the co-ordinates (x_3, y_3), where x_3 is the mean of the x co-ordinates of A, B and C and y_3 is the mean of their y co-ordinates.

(iii) What conclusion can you draw from your answer to part (ii)?

Q3 The points A, B and C are shown in the diagram.

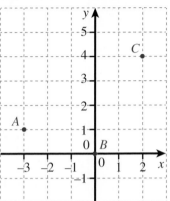

(a) Plot the point D so that $ABCD$ is a parallelogram.

(b) Are the diagonals, $[AC]$ and $[BD]$, of the parallelogram equal in length? Justify your answer.

(c) Find the area of **(i)** $\triangle ABC$ **(ii)** $\triangle ADC$.

(d) The answers to part (c) verify a theorem about parallelograms. State the theorem.

Q4 (a) Plot the points $P(-1, -2)$, $Q(8, 1)$ and $R(3, 6)$ on a co-ordinate plane.

(b) Find the co-ordinates of **(i)** A, the midpoint of $[PR]$ and **(ii)** B, the midpoint of $[RQ]$ and plot them on your diagram.

(c) Find the equation of line l_1, perpendicular to $[PR]$ and through the point A.

(d) Find the equation of line l_2, perpendicular to $[RQ]$ and through the point B.

(e) Plot l_1 and l_2 on your diagram.

(f) **(i)** Find the co-ordinates of C, the point of intersection of l_1 and l_2.

(ii) What is the geometric term for the point C?

(g) Draw the circle which passes through the points P, Q and R.

Q5 The diagram shows the triangle ABC.

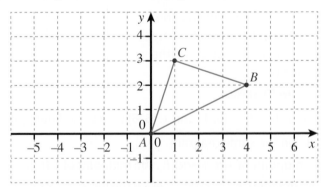

(a) Investigate whether or not the triangle ABC is isosceles.

(b) Find the equation of the line l, parallel to AB and passing through the point C.

(c) Find the co-ordinates of D, the point where l crosses the x-axis.

(d) Plot l and D on the diagram above.

(e) Find the ratio of the area of $\triangle ACD$ to the area of $\triangle ABC$.

Exercise C

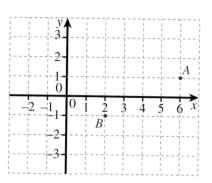

Q1 The points $A(6, 1)$ and $B(2, -1)$ are shown on the diagram.

   (a) Find the equation of the line AB.

   (b) The line AB crosses the y-axis at C. Find the co-ordinates of C.

   (c) Find the ratio $\dfrac{|AB|}{|AC|}$, giving your answer in the form $\dfrac{p}{q}$, where p and q are whole numbers.

                                                             (2011)

Q2 $A(6, -1)$, $B(12, -3)$, $C(8, 5)$ and $D(2, 7)$ are four points.

   (a) Plot the four points on the diagram below.

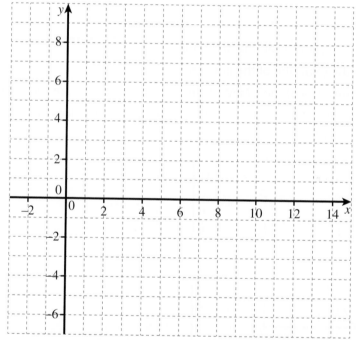

   (b) Describe two different ways of showing, using co-ordinate geometry techniques, that the points form a parallelogram $ABCD$.

   (c) Use one of the ways you have described to show that $ABCD$ is a parallelogram.

                                                             (2012)

Q3 (a) l is the line $3x + 2y + 18 = 0$. Find the slope of l.

   (b) The line k is perpendicular to l and cuts the x-axis at the point $(7, 0)$. Find the equation of k.

   (c) Find the co-ordinates of the point of intersection of the lines l and k.

                                                             (2013)

Q4 The points A, B, and C have co-ordinates as follows: $A(3, 5)$, $B(-6, 2)$ and $C(4, -4)$.

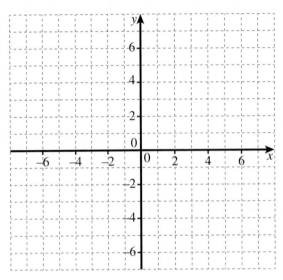

(a) Plot A, B, and C on the diagram.

(b) Find the equation of the line AB.

(c) Find the area of the triangle ABC.   *(SEC Sample Paper 2014)*

Q5 The points $A(-9, 3)$, $B(-4, 3)$, and $C(-4, 10)$ are the vertices of the triangle ABC, as shown.

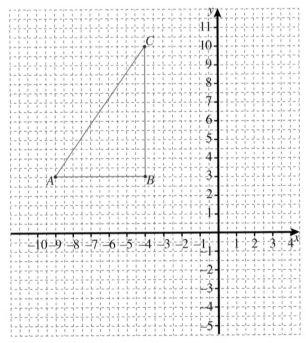

(a) (i) Find the length of $[AB]$.   (ii) Find the area of the triangle ABC.

(b) $X(2, -4)$ and $Y(2, 1)$ are two points.

(i) Draw, on the diagram above, a triangle, XYZ, which is congruent to the triangle ABC.

(ii) Write down the co-ordinates of Z and explain why the triangle XYZ is congruent to the triangle ABC.   *(2014)*

Solutions to Exercise A

Q1 (a) (b) This is a sample answer. It is possible to choose other values for the co-ordinates of B, C and D as long as they lie on the line shown.

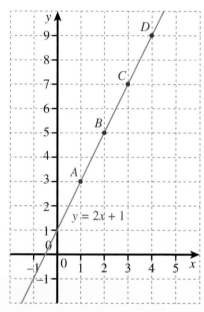

(c) The points lie on a line with equation $y = 2x + 1$.

Q2 (a) (b) As in Q1, this is a sample answer.

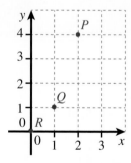

(c) The points are non-collinear. They lie on the quadratic curve $y = x^2$.

Q3 (a) $A(-1, 2) \to B(4, 3) \Rightarrow x \to x + 5$ and $y \to y + 1$

$\Rightarrow P(2, 5) \to P'(7, 6)$

(b)

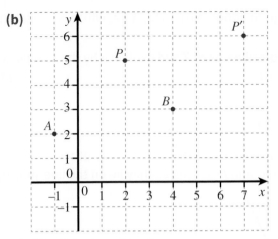

(c) (i) $A(-1, 2)$ $P'(7, 6)$
$\quad\quad (x_1, y_1)$ (x_2, y_2)

$$\text{midpoint} = \left(\frac{x_1 + x_2}{2}, \frac{y_1 + y_2}{2}\right) = \left(\frac{-1 + 7}{2}, \frac{2 + 6}{2}\right) = (3, 4)$$

(ii) $P(2, 5)$ $B(4, 3)$
$\quad\quad (x_1, y_1)$ (x_2, y_2)

$$\text{midpoint} = \left(\frac{x_1 + x_2}{2}, \frac{y_1 + y_2}{2}\right) = \left(\frac{2 + 4}{2}, \frac{5 + 3}{2}\right) = (3, 4)$$

(d) The midpoint of $[AP']$ is the same as the midpoint of $[PB]$. This means that they bisect each other. Thus, $ABP'P$ is a parallelogram.

Remember

If you are not explicitly asked to use the midpoint formula you may find it quicker to use means. The mean of the x co-ordinates of the end-points gives the x co-ordinate of the midpoint. The mean of the y co-ordinates of the end-points gives the y co-ordinate of the midpoint.

The choice is yours.

Q4 (a) $A(1, 3)$ $B(9, 7)$
$\quad\quad (x_1, y_1)$ (x_2, y_2)

$$\text{midpoint} = \left(\frac{x_1 + x_2}{2}, \frac{y_1 + y_2}{2}\right) = \left(\frac{1 + 9}{2}, \frac{3 + 7}{2}\right) = C(5, 5)$$

(b) $A(1, 3)$ $C(5, 5)$
$\quad\quad (x_1, y_1)$ (x_2, y_2)

$$\text{midpoint} = \left(\frac{x_1 + x_2}{2}, \frac{y_1 + y_2}{2}\right) = \left(\frac{1 + 5}{2}, \frac{3 + 5}{2}\right) = D(3, 4)$$

(c) $A(1, 3) \rightarrow B(9, 7) \Rightarrow x \rightarrow x + 8$ and $y \rightarrow y + 4 \Rightarrow B(9, 7) \rightarrow E(17, 11)$.

Q5 (a) $A(4,1) \quad B(6,5)$

$\qquad (x_1, y_1) \qquad (x_2, y_2)$

$$m_1 = \frac{y_2 - y_1}{x_2 - x_1} = \frac{5-1}{6-4} = \frac{4}{2} = 2$$

(b) $B(6,5) \quad C(8,4)$

$\qquad (x_1, y_1) \qquad (x_2, y_2)$

$$m_2 = \frac{y_2 - y_1}{x_2 - x_1} = \frac{4-5}{8-6} = -\frac{1}{2}$$

(c) $m_1 m_2 = (2)\left(-\frac{1}{2}\right) = -1 \implies AB \perp BC$

(d)

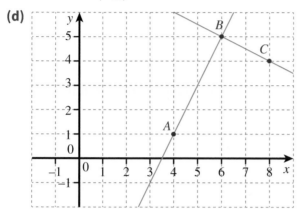

Q6 (a)

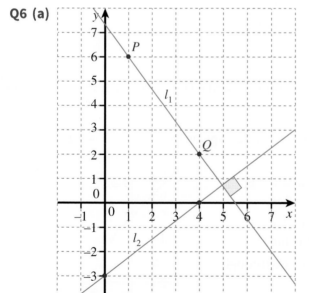

(b) From the diagram, using P and Q, $m_1 = \dfrac{\text{rise}}{\text{run}} = -\dfrac{4}{3}$.

Note that the line is going downhill, from left to right, so it has a negative rise, i.e. it falls.

Or, using the formula:

$P(1, 6)$ $Q(4, 2)$

(x_1, y_1) (x_2, y_2)

$$m_1 = \frac{y_2 - y_1}{x_2 - x_1} = \frac{2 - 6}{4 - 1} = -\frac{4}{3}$$

(c) $3x - 4y - 12 = 0$

$x = 0 \Rightarrow 3(0) - 4y - 12 = 0 \Rightarrow y = -3$. Thus, $(0, -3) \in l_2$.

$y = 0 \Rightarrow 3x - 4(0) - 12 = 0 \Rightarrow x = 4$. Thus, $(4, 0) \in l_2$.

See diagram for graph.

(d) The slope of l_2 is $m_2 = \dfrac{\text{rise}}{\text{run}} = \dfrac{3}{4}$.

$$m_1 m_2 = \left(-\frac{4}{3}\right)\left(\frac{3}{4}\right) = -1 \Rightarrow l_1 \perp l_2$$

Q7 (a) (i) A horizontal line has a rise of zero.   **(ii)** For example, $y = 12$.

(b) (i) A vertical line has a run of zero.   **(ii)** For example, $x = -4$.

(c) The converse is not true. Vertical lines are parallel, but their slopes are not defined.

(d) Bernard is wrong, the four points are collinear.

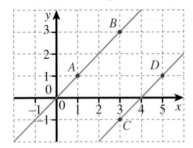

Consider the above diagram. AB and CD are parallel. Both have a slope given by $\dfrac{\text{rise}}{\text{run}} = \dfrac{2}{2} = 1$.

However, AC and BD have a slope given by $\dfrac{\text{rise}}{\text{run}} = -\dfrac{2}{2} = -1$.

Q8 (a) (i) $x + y = 6$

$x = 0 \Rightarrow 0 + y = 6 \Rightarrow y = 6$,
so $(0, 6)$ is on the line.

$y = 0 \Rightarrow x + 0 = 6 \Rightarrow x = 6$,
so $(6, 0)$ is on the line.

(ii) $x = 1$ is a vertical line through the point $(1, 0)$.

(iii) $y = 2$ is a horizontal line through the point $(0, 2)$.

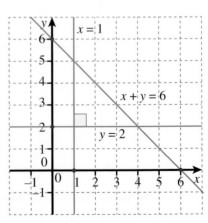

(b) Since the enclosed triangle is right-angled, $A = \dfrac{1}{2}ah = \dfrac{1}{2}(3)(3)$

$= 4\cdot5$ square units.

Q9 (a) (i) The line l_1 has equation $x - 3y = -3$.

$x = 0 \Rightarrow 0 - 3y = -3 \Rightarrow y = 1 \Rightarrow (0, 1) \in l_1$

$y = 0 \Rightarrow x - 3(0) = -3 \Rightarrow x = -3 \Rightarrow (-3, 0) \in l_1$

The line l_2 has equation $2x + y = 8$.

$x = 0 \Rightarrow 2(0) + y = 8 \Rightarrow y = 8 \Rightarrow (0, 8) \in l_2$

$y = 0 \Rightarrow 2x + 0 = 8 \Rightarrow x = 4 \Rightarrow (4, 0) \in l_2$

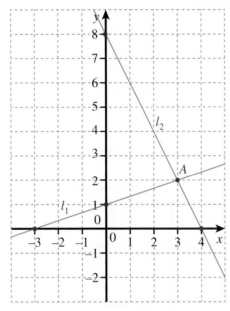

From the graph we see that A has co-ordinates $(3, 2)$.

(ii) l_1: $\qquad\qquad x - 3y = -3$

$3 \times l_2$: $\qquad \underline{6x + 3y = 24}$

Add: $\qquad\quad 7x \qquad = 21 \Rightarrow x = 3$

Substitute into l_2: $2(3) + y = 8 \Rightarrow 6 + y = 8 \Rightarrow y = 2$

Answer: $A(3, 2)$

(b) From the graph, we see that l_2 has slope $m = \dfrac{\text{rise}}{\text{run}} = -\dfrac{2}{1} = -2$.

We can also see from the equation $2x + y = 8$ that $m = -\dfrac{x \text{ coefficient}}{y \text{ coefficent}}$

$$= -\dfrac{2}{1} = -2.$$

Since l_3 is parallel to l_2, it also has a slope of $m = -2$.

$(5, 4) = (x_1, y_1)$

$y - y_1 = m(x - x_1) \Rightarrow y - 4 = -2(x - 5) = -2x + 10 \Rightarrow 2x + y - 14 = 0$

Q10 (a) $A(3, -1) \quad B(9, 7)$

$\quad (x_1, y_1) \qquad (x_2, y_2)$

$A = \dfrac{1}{2}|x_1 y_2 - x_2 y_1| = \dfrac{1}{2}|(3)(7) - (9)(-1)| = \dfrac{1}{2}|30| = 15$ square units

(b) $P(-1, -3) \rightarrow (0, 0) \Rightarrow x \rightarrow x + 1$ and $y \rightarrow y + 3$

$\Rightarrow Q(4, 1) \rightarrow (5, 4) = (x_1, y_1)$

$\Rightarrow R(2, 3) \rightarrow (3, 6) = (x_2, y_2)$

$\Rightarrow A = \dfrac{1}{2}|x_1 y_2 - x_2 y_1| = \dfrac{1}{2}|(5)(6) - (3)(4)| = \dfrac{1}{2}|18| = 9$ square units

Solutions to Exercise B

Q1 (a) All the lines are given in slope–intercept form: $y = mx + c$. The coefficient of x in each equation represents the slope. Thus Line 3, $y = 5x + 20$, has the greatest slope.

(b) Line 1 and Line 2 are parallel since they both have a slope of 3.

(c) A quick way to sketch Line 1, $y = 3x - 6$, is to notice that, since the y-intercept is −6, the line crosses the y-axis at $(0, -6)$. Since Line 1 has a slope of 3, a second point can be plotted by starting at $(0, -6)$, going across 1 step and up 3 steps.

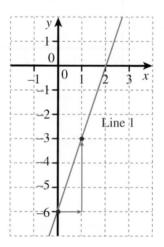

(d) Line 5, since its y-intercept is 4 and its slope is $m = \dfrac{\text{rise}}{\text{run}} = -\dfrac{4}{2} = -2$, i.e. it has equation $y = -2x + 4$.

(e) First use two of the points, any two since the three points are collinear, to find the slope. This will narrow down which line they lie on.

$(7, 12)\quad (9, 20)$

$(x_1, y_1)\quad (x_2, y_2)$

$m = \dfrac{y_2 - y_1}{x_2 - x_1} = \dfrac{20 - 12}{9 - 7} = \dfrac{8}{2} = 4$

Only Line 6 has a slope of 4.

If another of the lines had a slope of 4, we would have to substitute the points into each of the lines to see which one was correct.

(f) Line 4: $y = x - 7$, Line 6: $y = 4x - 16$.

Both have the same value for y when $4x - 16 = x - 7 \Rightarrow 3x = 9 \Rightarrow x = 3$.

The corresponding value of y is $y = 3 - 7 = -4$.

(g) Verify the solution $x = 3$ by substitution.

Line 4: $y = 3 - 7 = -4$, Line 6: $y = 4(3) - 16 = 12 - 16 = -4$.

Thus, $x = 3$ gives the same value for y for both lines.

Q2 (a)

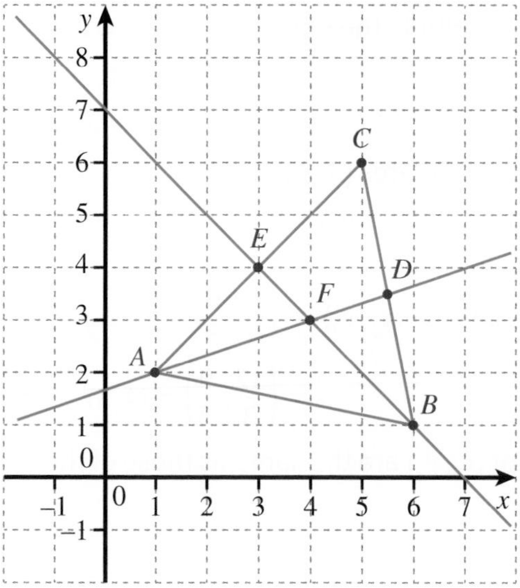

(b) **(i)** $B(6, 1)$ $C(5, 6)$

(x_1, y_1) (x_2, y_2)

$$D\left(\frac{x_1 + x_2}{2}, \frac{y_1 + y_2}{2}\right) = D\left(\frac{6 + 5}{2}, \frac{1 + 6}{2}\right) = D(5\cdot5, 3\cdot5)$$

$A(1, 2)$ $C(5, 6)$

(x_1, y_1) (x_2, y_2)

$$E\left(\frac{x_1 + x_2}{2}, \frac{y_1 + y_2}{2}\right) = E\left(\frac{1 + 5}{2}, \frac{2 + 6}{2}\right) = E(3, 4)$$

(ii) See diagram above.

(iii) AD and BE are called medians since they join the midpoint of one side of a triangle to the opposite vertex.

(c) **(i)** $A(1, 2)$ $D(5\cdot5, 3\cdot5)$

(x_1, y_1) (x_2, y_2)

$$m = \frac{y_2 - y_1}{x_2 - x_1} = \frac{3\cdot5 - 2}{5\cdot5 - 1} = \frac{1\cdot5}{4\cdot5} = \frac{1}{3}$$

$y - y_1 = m(x - x_1) \Rightarrow y - 2 = \frac{1}{3}(x - 1) \Rightarrow 3y - 6 = x - 1 \Rightarrow -5 = x - 3y$

(ii) BE has slope $m = \dfrac{\text{rise}}{\text{run}} = -\dfrac{3}{3} = -1$

$B(6, 1)$

(x_1, y_1)

$y - y_1 = m(x - x_1) \Rightarrow y - 1 = -1(x - 6) \Rightarrow y - 1 = -x + 6 \Rightarrow x + y = 7$

(d) **(i)** From the graph, $F(4, 3)$.

(ii) $x - 3y = -5$ The equation of AD.

$3x + 3y = 21$ Multiply the equation of BE by 3.

$4x = 16 \Rightarrow x = 4$ Add the equations to eliminate y.

Substituting in BE: $x + y = 7 \Rightarrow 4 + y = 7 \Rightarrow y = 3$.

So, again, F has co-ordinates $(4, 3)$.

(e) **(i)** The geometric term for F is the centroid, since it is the intersection of the medians.

(ii) $A(1, 2)$, $B(6, 1)$, $C(5, 6) \Rightarrow (x_3, y_3) = \left(\dfrac{1 + 6 + 5}{3}, \dfrac{2 + 1 + 6}{3} \right)$

$$= \left(\dfrac{12}{3}, \dfrac{9}{3} \right) = (4, 3)$$

(iii) The co-ordinates of (x_3, y_3) are the same as those of the centroid, F.

Q3 (a)

(b) $A(-3, 1)$ $C(2, 4)$

(x_1, y_1) (x_2, y_2)

$|AC| = \sqrt{(x_2 - x_1)^2 + (y_2 - y_1)^2} = \sqrt{(2 - (-3))^2 + (4 - 1)^2} = \sqrt{(5)^2 + (3)^2}$

$= \sqrt{34}$

From Pythagoras' theorem: $|BD| = \sqrt{1^2 + 5^2} = \sqrt{26}$

Thus $|AC| \neq |BD|$.

(c) **(i)** $A(-3, 1)$ $C(2, 4)$

(x_1, y_1) (x_2, y_2)

$A = \dfrac{1}{2}\left|x_1 y_2 - x_2 y_1\right| = \dfrac{1}{2}\left|(-3)(4) - (2)(1)\right| = \dfrac{1}{2}\left|-12 - 2\right| = \dfrac{1}{2}\left|-14\right|$

$= 7$ square units

(ii) $A(-3, 1) \rightarrow (0, 0) \Rightarrow x \rightarrow x + 3$ and $y \rightarrow y - 1$

$\Rightarrow D(-1, 5) \rightarrow (2, 4) = (x_1, y_1)$ and $C(2, 4) \rightarrow (5, 3) = (x_2, y_2)$

$A = \frac{1}{2}|x_1 y_2 - x_2 y_1| = \frac{1}{2}|(2)(3) - (5)(4)| = \frac{1}{2}|6 - 20| = \frac{1}{2}|-14|$

$= 7$ square units

(d) A diagonal of a parallelogram bisects its area.

Q4

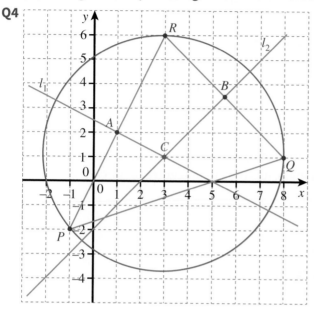

(a) See diagram above.

(b) **(i)** $P(-1, -2)$ $R(3, 6)$
   (x_1, y_1) (x_2, y_2)

$A = \left(\dfrac{x_1 + x_2}{2}, \dfrac{y_1 + y_2}{2}\right) = \left(\dfrac{(-1) + 3}{2}, \dfrac{(-2) + 6}{2}\right) = (1, 2)$

(ii) $Q(8, 1)$ $R(3, 6)$
   (x_1, y_1) (x_2, y_2)

$B = \left(\dfrac{x_1 + x_2}{2}, \dfrac{y_1 + y_2}{2}\right) = \left(\dfrac{8 + 3}{2}, \dfrac{1 + 6}{2}\right) = (5 \cdot 5, 3 \cdot 5)$

(c) $P(-1, -2)$ $R(3, 6)$
   (x_1, y_1) (x_2, y_2)

$m_{PR} = \dfrac{y_2 - y_1}{x_2 - x_1} = \dfrac{6 - (-2)}{3 - (-1)} = \dfrac{8}{4} = 2$

Thus the slope of l_1 is $-\dfrac{1}{2}$. Remember, $A(1, 2) = (x_1, y_1)$.

$y - y_1 = m(x - x_1) \Rightarrow y - (2) = -\dfrac{1}{2}(x - (1))$

$\Rightarrow 2y - 4 = -x + 1 \Rightarrow x + 2y = 5$

(d) $R(3, 6)$ $Q(8, 1)$
   (x_1, y_1) (x_2, y_2)

$$m_{RQ} = \frac{y_2 - y_1}{x_2 - x_1} = \frac{1 - 6}{8 - 3} = \frac{-5}{5} = -1$$

Thus the slope of l_2 is 1. Remember, $B(5\cdot 5, 3\cdot 5) = (x_1, y_1)$.

$y - y_1 = m(x - x_1) \Rightarrow y - 3\cdot 5 = 1(x - 5\cdot 5) \Rightarrow x - y = 2$

(e) See diagram above.

(f) (i) l_1: $x + 2y = 5$

   $2l_2$: $2x - 2y = 4$

   $l_1 + 2l_2$: $3x \qquad\;\; = 9 \Rightarrow x = 3$

   Substitute in l_1: $3 + 2y = 5 \Rightarrow y = 1$

   Thus C has co-ordinates $(3, 1)$.

  (ii) Since C is the intersection of the perpendicular bisectors of the sides of the triangle, it is the circumcentre of $\triangle PQR$.

(g) See diagram above.

Q5 (a) $A(0, 0)$ $C(1, 3)$

   (x_1, y_1) (x_2, y_2)

   $|AC| = \sqrt{(1 - 0)^2 + (3 - 0)^2} = \sqrt{10}$

   $B(4, 2)$ $C(1, 3)$

   (x_1, y_1) (x_2, y_2)

   $|BC| = \sqrt{(4 - 1)^2 + (2 - 3)^2} = \sqrt{3^2 + (-1)^2} = \sqrt{10}$

   Since $|AC| = |BC| = \sqrt{10}$, $\triangle ABC$ is isosceles.

(b) $A(0, 0)$ $B(4, 2)$

   (x_1, y_1) (x_2, y_2)

$$m = \frac{y_2 - y_1}{x_2 - x_1} = \frac{2 - 0}{4 - 0} = \frac{1}{2}$$

Since l is parallel to AB, it also has a slope of $m = \frac{1}{2}$.

$C(1, 3) = (x_1, y_1)$, $y - y_1 = m(x - x_1) \Rightarrow y - 3 = \frac{1}{2}(x - 1) \Rightarrow 2y - 6 = x - 1$
$\Rightarrow x - 2y + 5 = 0$.

(c) l crosses the x-axis when its y co-ordinate is zero.

   $x - 2(0) + 5 = 0 \Rightarrow x = -5$, i.e. D has co-ordinates $(-5, 0)$.

(d)

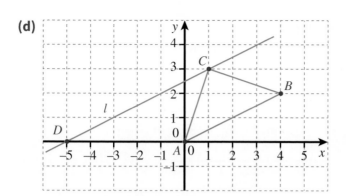

(e) $C(1, 3)$ $D(-5, 0)$

(x_1, y_1) (x_2, y_2)

$A = \dfrac{1}{2}\left|x_1 y_2 - x_2 y_1\right| = \dfrac{1}{2}\left|(1)(0) - (-5)(3)\right| = \dfrac{1}{2}\left|15\right| = 7{\cdot}5$ square units

$B(4, 2)$ $C(1, 3)$

(x_1, y_1) (x_2, y_2)

$A = \dfrac{1}{2}\left|x_1 y_2 - x_2 y_1\right| = \dfrac{1}{2}\left|(4)(3) - (1)(2)\right| = \dfrac{1}{2}\left|10\right| = 5$ square units.

Thus, the required ratio is $7{\cdot}5 : 5 = 3 : 2$.

Solutions to Exercise C

Q1 (a) Label the points:

$A(6, 1)$ $B(2, -1)$

(x_1, y_1) (x_2, y_2)

Substitute and simplify:

$m = \dfrac{y_2 - y_1}{x_2 - x_1} = \dfrac{-1 - 1}{2 - 6} = \dfrac{-2}{-4} = \dfrac{1}{2}$

$y - y_1 = m(x - x_1) \Rightarrow y - 1 = \dfrac{1}{2}(x - 6) = \dfrac{1}{2}x - 3 \Rightarrow y = \dfrac{1}{2}x - 2$

(b) The line $y = mx + c$ crosses the y-axis at the point $(0, c)$.

Thus the line $y = \dfrac{1}{2}x - 2$ crosses the y-axis at $C(0, -2)$.

(c) Label the points:

$A(6, 1)$ $B(2, -1)$

(x_1, y_1) (x_2, y_2)

Substitute and simplify:

$|AB| = \sqrt{(x_2 - x_1)^2 + (y_2 - y_1)^2} = \sqrt{(2 - 6)^2 + (-1 - 1)^2} = 2\sqrt{5}$

Label the points:

$A(6, 1)$ $C(0, -2)$

(x_1, y_1) (x_2, y_2)

Substitute and simplify:

$$|AC| = \sqrt{(x_2-x_1)^2+(y_2-y_1)^2} = \sqrt{(0-6)^2+(-2-1)^2} = 3\sqrt{5}$$

Thus, $\dfrac{|AB|}{|AC|} = \dfrac{2\sqrt{5}}{3\sqrt{5}} = \dfrac{2}{3}.$

Top Tip

In Q1 (c), you have to use the same formula twice.

The most common error in this type of question is to substitute incorrectly. Labelling the points as shown dramatically reduces the risk of losing marks in this way.

Q2 (a)

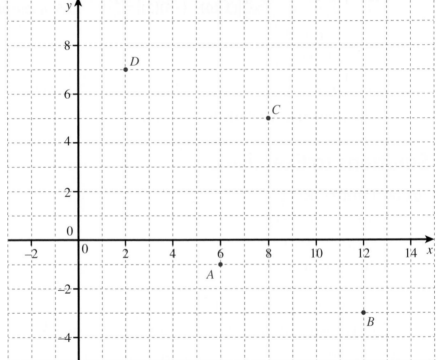

(b) You could show that

(i) $AB \parallel DC$ and $DA \parallel CB$

(ii) $|AB| = |DC|$ and $|AD| = |BC|$ or

(iii) the diagonals bisect each other, e.g. the midpoint of $[DB]$ is the same as the midpoint of $[AC]$.

Note: you only have to give two reasons here.

(c) The slope of $AB = \dfrac{\text{rise}}{\text{run}} = \dfrac{-2}{6} = -\dfrac{1}{3} =$ the slope of DC. Thus, $AB \parallel DC$.

The slope of $DA = \dfrac{\text{rise}}{\text{run}} = \dfrac{-8}{4} = -2 =$ the slope of CB. Thus, $DA \parallel CB$.

Thus, $ABCD$ is a parallelogram since opposite sides are parallel.

Q3 (a) Since $ax + by + c = 0$ has slope $-\dfrac{a}{b}$, the line $3x + 2y + 18 = 0$ has slope $-\dfrac{3}{2}$.

(b) l has slope $-\dfrac{3}{2}$, and since $k \perp l$, k has slope $-1 \div \left(-\dfrac{3}{2}\right) = \dfrac{2}{3}$.

Label the point:

$(7, 0) = (x_1, y_1)$

Substitute and simplify:

$y - y_1 = m(x - x_1) \Rightarrow y - 0 = \dfrac{2}{3}(x - 7) \Rightarrow 3y = 2x - 14 \Rightarrow 0 = 2x - 3y - 14$

(c) l: $3x + 2y + 18 = 0$

k: $2x - 3y - 14 = 0$

Eliminate one variable by multiplying each equation then adding them.

$3l$: $9x + \cancel{6y} + 54 = 0$

$2k$: $\underline{4x - \cancel{6y} - 28 = 0}$

$\qquad 13x \qquad + 26 = 0$

$\Rightarrow 13x = -26 \Rightarrow x = -2$

Substitute to find the second variable.

l: $3(-2) + 2y + 18 = 0 \Rightarrow -6 + 2y + 18 = 0 \Rightarrow 2y + 12 = 0 \Rightarrow y = -6$

Thus the two lines intersect at $(-2, -6)$.

Q4 (a)

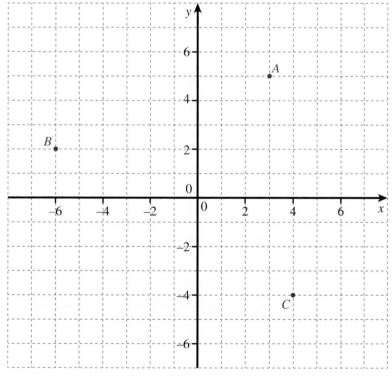

(b) Label the points:

$A(3, 5)$ $B(-6, 2)$

(x_1, y_1) (x_2, y_2)

Substitute:

$$m = \frac{y_2 - y_1}{x_2 - x_1} = \frac{2 - 5}{-6 - 3} = \frac{-3}{-9} = \frac{1}{3}$$

$y - y_1 = m(x - x_1) \Rightarrow y - 5 = \frac{1}{3}(x - 3) \Rightarrow 3y - 15 = x - 3 \Rightarrow 0 = x - 3y + 12$

(c) Translate the triangle so that one vertex is $(0, 0)$.

$A(3, 5) \rightarrow (0, 0) \Rightarrow x \rightarrow x - 3$ and $y \rightarrow y - 5$

$\Rightarrow B(-6, 2) \rightarrow (-9, -3)$ and $C(4, -4) \rightarrow (1, -9)$

Label the points:

$(-9, -3)$ $(1, -9)$

(x_1, y_1) (x_2, y_2)

Substitute:

$A = \frac{1}{2}|x_1 y_2 - x_2 y_1| = \frac{1}{2}|(-9)(-9) - (1)(-3)| = 42$ square units

Q5 (a)   **(i)** $|AB| = |-9 - (-4)| = 5$

(ii) $|BC| = 10 - 3 = 7$. In a right-angled triangle, $A = \frac{1}{2}bh = \frac{1}{2}(5)(7)$

= 17·5 square units.

(b)   **(i)**

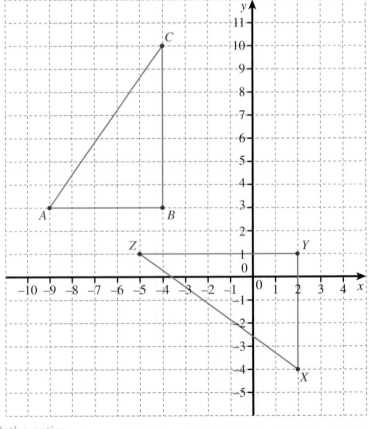

(ii) $Z(-5, 1)$

(Another solution is $Z(-5, -4)$. You only have to give one answer here.)

The two triangles are congruent since corresponding sides are equal in length,

i.e. $|AB| = |XY| = 5$, $|BC| = |ZY| = 7$ and
$|AC| = |ZX| = \sqrt{7^2 + 5^2} = \sqrt{74}$, SSS.

Top-Tip

If two points are on the same horizontal or vertical line, their distance apart can be worked out by simple subtraction as in Q5.

Similarly, the area of the triangle was worked out using $A = \dfrac{1}{2}bh$ which was quicker than translating one point to the origin and using the formula $A = \dfrac{1}{2}|x_1 y_2 - x_2 y_1|$.

Exam questions are sometimes set up with shortcuts like this. Be on the lookout for them as time is precious.

6 The Circle

In this chapter you will learn how to:

- Find the equation of a circle
- Find the equation of a tangent to a circle at a given point
- Prove whether a given line is a tangent to a given circle or not
- Find the point or points of intersection of a line and a circle with the origin as centre.

Two forms of the equation of a circle

Suppose a circle, c, is drawn with a centre (h, k) and a radius of length r. What is necessary for a point (x, y) to be on the circle?

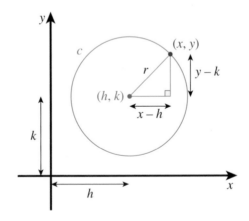

From the diagram, we see that (x, y) can only be on the circle if its distance from (h, k) is equal to the radius, r. Using Pythagoras' theorem, we get $(x - h)^2 + (y - k)^2 = r^2$. This is the equation of the circle, c, above.

A special case of this equation occurs when the circle has the origin as centre, i.e. $h = 0$ and $k = 0$. Substituting, we get $x^2 + y^2 = r^2$.

Tangents

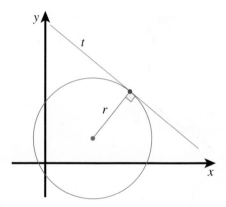

There are three very important properties of a tangent:

- It is a line.
- It intersects the circle at a single point.
- It is perpendicular to the radius at the point of contact.

How do these properties turn up in questions?

- Remember, a tangent is a line, so you may have to use the equation $y - y_1 = m(x - x_1)$.

- You may have to solve a line equation and a circle equation to see if the solution is a single point.

- You may have to find the slope of the radius at the point of contact. Then you will use $m_1 m_2 = -1$ to find the slope of the tangent at that point.

Example

The circle c has centre $(0, 0)$. The point $P(-2, 1)$ is on c.

(a) Find the radius of c.

(b) Find the equation of c.

(c) Find the equation of the tangent t to c at the point P.

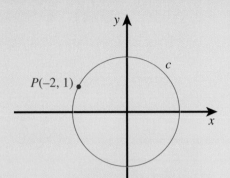

Solution

(a) The radius is equal to the distance between $(0, 0)$ and $P(-2, 1)$.

$$r = \sqrt{(x_2 - x_1)^2 + (y_2 - y_1)^2} = \sqrt{((-2) - 0)^2 + (1 - 0)^2} = \sqrt{4 + 1} = \sqrt{5}$$

(b) $x^2 + y^2 = r^2 \Rightarrow x^2 + y^2 = (\sqrt{5})^2 = x^2 + y^2 = 5$

(c) The radius at P has slope $m_r = \dfrac{1 - 0}{(-2) - 0} = -\dfrac{1}{2}$.

Thus, the tangent at P has slope $m = 2$ (flip the fraction and change the sign).

$$y - y_1 = m(x - x_1) \Rightarrow y - 1 = 2(x - (-2)) \Rightarrow y - 1 = 2x + 4 \Rightarrow 2x - y + 5 = 0$$

Point to note

Suppose a circle c with centre A has a tangent at a point P. Then there is a parallel tangent at the point Q as shown in the diagram.

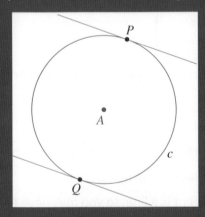

To find the co-ordinates of Q, notice that it is the image of P under a central symmetry in A. That is, $P \rightarrow A \rightarrow Q$.

Intersecting lines and circles

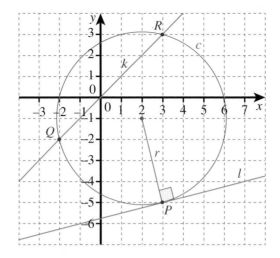

In the diagram above, you can see that the line, l, intersects the circle, c, at a single point $P(3, -5)$. The line l is a tangent. Notice that l is perpendicular to the radius at the point P.

The line k intersects c at two points, $Q(-2, -2)$ and $R(3, 3)$. The line k is a **secant**.

You may be asked to find such points of intersection:

- graphically, from a diagram, or

- algebraically, using simultaneous equations.

As you may remember from your studies for Paper 1, solving a simultaneous linear and non-linear equation can be quite a task. To simplify matters, if such a question comes up, the only type of circle it will involve is one with centre $(0, 0)$.

Example

(a) Draw a diagram of the circle, c, which has equation $x^2 + y^2 = 25$, on co-ordinate axes.

(b) On the same diagram, graph the line, l, with equation $2x + y = 5$.

(c) Use your diagram to find the points of intersection of l and c.

Solution

(a) A circle with equation $x^2 + y^2 = 25$ has centre $(0, 0)$ and radius $r = \sqrt{25} = 5$. Use a compass to draw it.

(b) We need to find two points on the line *l*, given by the equation $2x + y = 5$.

$x = 0 \Rightarrow 2(0) + y = 5 \Rightarrow y = 5$, i.e. $(0, 5)$ is on the line.

$y = 0 \Rightarrow 2x + 0 = 5 \Rightarrow x = 2\cdot5$, i.e. $(2\cdot5, 0)$ is on the line.

Graphing these we get the following:

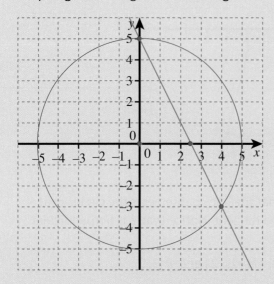

(c) From the diagram we see that the points of intersection are $(0, 5)$ and $(4, -3)$.

Example

Use algebra to investigate whether or not the line $x = 5$ is a tangent to the circle $x^2 + y^2 = 169$.

Solution

Substitute $x = 5$ into the circle equation.

$\Rightarrow (5)^2 + (y)^2 = 169 \Rightarrow 25 + y^2 = 169 \Rightarrow y^2 = 169 - 25 = 144 \Rightarrow y = \pm\sqrt{144}$,

i.e. $y = 12$ or $y = -12$.

Thus the points of intersection are $(5, 12)$ and $(5, -12)$.

Since there are two points of intersection, the line is *not* a tangent. It is a *secant*.

Exercise A

Q1 (a) Find the equation of the circle with:

     (i) centre $(3, 2)$ and radius 4

     (ii) centre $(-1, -4)$ and radius 7

     (iii) centre $(0, -5)$ and radius $\sqrt{3}$.

  (b) Find the equation of the circle with centre $(0, 0)$ and radius:

     (i) 2   **(ii)** 1   **(iii)** $\sqrt{5}$ **(iv)** $\frac{2}{3}$.

Q2 The segment $[AB]$, where $A(-3, 1)$ and $B(5, 7)$, is a diameter of a circle, c.

  (a) Find the co-ordinates of the centre of c.

  (b) Calculate the length of the radius of c.

  (c) Find the equation of c.

Q3 The circle c has equation $x^2 + y^2 = 36$.

  (a) Write down the co-ordinates of the centre and the radius of c.

  (b) The line l, $x = -6$, is a vertical tangent to c. Show c and l on a co-ordinate plane.

  (c) Write down the equation of the other vertical tangent to c.

Q4 The circle c has equation $x^2 + y^2 = 289$.

  (a) Write down the co-ordinates of the centre and the radius of c.

  (b) Show that the point $P(8, 15)$ lies on c.

  (c) Find the slope of the radius at P.

  (d) Find the equation of the tangent to c which passes through P.

Q5 The circle c_1 has equation $x^2 + y^2 = 4$. The circle c_2 has equation $(x + 3)^2 + y^2 = 25$.

  (a) Write down the co-ordinates of the centre and the radius of **(i)** c_1 **(ii)** c_2.

  (b) Show c_1 and c_2 on a co-ordinate plane.

  (c) Use your diagram to show that the distance between the centres of the two circles is equal to $r_2 - r_1$.

  (d) Use your diagram to find the point of contact of c_1 and c_2.

  (e) Write down the equation of t, the common tangent to c_1 and c_2. Show the tangent on your diagram.

Q6 The circle c has equation $(x - 3)^2 + (y - 4)^2 = 25$.

  (a) Write down the co-ordinates of the centre and the radius of c.

  (b) Find the equation of the tangent to c at the point $(6, 8)$.

  (c) Find the co-ordinates of the points where c crosses the y-axis.

Exercise B

Q1 Prove that the line $x - 3y = 10$ is a tangent to the circle with equation $x^2 + y^2 = 10$ and find the co-ordinates of the point of contact.

Q2 Write down the co-ordinates of any three points that lie on the circle with equation $x^2 + y^2 = 100$.

Q3 (a) Joan wants to prove that the triangle ABC is right-angled. Can she use the equation $m_1 m_2 = -1$ in her proof? Justify your answer.

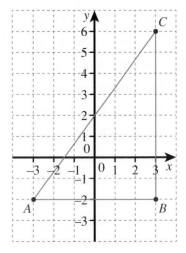

(b) Prove that the triangle ABC is right-angled without using slopes.

(c) Find the midpoint of $[AC]$.

(d) Find the equation of the circumcircle of $\triangle ABC$.

Q4 l_1 has equation $2x + 3y = -6$ and l_2 has equation $2x - 3y = 18$. P is the point of intersection of l_1 and l_2.

(a) Find the co-ordinates of P.

(b) The circle c has the origin as centre. P lies on c. Find the radius of c.

(c) Write down the equation of c.

(d) Say whether each of the following points is **(i)** on c **(ii)** inside c **(iii)** outside c:

$A(4, 3)$ $B(1·5, 4·5)$ $C(\sqrt{7}, \sqrt{17})$ $D(-3·6, 3·6)$ $E(\sqrt{15}, \sqrt{10})$ $F(\sqrt{11}, 4)$.

Q5 l_1 has equation $x = 2$, l_2 has equation $x = 6$, l_3 has equation $y = -1$ and l_4 has equation $y = 3$.

(a) Show the lines l_1, l_2, l_3 and l_4 on a co-ordinate diagram.

(b) The four lines in part (a) are tangents to a circle c.

   (i) Write down the co-ordinates of the centre and the radius of c.

   (ii) Show c on your diagram.

(c) Write down the equation of c.

(d) A line k has a positive slope. It divides c into two regions of equal area.

   (i) Show such a line k on your diagram.   **(ii)** Find the equation of k.

Exercise C

Q1 A circle, c_1, has centre $(0, 0)$ and diameter 8 units.

(a) Show c_1 on a co-ordinate diagram.

(b) Find the equation of c_1.

(c) Prove that the point $(3, 2)$ is inside c_1 and $(3, 3)$ is outside it.

(d) Another circle, c_2, has centre $(0, 1)$ and just touches the circle c_1. Show c_2 on your diagram in part (a) above and find the equation of c_2.

(2011)

Q2 The diagram shows two circles, c_1 and c_2, of equal radius.

c_1 has centre $(0, 0)$ and it cuts the x-axis at $(5, 0)$.

(a) Find the equation of c_1.

(b) Show that the point $P(-3, 4)$ is on c_1.

(c) The two circles touch at $P(-3, 4)$. P is on the line joining the two centres.

Find the equation of c_2.

(d) Find the equation of the common tangent at P.

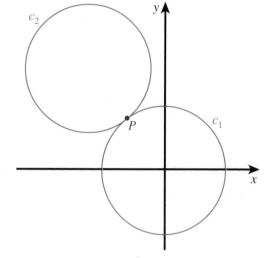

(2012)

Q3 The point A has co-ordinates $(8, 6)$ and O is the origin. The diagram shows two circles c_1 and c_2.

c_1 has centre $(0, 0)$ and radius $|OA|$.

c_2 has a diameter of $[OA]$.

(a) Find the equation of c_1.

(b) Find the equation of c_2.

(c) The circle c_2 cuts the x-axis at the point P. Find the co-ordinates of P.

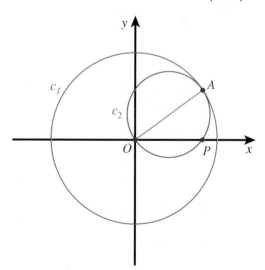

(2013)

Q4 The circle c has centre $P(-2, -1)$ and passes through the point $Q(3, 1)$.

(a) Show c, P, and Q on a co-ordinate diagram.

(b) Find the radius of c and hence write down its equation.

(c) R is the point $(1, 6)$. By finding the slopes of PQ and QR, show that QR is a tangent to c.

(SEC Sample Paper 2014)

Q5 The circle, c, has equation $(x+2)^2 + (y-3)^2 = 100$.

(a) (i) Write down the co-ordinates of A, the centre of c.

Write down r, the length of the radius of c.

(ii) Show that the point $P(-8, 11)$ is on the circle c.

(b) (i) Find the slope of the radius $[AP]$.

(ii) Hence, find the equation of t, the tangent to c at P.

(c) A second line, k, is a tangent to c at the point Q, and $k \parallel t$. Find the co-ordinates of Q.

(2014)

Solutions to Exercise A

Q1 (a) (i) $(x-3)^2 + (y-2)^2 = 16$ (ii) $(x+1)^2 + (y+4)^2 = 49$

(iii) $x^2 + (y+5)^2 = 3$

(b) (i) $x^2 + y^2 = 4$ (ii) $x^2 + y^2 = 1$ (iii) $x^2 + y^2 = 5$

(iv) $x^2 + y^2 = \dfrac{4}{9}$ or $9x^2 + 9y^2 = 4$

Q2 (a) The centre of c will be the midpoint of $[AB]$.

$A(-3, 1) \qquad B(5, 7)$

$(x_1, y_1) \qquad (x_2, y_2)$

$\left(\dfrac{x_1 + x_2}{2}, \dfrac{y_1 + y_2}{2} \right) = \left(\dfrac{(-3) + 5}{2}, \dfrac{1 + 7}{2} \right) = \left(\dfrac{2}{2}, \dfrac{8}{2} \right) = (1, 4)$

(b) $(1, 4) \qquad B(5, 7)$

$(x_1, y_1) \quad (x_2, y_2)$

$r = \sqrt{(x_2 - x_1)^2 + (y_2 - y_1)^2} = \sqrt{(5-1)^2 + (7-4)^2} = \sqrt{4^2 + 3^2} = 5$

(c) $(x-h)^2 + (y-k)^2 = r^2 \Rightarrow (x-1)^2 + (y-4)^2 = 25$

Q3 (a) Centre $(0, 0)$, $r = \sqrt{36} = 6$.

(b)

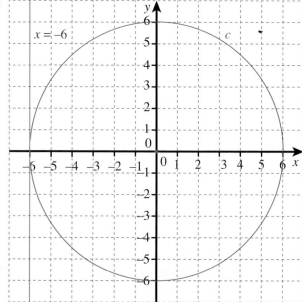

(c) The other vertical tangent has equation $x = 6$.

Q4 (a) Centre $(0, 0)$, $r = \sqrt{289} = 17$.

(b) We need to show that $P(8, 15)$ satisfies the equation $x^2 + y^2 = 289$.
$(8)^2 + (15)^2 = 64 + 225 = 289$. Thus, P lies on c.

(c) $(0, 0)$ $P(8, 15)$
(x_1, y_1) (x_2, y_2)
$$m_{OP} = \frac{y_2 - y_1}{x_2 - x_1} = \frac{15 - 0}{8 - 0} = \frac{15}{8}$$

(d) Since the tangent at P is perpendicular to OP, its slope is $m = -\frac{8}{15}$.
$(x_1, y_1) = (8, 15) \Rightarrow y - y_1 = m(x - x_1)$
$\Rightarrow y - 15 = -\frac{8}{15}(x - 8)$
$\Rightarrow 15y - 225 = -8x + 64 \Rightarrow 8x + 15y = 289$

Q5 (a) **(i)** c_1 has centre $(0, 0)$, $r = \sqrt{4} = 2$.

(ii) c_2 has centre $(-3, 0)$, $r = \sqrt{25} = 5$.

(b)

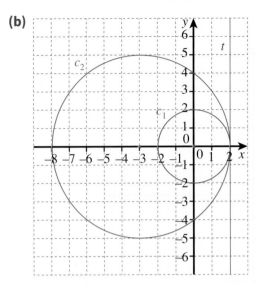

(c) The distance between the centres is 3, $r_2 - r_1 = 5 - 2 = 3$.

(d) The point of contact has co-ordinates $(2, 0)$.

(e) The equation of the common tangent t is $x = 2$.

Q6 (a) c has centre $(3, 4)$, $r = \sqrt{25} = 5$.

(b) First find the slope of the radius at the point of contact.

$$(3, 4) \quad (6, 8)$$
$$(x_1, y_1) \quad (x_2, y_2)$$

$$m_{radius} = \frac{y_2 - y_1}{x_2 - x_1} = \frac{8 - 4}{6 - 3} = \frac{4}{3}$$

Thus the slope of the tangent at $(6, 8) = (x_1, y_1)$ is $m = -\frac{3}{4}$.

$$y - y_1 = m(x - x_1) \Rightarrow y - 8 = -\frac{3}{4}(x - 6)$$
$$\Rightarrow 4y - 32 = -3x + 18 \Rightarrow 3x + 4y = 50$$

(c) A diagram is very helpful in this kind of question.

c crosses the y-axis at $(0, 0)$ and $(0, 8)$.

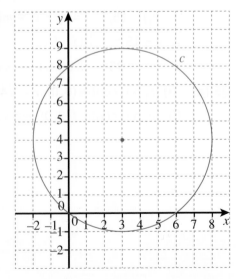

Solutions to Exercise B

Q1 $x - 3y = 10 \Rightarrow x = 3y + 10$. Substitute this into the circle equation.

$x^2 + y^2 = 10 \Rightarrow (3y + 10)^2 + y^2 = 10 \Rightarrow 9y^2 + 60y + 100 + y^2 = 10$

$\Rightarrow 10y^2 + 60y + 90 = 0 \Rightarrow y^2 + 6y + 9 = 0 \Rightarrow (y + 3)(y + 3) = 0 \Rightarrow y = -3.$

Substitute this into $x = 3y + 10 \Rightarrow x = 3(-3) + 10 = 1.$

Since the simultaneous equations have only one solution, the line is a tangent and the point of contact has co-ordinates $(1, -3)$.

Q2 Any points on the circle must satisfy the equation $x^2 + y^2 = 100$.

For example, $(6)^2 + (8)^2 = 100 \Rightarrow (6, 8)$ is on the circle, $(8)^2 + (6)^2 = 100$ $\Rightarrow (8, 6)$ is on the circle and $(-6)^2 + (-8)^2 = 100 \Rightarrow (-6, -8)$ is on the circle. Similarly, $(-8, -6)$, $(8, -6)$, $(-8, 6)$, $(6, -8)$ and $(-6, 8)$ are on the circle. These are just the points with integer co-ordinates. Irrational possibilities would include $(\sqrt{3}, \sqrt{97})$. There are infinitely many points on the circle. You only have to give three in your answer.

Q3 (a) AB is perpendicular to BC. Since BC is vertical its slope is undefined so the equation $m_1 m_2 = -1$ cannot be used.

(b) From the diagram, $|AB| = 6$. (Count the horizontal steps apart.) Similarly $|BC| = 8$.

$\begin{array}{cc} A(-3, -2) & C(3, 6) \\ (x_1, y_1) & (x_2, y_2) \end{array}$

$|AC| = \sqrt{(x_2 - x_1)^2 + (y_2 - y_1)^2} = \sqrt{(3 - (-3))^2 + (6 - (-2))^2} = \sqrt{6^2 + 8^2} = 10.$

Thus, $|AC|^2 = 100 = |AB|^2 + |BC|^2 = 36 + 64$. That is, by the converse of Pythagoras' theorem, the triangle ABC is right-angled.

(c) $\begin{array}{cc} A(-3, -2) & C(3, 6) \\ (x_1, y_1) & (x_2, y_2) \end{array}$

$\left(\dfrac{x_1 + x_2}{2}, \dfrac{y_1 + y_2}{2} \right) = \left(\dfrac{(-3) + 3}{2}, \dfrac{(-2) + 6}{2} \right) = (0, 2)$

(d) $[AC]$ is the hypotenuse of a right-angled triangle.

The angle standing on a diameter of a circle is a right angle.
Thus, $[AC]$ is the diameter of the circumcircle.

Its centre is the midpoint of $[AC]$, $(0, 2)$.

Its radius is $\dfrac{|AC|}{2} = \dfrac{10}{2} = 5.$

Thus, the circumcircle has the equation $x^2 + (y - 2)^2 = 25.$

Q4 (a) $2x + 3y = -6$

$\underline{2x - 3y = 18}$

$4x \qquad = 12 \Rightarrow x = 3$

Substitute: $2(3) + 3y = -6 \Rightarrow 3y = -12 \Rightarrow y = -4$.

P has co-ordinates $(3, -4)$.

(b) $(0, 0) \quad (3, -4)$

$(x_1, y_1) \quad (x_2, y_2)$

$r = \sqrt{(3-0)^2 + (-4-0)^2} = \sqrt{9 + 16} = 5$

(c) c has equation $x^2 + y^2 = 25$.

(d) In each case, substitute the co-ordinates of the point into the left-hand side of the equation $x^2 + y^2 = 25$.

$A\,(4, 3)$: $4^2 + 3^2 = 25$, so A is on c.

$B\,(1{\cdot}5, 4{\cdot}5)$: $1{\cdot}5^2 + 4{\cdot}5^2 = 22{\cdot}5 < 25$, so B is inside c.

$C\left(\sqrt{7}, \sqrt{17}\right)$: $\left(\sqrt{7}\right)^2 + \left(\sqrt{17}\right)^2 = 24 < 25$, so C is inside c.

$D\,(-3{\cdot}6, 3{\cdot}6)$: $(-3{\cdot}6)^2 + (3{\cdot}6)^2 = 25{\cdot}92 > 25$, so D is outside c.

$E\left(\sqrt{15}, \sqrt{10}\right)$: $\left(\sqrt{15}\right)^2 + \left(\sqrt{10}\right)^2 = 25$, so E is on c.

$F\left(\sqrt{11}, 4\right)$: $\left(\sqrt{11}\right)^2 + 4^2 = 27 > 25$, so F is outside c.

Q5 (a)

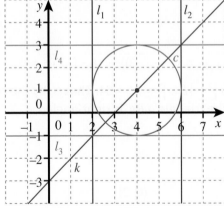

(b) **(i)** Centre $(4, 1)$, radius, $r = 2$. **(ii)** See diagram above.

(c) $(x - 4)^2 + (y - 1)^2 = 4$

(d) **(i)** See diagram above.

(ii) From the diagram, k has a y-intercept $c = -3$

and slope $m = \dfrac{\text{rise}}{\text{run}} = \dfrac{2}{2} = 1$.

$y = mx + c \Rightarrow y = x - 3$ is the equation of k.

Note that the line k shown is just one example. It could be rotated to almost horizontal or almost vertical and still meet the criteria, as long as it passes through the centre of c.

Solutions to Exercise C

Q1 (a)

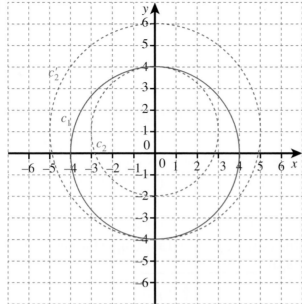

(b) $d = 8 \Rightarrow r = 4$. $x^2 + y^2 = r^2 \Rightarrow x^2 + y^2 = 16$.

(c) $3^2 + 2^2 = 9 + 4 = 13 < 16$, thus $(3, 2)$ is inside c_1.

$3^2 + 3^2 = 9 + 9 = 18 > 16$, thus $(3, 3)$ is outside c_1.

(d) There are two possible circles, as shown. One is inside c_1 and the other is outside c_1.

The inner solution has centre $(0, 1)$ and radius 3.

$(x - h)^2 + (y - k)^2 = r^2 \Rightarrow (x - 0)^2 + (y - 1)^2 = 3^2 \Rightarrow x^2 + (y - 1)^2 = 9$

The outer solution has centre $(0, 1)$ and radius 5.

$(x - 0)^2 + (y - 1)^2 = 5^2 \Rightarrow x^2 + (y - 1)^2 = 25$.

Q2 (a) $x^2 + y^2 = r^2 \Rightarrow x^2 + y^2 = 25$

(b) $(-3)^2 + (4)^2 = 9 + 16 = 25 = r^2$, thus $P(-3, 4)$ is on c_1.

(c) The centre of c_2 is the image of the centre of c_1 under central symmetry in the point P.

$(0, 0) \rightarrow P(-3, 4) \Rightarrow x \rightarrow x - 3$ and $y \rightarrow y + 4$

$P(-3, 4) \rightarrow (-3 - 3, 4 + 4) = (-6, 8)$

$(x - h)^2 + (y - k)^2 = r^2 \Rightarrow (x - (-6))^2 + (y - 8)^2 = 5^2 \Rightarrow (x + 6)^2 + (y - 8)^2 = 25$

(d) The line joining the centres has slope $\dfrac{y_2 - y_1}{x_2 - x_1} = \dfrac{0 - 8}{0 - (-6)} = \dfrac{-8}{6} = -\dfrac{4}{3}$.

The tangent at $P(-3, 4)$ is perpendicular to that line so its slope is $-1 \div \left(-\frac{4}{3}\right) = \frac{3}{4}$.

$y - y_1 = m(x - x_1) \Rightarrow y - 4 = \frac{3}{4}(x - (-3))$

$\Rightarrow 4y - 16 = 3x + 9 \Rightarrow 0 = 3x - 4y + 25$

Q3 (a) $r = |OA| = \sqrt{(8-0)^2 + (6-0)^2} = 10.$ $x^2 + y^2 = r^2 \Rightarrow x^2 + y^2 = 100.$

(b) The midpoint of $[OA]$, $\left(\frac{8+0}{2}, \frac{6+0}{2}\right) = (4, 3)$, is the centre of c_2.

Since its diameter is $|OA| = 10$, its radius is $r = 5$.

$(x - h)^2 + (y - k)^2 = r^2 \Rightarrow (x - 4)^2 + (y - 3)^2 = 5^2 \Rightarrow (x - 4)^2 + (y - 3)^2 = 25$

(c) The y co-ordinate of any point on the x-axis is 0.

$y = 0 \Rightarrow (x - 4)^2 + (0 - 3)^2 = 25 \Rightarrow (x - 4)^2 + 9 = 25 \Rightarrow (x - 4)^2 = 16$

$\Rightarrow x - 4 = \pm \sqrt{16} = \pm 4.$

$x - 4 = 4 \Rightarrow x = 8$ and $x - 4 = -4 \Rightarrow x = 0.$

Thus, c_2 cuts the x-axis at $(0, 0)$ and at $(8, 0)$, so the point P has co-ordinates $(8, 0)$.

Q4 (a)

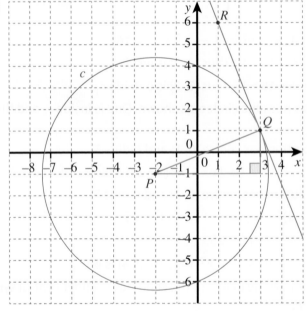

(b) Using the right-angled triangle shown and Pythagoras' theorem:

$r = \sqrt{5^2 + 2^2} = \sqrt{29}$

$(x - h)^2 + (y - k)^2 = r^2 \Rightarrow (x - (-2))^2 + (y - (-1))^2 = (\sqrt{29})^2$

$\Rightarrow (x + 2)^2 + (y + 1)^2 = 29.$

(c) $P(-2, -1) \quad Q(3, 1)$

$ (x_1, y_1) \quad (x_2, y_2) \Rightarrow m_{PQ} = \frac{y_2 - y_1}{x_2 - x_1} = \frac{1 - (-1)}{3 - (-2)} = \frac{2}{5}$

$Q(3, 1) \quad R(1, 6)$

$(x_1, y_1) \quad (x_2, y_2) \Rightarrow m_{QR} = \frac{y_2 - y_1}{x_2 - x_1} = \frac{6 - 1}{1 - 3} = -\frac{5}{2}$

$$m_{PQ}\,m_{QR} = \left(\frac{2}{5}\right)\left(-\frac{5}{2}\right) = -1 \Rightarrow PQ \perp QR$$

Thus, QR is a tangent to c since it is perpendicular to the radius PQ at the point of contact Q.

> **Remember**
>
> The distance formula is based on Pythagoras' theorem.
>
> If you have a diagram it may be quicker to just draw the relevant right-angled triangle, as in Q4 (b), to get the radius of a circle.

Q5 (a) **(i)** $A(-2, 3)$, $r = \sqrt{100} = 10$.

   (ii) $P(-8, 11)$, $(-8 + 2)^2 + (11 - 3)^2 = (-6)^2 + 8^2 = 100$. Thus, P is on the circle c since it satisfies its equation.

(b) **(i)** $A(-2, 3)$ $P(-8, 11)$
   (x_1, y_1) (x_2, y_2) $\Rightarrow m_{AP} = \dfrac{y_2 - y_1}{x_2 - x_1} = \dfrac{11 - 3}{-8 - (-2)} = \dfrac{8}{-6} = -\dfrac{4}{3}$

   (ii) Since the tangent at P is perpendicular to AP its slope is
   $$m = -1 \div \left(-\frac{4}{3}\right) = \frac{3}{4}.$$
   $P(-8, 11) = (x_1, y_1)$,
   $$y - y_1 = m(x - x_1) \Rightarrow y - 11 = \frac{3}{4}(x - (-8)) \Rightarrow 4y - 44 = 3x + 24$$
   $$\Rightarrow 3x - 4y + 68 = 0$$

(c) Use the central symmetry $P \to A \to Q$.
   $P(-8, 11) \to A(-2, 3) \Rightarrow x \to x + 6$ and $y \to y - 8 \Rightarrow A(-2, 3) \to Q(4, -5)$.

7 Trigonometry and Enlargements

Learning objectives

In this chapter you will learn how to find:

- The length of a side of a right-angled triangle using Pythagoras' theorem or SOHCAHTOA

- An angle in a right-angled triangle using SOHCAHTOA

- The area of a right-angled triangle

- The length of a side of a non-right-angled triangle using the sine rule (given two angles and a side)

- An angle in a non-right-angled triangle using the sine rule (given two sides and an angle)

- A side of a non-right-angled triangle using the cosine rule (given two sides and the included angle)

- An angle in a non-right-angled triangle using the cosine rule (given three sides)

- The area of a non-right-angled triangle

- The image of a figure under an enlargement given a centre point and a scale factor

- The centre or scale factor of an enlargement given a figure and its image and you will learn that the area of an image is k^2 times the area of the figure that was enlarged.

Trigonometry

Solving right-angled triangles

A hexagon is a six-sided figure. A trigon has three sides. The word **trigonometry** derives from Greek and means 'measuring triangles'.

We will use trigonometry to find:

- the lengths of sides
- the measures of angles
- the areas of triangles.

Trigonometry is based on a property of similar triangles: ratios of corresponding sides are equal.

Imagine you drew a right-angled triangle where one angle was, for example, 30°. Suppose you then repeatedly enlarged it on a photocopier. Copies of all sorts of sizes could be made.

The angles in each triangle would all match up, even though the corresponding sides would have different lengths.

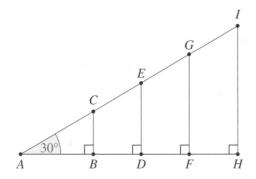

Suppose you put the triangles on top of each other as in the diagram above. If you measured them carefully enough, you would find that **ratios of corresponding sides would be equal**.

In trigonometry, each ratio is given a name: **sine, cosine** or **tangent** (**sin, cos** and **tan** for short).

$$\sin(30°) = \frac{|BC|}{|AC|} = \frac{|DE|}{|AE|} = \frac{|FG|}{|AG|} = \frac{|HI|}{|AI|} = \frac{|\text{side opposite } 30°|}{|\text{hypotenuse}|} = 0 \cdot 5$$

$$\cos(30°) = \frac{|AB|}{|AC|} = \frac{|AD|}{|AE|} = \frac{|AF|}{|AG|} = \frac{|AH|}{|AI|} = \frac{|\text{adjacent}|}{|\text{hypotenuse}|} = 0 \cdot 866$$

$$\tan(30°) = \frac{|BC|}{|AB|} = \frac{|DE|}{|AD|} = \frac{|FG|}{|AF|} = \frac{|HI|}{|AH|} = \frac{|\text{opposite}|}{|\text{adjacent}|} = 0 \cdot 5774$$

To save you drawing diagrams and measuring each time, these three ratios are programmed into your calculator.

Students often use the mnemonic SohCahToa to remember the trigonometric ratios.

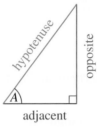

$$\text{Sin } A = \frac{o}{h}, \quad \text{Cos } A = \frac{a}{h}, \quad \text{Tan } A = \frac{o}{a}.$$

If a triangle is right-angled, use:

- Pythagoras' theorem to find a side given two other sides
- SOHCAHTOA to find a side given an angle and a side
- SOHCAHTOA to find an angle given two sides
- $A = \frac{1}{2}ah$ (area equals half the base by the height) to find the area.

The following information for right-angled triangles can be found on page 16 of the *Formulae and Tables* booklet.

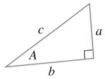

$$\sin A = \frac{a}{c} \qquad \cos A = \frac{b}{c} \qquad \tan A = \frac{a}{b}$$

$c^2 = a^2 + b^2$ Pythagoras' theorem

The area formula for a right-angled triangle is on page 9 of the booklet.

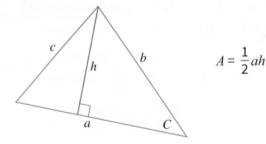

$$A = \frac{1}{2}ah$$

In the examples below, we will match the formula triangle from the *Formulae and Tables* booklet with the triangle in each question. This will help later when it comes to solving non-right-angled triangles. Learn how to do this as well as using SOHCAHTOA.

Example

Find:

(a) the length of the side x

(b) the length of the side y

(c) the measure of the angle A, correct to the nearest degree

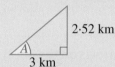

(d) the area of the triangle (i) ABC (ii) ABD (iii) ABE.

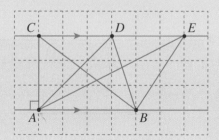

Note that each square on the grid represents 1 cm.

Solutions

(a) $c^2 = a^2 + b^2 \Rightarrow 8{\cdot}5^2 = 4^2 + x^2 \Rightarrow \sqrt{8{\cdot}5^2 - 4^2} = x = 7{\cdot}5$ m

(b)

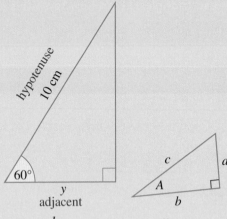

$$\cos A = \frac{b}{c} \Rightarrow \cos(60°) = \frac{y}{10} \Rightarrow 10 \times \cos(60°) = y = 5 \text{ cm}$$

(c)

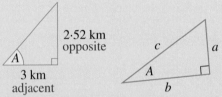

$$\tan A = \frac{a}{b} \Rightarrow \tan A = \frac{2{\cdot}52}{3} \Rightarrow A = \tan^{-1}\!\left(\frac{2{\cdot}52}{3}\right) = 40°$$

(d) (i) Triangle ABC has a height of 3 cm and a base of length 4 cm.

$$A = \frac{1}{2}ah = \frac{1}{2}(4)(3) = 6 \text{ cm}^2$$

(ii) and (iii)

Since $CD \parallel AB$ (notice the arrows on the lines) the triangles ABD and ABE have the same height as triangle ABC. Since they also have the same base, the three triangles have the same area, i.e. $A = 6 \text{ cm}^2$.

Point to note

$\sin^{-1}$ is the inverse of sin.

$\cos^{-1}$ is the inverse of cos.

$\tan^{-1}$ is the inverse of tan.

These inverse functions are used to find angles. For $\sin^{-1}(x)$, say 'sine inverse x', or 'the angle whose sine is x', etc.

Solving triangles which don't contain a right angle

Page 16 of the *Formulae and Tables* booklet deals with triangles which do not contain a right angle. The following information is given on that page:

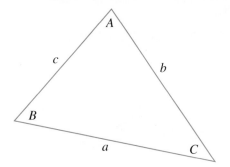

area: $A = \dfrac{1}{2} ab \sin C$

sine rule: $\dfrac{a}{\sin A} = \dfrac{b}{\sin B} = \dfrac{c}{\sin C}$

cosine rule: $a^2 = b^2 + c^2 - 2bc \cos A$

> ### Point to note
>
> It is very important to be aware that the side a is *opposite* the angle A in the formula diagram above. The sine rule is about a pair of angles and their opposite sides (you can ignore the third ratio).
>
> Quite often, you will be given a pair of angles, one of which is *not* opposite to one of the sides in the question. You will have to work out the third angle using, for example, the fact that the three interior angles of a triangle add up to 180°.

If a triangle is not right-angled, use:

- the sine rule to find a side given the opposite angle and another side and its opposite angle

- the sine rule to find an angle given its opposite side and another angle and its opposite side

- the cosine rule to find a side given two sides and their included angle

- the cosine rule to find an angle given three sides

- the formula $A = \dfrac{1}{2} ab \sin C$ to find the area given two sides and the included angle.

Pythagoras' theorem is great. If you know two sides of a right-angled triangle, you can work out the third side. But it only works for right-angled triangles.

How can we make it work for non-right-angled triangles? Add vitamins!

$$a^2 = b^2 + c^2 \boxed{- 2bc \cos A}$$

Added vitamins

The cosine rule is a new, improved version of Pythagoras' theorem. Now you can solve *any* triangle!

Example

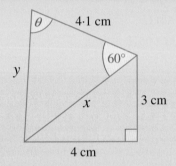

Find **(a)** x **(b)** y, correct to two decimal places
(c) θ, correct to the nearest degree.

Solution

(a) x is the hypotenuse of a right-angled triangle.
Thus, $x^2 = 3^2 + 4^2 = 25 \implies x = 5$ cm.

(b) To find y, draw a formula triangle beside the problem triangle.

Since the problem involves *three* sides of a non-right-angled triangle, it is a cosine rule problem.

Match the unknown, y, with a.
The opposite angle will then be A.
It doesn't particularly matter which side you make b or c.

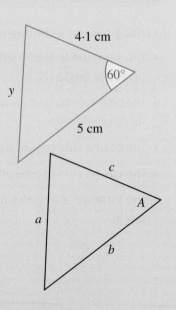

$$a^2 = b^2 + c^2 - 2bc \cos A \Rightarrow y^2 = (5)^2 + (4\cdot1)^2 - 2(5)(4\cdot1) \cos(60°) = 21\cdot31$$
$$\Rightarrow y = \sqrt{21\cdot31} = 4\cdot62 \text{ cm}$$

(c) Again, draw the relevant parts of the problem diagram.

Draw a formula diagram beside it. Make sure to match the unknown, θ, with A.

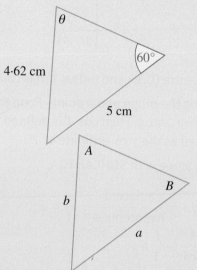

$$\frac{\sin A}{a} = \frac{\sin B}{b} \Rightarrow \frac{\sin \theta}{5} = \frac{\sin 60°}{4\cdot62} \Rightarrow \sin \theta = 5 \times \frac{\sin 60°}{4\cdot62} = 0\cdot9373$$
$$\Rightarrow \theta = \sin^{-1}(0\cdot9373) = 70°.$$

Top Tip

Always draw a formula triangle along with the relevant parts of the problem triangle.

If you are looking for a side, label the unknown a.

If you are looking for an angle, label the unknown A.

As you saw in the above example, you may have to draw different formula triangles for different parts of the same question.

All the angles

Type 'cos(300°)' into your calculator. It should give an answer of $\frac{1}{2}$.

Hold on! We defined $\cos A$ as the ratio, $\dfrac{\text{adjacent}}{\text{hypotenuse}}$, of two sides of

a right-angled triangle. You'd have a hard time getting an angle of 300° into a right-angled triangle. What's going on?

Page 13 of the *Formulae and Tables* booklet has the answer.

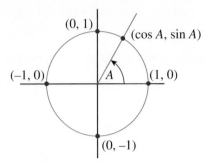

The circle shown has centre $(0, 0)$ and radius 1. It is called the **unit circle**.

Suppose the line joining the origin and a point, P, on the unit circle makes an angle A with the positive x-axis. Then $\cos A$ is defined as the x co-ordinate of P and $\sin A$ is defined as the y co-ordinate of P.

These new definitions agree with SOHCAHTOA, for acute angles.

From the diagram, $\cos A = \dfrac{\text{adjacent}}{\text{hypotenuse}} = \dfrac{x}{1} = x$

and $\sin A = \dfrac{\text{opposite}}{\text{hypotenuse}} = \dfrac{y}{1} = y.$

Clearly, the angle A can take any value, so $\cos A$ and $\sin A$ are now defined for all angles.

Since we have moved on from acute angles in a right-angled triangle, we also need a new definition for $\tan A$. It is defined as the ratio of $\sin A$ to $\cos A$, i.e. $\tan A = \dfrac{\sin A}{\cos A}.$

Page 13 of the *Formulae and Tables* booklet also contains the following table.

A (degrees)	0°	90°	180°	270°	30°	45°	60°
A (radians)	0	$\dfrac{\pi}{2}$	π	$\dfrac{3\pi}{2}$	$\dfrac{\pi}{6}$	$\dfrac{\pi}{4}$	$\dfrac{\pi}{3}$
cos A	1	0	−1	0	$\dfrac{\sqrt{3}}{2}$	$\dfrac{1}{\sqrt{2}}$	$\dfrac{1}{2}$
sin A	0	1	0	−1	$\dfrac{1}{2}$	$\dfrac{1}{\sqrt{2}}$	$\dfrac{\sqrt{3}}{2}$
tan A	0	Not defined	0	Not defined	$\dfrac{1}{\sqrt{3}}$	1	$\sqrt{3}$

Ignore the second row, which uses radians. They're not on the ordinary syllabus.

Notice that some of the values are given in surd form, e.g. $\tan(60°) = \sqrt{3}$.

Any DAL (direct algebraic logic) calculator can also express these values in surd form, where applicable.

Angles of elevation, angles of depression, compass bearings

Suppose a telescope is set up for viewing something straight ahead.

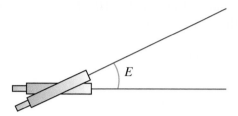

If the telescope is rotated upwards, the angle marked E is called the **angle of elevation**.

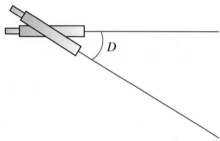

If it is rotated downwards, the angle marked D is called the **angle of depression**.

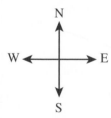

The four cardinal points of the compass, North, South, East and West, are shown.

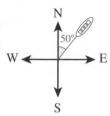

The direction of the boat in the diagram above is N 50° E, that is, face North then turn 50° in the direction of East. It could also be described as E 40° N.

Enlargements

If you enlarge a drawing of a triangle on a photocopier, you get a similar triangle. To enlarge an object in maths you use a point and a number.

The point, usually denoted by O, is called the **centre of the enlargement**. The number, usually denoted by k, is called the **scale factor**.

Suppose we want to enlarge the triangle ABC below, using O as the centre of the enlargement, with a scale factor of $k = 2$.

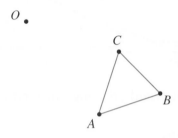

Draw a line segment from O to C. Continue until you get to a point C' where $|OC'| = 2|OC|$. Repeat this for points A and B.

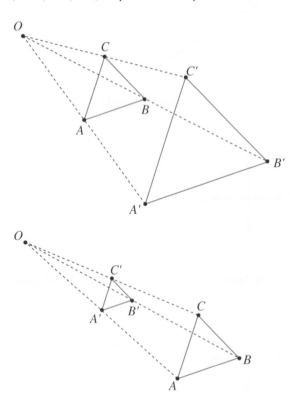

Notice that each side of the new triangle $A'B'C'$ is twice the length of the corresponding side in triangle ABC. This is because we chose $k = 2$. This means that the area of $A'B'C'$ is 4 times the area of ABC, since the height and base are both doubled.

What happens if we choose a scale factor less than 1?

Let's look at $k = \dfrac{1}{2}$.

Notice that the sides of $A'B'C'$ are now all half the length of the corresponding sides in triangle ABC. It is important to note that the area of $A'B'C'$ is $k^2 = \left(\dfrac{1}{2}\right)^2 = \dfrac{1}{4}$ of the area of ABC.

Exercise A

Q1

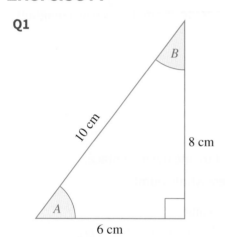

(a) Use the diagram to write down (i) $\sin A$ (ii) $\cos A$
    (iii) $\tan A$ as a ratio in its simplest terms.

(b) Use the diagram to write down (i) $\sin B$ (ii) $\cos B$
    (iii) $\tan B$ as a ratio in its simplest terms.

(c) Find $A + B$.

(d) Write down some generalisations based on the answers above.

Q2 Find the measure of the angles **(a)** A **(b)** B **(c)** C **(d)** D below.
Give your answers correct to the nearest degree where appropriate.

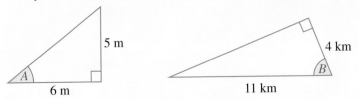

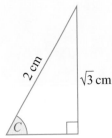

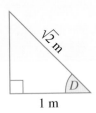

Q3 The angle A of a right-angled triangle is acute. If $\sin A = \dfrac{3}{5}$, use a diagram
to find **(a)** $\cos A$ **(b)** $\tan A$ **(c)** $\tan(90° - A)$.

Q4

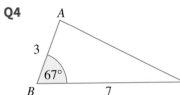

(a) Calculate the area of $\triangle ABC$, correct to one decimal place.

(b) Calculate $|AC|$, correct to the nearest whole number.

Q5 A lighthouse, H, is observed from a ship sailing a straight
course due North. P and Q are points on the ship's route.
The distance from P to H is 2 km and the bearing of the
lighthouse from P is N 41·3° E. The distance from Q to H
is 2·64 km.

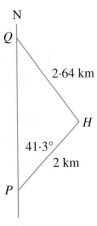

(a) Find the bearing of the lighthouse from Q.

(b) Find $|\angle PHQ|$, correct to one decimal place.

(c) Find $|PQ|$, correct to one decimal place.

(d) The ship is sailing at a speed of 19 km/h. Find,
correct to the nearest minute, the time taken to sail
from P to Q.

Q6

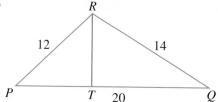

The lengths of the sides of the triangle PQR are $|PQ| = 20, |QR| = 14$ and $|PR| = 12$.

(a) Find $|\angle RPQ|$, correct to one decimal place.

(b) Find the area of the triangle PQR, correct to one decimal place.

(c) Find $|RT|$, where $PQ \perp RT$. Give your answer correct to the nearest whole number.

Q7 David is speaking at a conference. He wishes to project images from his laptop onto a large screen.

The dimensions of his laptop screen are 34·5 cm by 19·3 cm. The enlargement of David's images will fill the large screen exactly. The scale factor of the enlargement is 5.

(a) Find the width of the large screen.

(b) Find the height of the large screen.

(c) Find the area of the large screen.

(d) Find the area of David's laptop screen.

(e) Find the ratio, area of the large screen: area of David's laptop screen.

Exercise B

Q1 The trapezium below has right angles at points A and B, and $|\angle C| = 102°$. $|AB| = 9·1$ m and $|BC| = 2·3$ m.

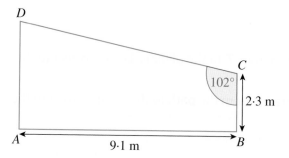

(a) Find $|AD|$, correct to one decimal place.

(b) Find the area of the trapezium $ABCD$, correct to three significant figures.

Q2 In the diagram, AD and BC are horizontal and AC is vertical. CE is perpendicular to AB.

$|AC| = 4{\cdot}2$ m, $|CD| = 5{\cdot}6$ m and $|\angle BAC| = 55°$.

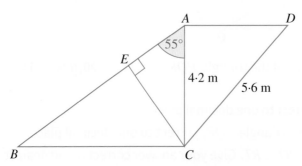

Calculate, correct to one decimal place, **(a)** $|AD|$ **(b)** $|\angle ACD|$ **(c)** $|CE|$ and **(d)** $|AB|$.

Q3 S and T are two points 300 m apart on a straight path due North. From S the bearing of a pillar is N 40° E. From T the bearing of the pillar is N 70° E.

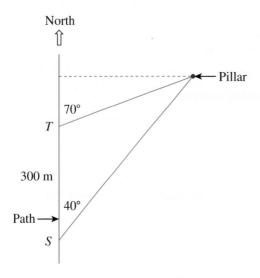

(a) Show that the distance from T to the pillar is 386 m, correct to the nearest metre.

(b) Find the shortest distance from the path to the pillar, correct to the nearest metre.

Q4 A harbour is 6 km due East of a lighthouse. A boat is 4 km from the lighthouse. The bearing of the boat from the lighthouse is N 40° W.

(a) How far is the boat from the harbour? Give your answer correct to one decimal place.

(b) Find the bearing of the boat from the harbour. Give your answer correct to the nearest degree.

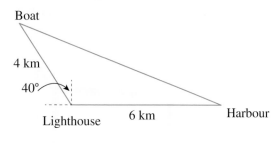

Q5 Alan has four sticks which are of length 2 cm, 4 cm, 6 cm and 8 cm.

(a) Three of the sticks are chosen at random. List the resulting sample space.

(b) What is the probability that a triangle can be formed using the three sticks chosen in part (a)?

(c) Calculate the smallest angle in the largest triangle that can be formed using the sticks. Give your answer correct to the nearest integer.

Q6 Crime has struck Goatham city again. Inspector Gormless beams the Cat-signal onto a cloud to inform Catman.

The searchlight is on the top of a building 400 m high. The angle of elevation of the cloud from the searchlight is 60°. The vertical distance of the cloud from the ground is 2000 m.

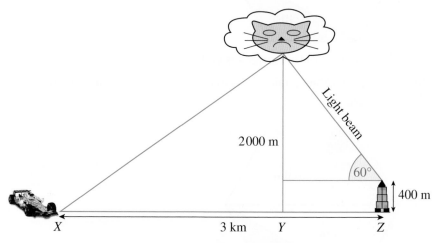

(a) Find the length of the light beam, correct to three significant figures.

(b) Catman is at point X, 3 km away, when he sees the signal. Calculate the angle of elevation of the Cat-signal from the point X. Give your answer correct to one decimal place.

Exercise C

Q1 The tables in a primary school classroom are like the one in the picture.
The top of the table is in the shape of a trapezium, as shown in the diagram.

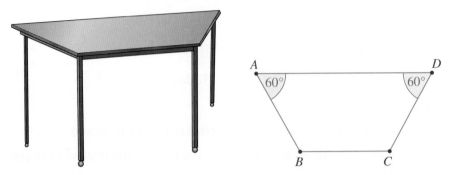

The measurements are as follows: $|AD|$ = 140 cm, $|BC|$ = 70 cm,
$|AB|$ = $|DC|$, $|\angle ADC|$ = $|\angle DAB|$ = 60°.

(a) Show that $|AB|$ = 70 cm.

(b) Find the distance between the parallel sides $[AD]$ and $[BC]$. Give your
answer in centimetres, correct to one decimal place.

(c) Some of the tables are painted with a yellow and blue pattern as
shown.

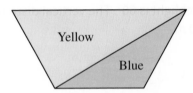

What fraction of the surface is yellow? Show your work.

(d) Two of the tables, painted as in part (c) above, are arranged to form a
hexagon.

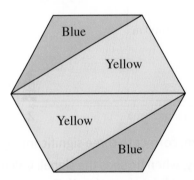

Prove that the yellow area is a rectangle.

(e) Twelve of the tables are arranged as six hexagons in a classroom, as shown in the diagram.

The clearance between neighbouring tables is 2 metres and the clearance to the side walls is 1·5 metres, as shown.

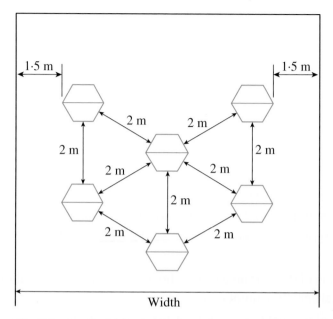

Find the total width of the classroom, in metres, correct to two decimal places.

(f) The tops of the trapezium tables are made of wood. The wood is 1·6 cm thick. Each cubic centimetre of the wood weighs 0·75 grams. Each table also has a metal frame weighing 6 kilograms. How much does each table weigh? Give your answer in kilograms, correct to one decimal place. *(2011)*

Q2 The planned supports for the roof of a building form scalene triangles of different sizes.

(a) Explain what is meant by a **scalene triangle**.

The triangle EFG is the image of the triangle CDE under an enlargement and the triangle CDE is the image of the triangle ABC under the same enlargement.

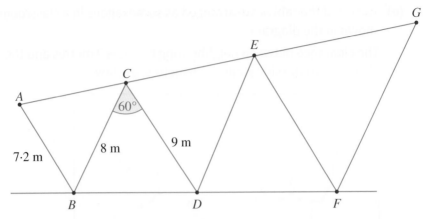

The proposed dimensions for the structure are $|AB| = 7{\cdot}2$ m, $|BC| = 8$ m, $|CD| = 9$ m and $|\angle DCB| = 60°$.

(b) Find the length of $[FG]$.

(c) Find the length of $[BD]$, correct to three decimal places.

(d) The centre of the enlargement is O. Find the distance from O to the point B.

(e) A condition of the planning is that the height of the point G above the horizontal line BF cannot exceed 11·6 m.

Does the plan meet this condition? Justify your answer by calculation.

(2012)

Q3 A search is begun for a buoy that has become detached from its mooring at sea. The area to be searched is a circle of radius 30 km from the last known position, K, of the buoy. The search area is divided into six equal sectors as indicated by the letters A, B, C, D, E and F.

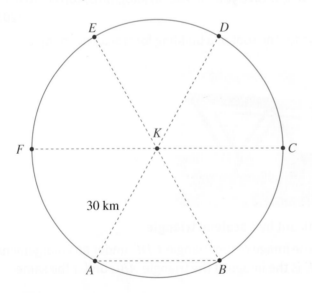

(a) Fishing boats search the triangular area KAB.

   (i) Find $|\angle BKA|$.

  (ii) Find the area of the triangle KAB.

 (iii) Write the area of the triangle KAB as a percentage of the area of the sector KAB.

 (iv) Use the cosine rule to find the length of $[AB]$.

  (v) What does your answer to (iv) above show about the triangle KAB?

(b) A helicopter took part in the search.

   (i) The helicopter flew from the point F around the perimeter of the search area. What distance did the helicopter fly, correct to the nearest km?

  (ii) The helicopter then flew in a straight line from F to D and from D on to C, also in a straight line. Draw the path of the helicopter on the diagram.

 (iii) A theorem on your course can be used to find $|\angle FDC|$. Write down $|\angle FDC|$ and state the theorem.

 (iv) The helicopter flew at a speed of 80 km/h. How long did it take to fly from F to D and on to C?

(c) A lifeboat taking part in the search sailed, in a straight line, from the point K until it reached a point X, the midpoint of $[ED]$.

   (i) Calculate $|KX|$.

  (ii) The buoy was located at the point where the path, KX, of the lifeboat crossed the path FD of the helicopter. How far was the buoy from X?   (2013)

 Q4

A stand is being used to prop up a portable solar panel. It consists of a support that is hinged to the panel near the top, and an adjustable strap joining the panel to the support near the bottom.

By adjusting the length of the strap, the angle between the panel and the ground can be changed.

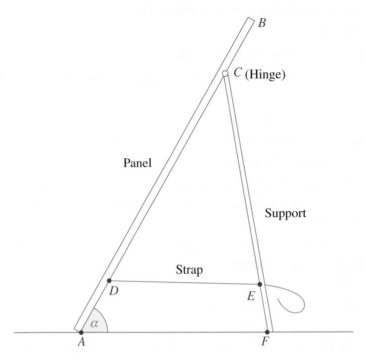

The dimensions are as follows: $|AB|$ = 30 cm, $|AD|$ = $|CB|$ = 5 cm, $|CF|$ = 22 cm, $|EF|$ = 4 cm.

We want to find out how long the strap has to be in order to make the angle α between the panel and the ground equal to 60°.

(a) Two diagrams are given below – one showing triangle CAF and the other showing triangle CDE. Use the measurements given above to record on the two diagrams below the lengths of two of the sides in each triangle.

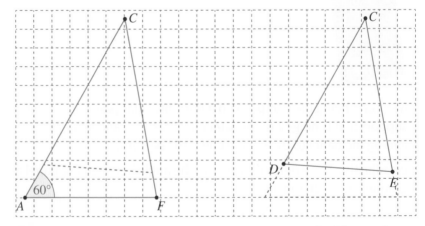

(b) Taking α = 60°, as shown, use the triangle CAF to find $|\angle CFA|$, correct to one decimal place.

(c) Hence find $|\angle ACF|$, correct to one decimal place.

(d) Use triangle CDE to find $|DE|$, the length of the strap, correct to one decimal place.

(SEC Sample Paper 2014)

Q5 (a) A wind turbine, used to generate electricity, has three equally spaced blades 65 metres long.

    (i) Write down the size of the angle between two blades.

   (ii) Find the area of the disc traced out by one full rotation of the blades, correct to the nearest whole number.

  (iii) Find the area of the triangle formed by joining the tips of the three blades, correct to the nearest whole number.

  (iv) The expected lifetime of the turbine is 25 years. On average, the turbine operates 31% of the time. The blades rotate 15 times per minute when the turbine is operating. Find the number of times the blades will rotate during the expected lifetime of the turbine (ignore leap years). Write your answer in the form $a \times 10^n$, where $1 < a \le 10$ and $n \in \mathbb{N}$.

(b)

Gráinne stood at a point B, which is on level ground 100 metres from the base of the tower supporting the blades, as shown. From there, she measured the angle of elevation to the top of the tower as 60°. Find the height of the tower, using Gráinne's measurements. Give your answer correct to the nearest metre.

(c) Gráinne recognises that her measurement of the angle may not be totally accurate. She read elsewhere that the actual height of the tower is 154 m.

(i) If Gráinne measured the 100 m accurately, find the actual size of the angle at B, correct to the nearest degree.

(ii) Find the percentage error in Grainne's measurement of the angle of elevation, correct to one decimal place. *(2014)*

Q6 At an activity centre a zip-line, $[BD]$, runs between two vertical poles, $[AB]$ and $[CD]$, on level ground, as shown. The point E is on the ground, directly below the zip-line.

$|AE| = 12$ m, $|BE| = 14$ m, $|CD| = 1.95$ m and $|EC| = 10$ m.

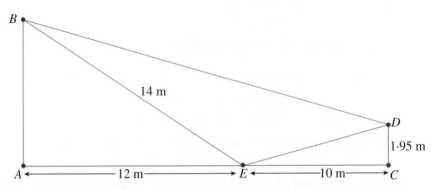

(a) (i) Find the distance $|ED|$, correct to one decimal place.

(ii) Find $|\angle AEB|$, correct to the nearest degree.

(b) (i) Find $|\angle DEB|$, given that $|\angle CED| = 11°$, correct to the nearest degree.

(ii) Hence, or otherwise, find the distance $|DB|$. Give your answer correct to one decimal place. *(2014)*

Solutions to Exercise A

Q1 (a) (i) $\sin A = \dfrac{8}{10} = \dfrac{4}{5}$ (ii) $\cos A = \dfrac{6}{10} = \dfrac{3}{5}$ (iii) $\tan A = \dfrac{8}{6} = \dfrac{4}{3}$

(b) (i) $\sin B = \dfrac{6}{10} = \dfrac{3}{5}$ (ii) $\cos B = \dfrac{8}{10} = \dfrac{4}{5}$ (iii) $\tan B = \dfrac{6}{8} = \dfrac{3}{4}$

(c) $A + B = 90°$. (The acute angles in a right-angled triangle are complementary.)

(d) If A and B are complementary:

(i) $\sin A = \cos B$ (ii) $\cos A = \sin B$ (iii) $\tan A = \dfrac{1}{\tan B}$.

Q2 (a) $\tan A = \dfrac{5}{6} \Rightarrow A = \tan^{-1}\left(\dfrac{5}{6}\right) = 40°$

(b) $\cos B = \dfrac{4}{11} \Rightarrow B = \cos^{-1}\left(\dfrac{4}{11}\right) = 69°$

(c) $\sin C = \dfrac{\sqrt{3}}{2} \Rightarrow B = \sin^{-1}\left(\dfrac{\sqrt{3}}{2}\right) = 60°$

(d) $\cos D = \dfrac{1}{\sqrt{2}} \Rightarrow D = \cos^{-1}\left(\dfrac{1}{\sqrt{2}}\right) = 45°$

Q3

Using Pythagoras' theorem, we can see that if the opposite side to A has length 3, and the hypotenuse has length 5, then the adjacent to A has length 4.

The angle B is marked in as it is equal to $90° - A$ and will be needed in part (c). (Recall that the acute angles in a right-angled triangle are complementary, i.e. they add up to $90°$.)

(a) $\cos A = \dfrac{4}{5}$ **(b)** $\tan A = \dfrac{3}{4}$ **(c)** $\tan(90° - A) = \tan B = \dfrac{4}{3}$

Q4 (a) Use a formula triangle to match the letters in the area formula with the numbers in the question.

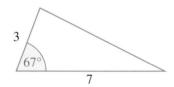 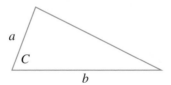

$A = \dfrac{1}{2}ab\sin C = \dfrac{1}{2}(3)(7)\sin(67°) = 9{\cdot}7$ square units

(b) Use a new formula triangle for the new formula. Make sure that the unknown is marked A or a, depending on if you are looking for an angle or a side, when applying the sine or cosine rule.

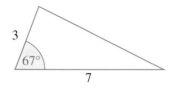 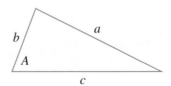

$a^2 = b^2 + c^2 - 2bc\cos A = (3)^2 + (7)^2 - 2(3)(7)\cos(67°) = 41{\cdot}589$

$\Rightarrow a = \sqrt{41{\cdot}589} = 6$ units

Q5 (a) Use the sine rule. Make A the unknown angle in the formula triangle.

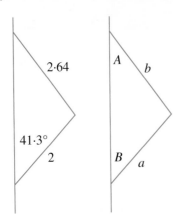

$$\frac{\sin A}{a} = \frac{\sin B}{b} \Rightarrow \frac{\sin A}{2} = \frac{\sin(41\cdot3°)}{2\cdot64} \Rightarrow A = \sin^{-1}\left[\frac{2\sin(41\cdot3°)}{2\cdot64}\right] = 30°.$$

This would be S 30° E.

(b) The sum of the interior angles is 180°,

$$\Rightarrow |\angle PHQ| = 180° - 30° - 41\cdot3° = 108\cdot7°.$$

(c) Use the cosine rule. Draw a formula triangle, marking the unknown as a.

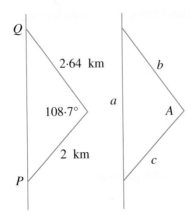

$$|PQ|^2 = a^2 = b^2 + c^2 - 2bc\cos A$$
$$= (2\cdot64)^2 + (2)^2 - 2(2\cdot64)(2)\cos(108\cdot7°) = 14\cdot36$$
$$\Rightarrow |PQ| = \sqrt{14\cdot36} = 3\cdot8 \text{ km}$$

(d) time $= \dfrac{\text{distance}}{\text{speed}} = \dfrac{3\cdot8}{19} = 0\cdot2$ hours $= 0\cdot2 \times 60 = 12$ minutes

Q6 (a) Use the cosine rule. Mark the unknown angle as A.

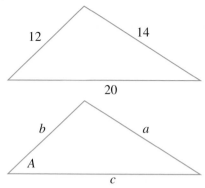

$a^2 = b^2 + c^2 - 2bc \cos A \Rightarrow (14)^2 = (12)^2 + (20)^2 - 2(12)(20) \cos A$

$\Rightarrow 196 = 144 + 400 - 480 \cos A$

$\Rightarrow 480 \cos A = 144 + 400 - 196 = 348$

$\Rightarrow \cos A = \dfrac{348}{480} \Rightarrow A = \cos^{-1}\left(\dfrac{348}{480}\right) = 43 \cdot 5°$

(b)

$A = \dfrac{1}{2} ab \sin C = \dfrac{1}{2}(12)(20)\sin(43 \cdot 5°) = 82 \cdot 6$ square units.

(c) $\dfrac{1}{2} \times$ base $\times$ height = area $\Rightarrow \dfrac{1}{2} \times 20 \times |RT| = 82 \cdot 6$

$\Rightarrow |RT| = \dfrac{2 \times 82 \cdot 6}{20} = 8$ units

Q7 (a) $34 \cdot 5 \times 5 = 172 \cdot 5$ cm

(b) $19 \cdot 3 \times 5 = 96 \cdot 5$ cm

(c) $A = 172 \cdot 5 \times 96 \cdot 5 = 16\,646 \cdot 25$ cm^2

(d) $A = 34 \cdot 5 \times 19 \cdot 3 = 665 \cdot 85$ cm^2

(e) $\dfrac{16\,646 \cdot 25}{665 \cdot 85} = 25$. That is, the ratio is $25:1$.

(Note that you could also write the solution as $k^2 = 5^2 = 25$.)

Solutions to Exercise B

Q1 (a) Modify the diagram as shown to obtain a right-angled triangle.

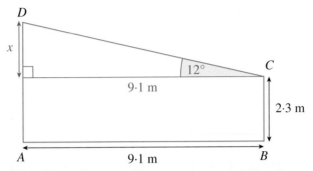

$$\frac{x}{9\cdot1} = \tan 12° \Rightarrow x = 9\cdot1 \times \tan 12° = 1\cdot9 \text{ m}$$

$$|AD| = x + |BC| = 1\cdot9 + 2\cdot3 = 4\cdot2 \text{ m}$$

(b) $A = \left(\dfrac{a+b}{2}\right)h = \left(\dfrac{4\cdot2 + 2\cdot3}{2}\right)(9\cdot1) = 29\cdot6 \text{ m}^2$

Q2 (a) $|AD|^2 + 4\cdot2^2 = 5\cdot6^2 \Rightarrow |AD| = \sqrt{5\cdot6^2 - 4\cdot2^2} = 3\cdot7 \text{ m}$

(b) $\cos(\angle ACD) = \dfrac{4\cdot2}{5\cdot6} \Rightarrow |\angle ACD| = \cos^{-1}\left(\dfrac{4\cdot2}{5\cdot6}\right) = 41\cdot4°$

(c) $\dfrac{|CE|}{4\cdot2} = \sin 55° \Rightarrow |CE| = 4\cdot2 \sin 55° = 3\cdot4 \text{ m}$

(d) $\cos 55° = \dfrac{4\cdot2}{|AB|} \Rightarrow |AB| = \dfrac{4\cdot2}{\cos 55°} = 7\cdot3 \text{ m}$

Q3 (a)

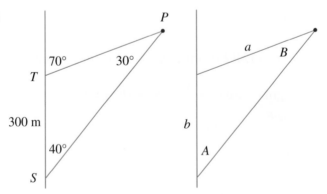

$70° = |\angle TPS| + 40° \Rightarrow |\angle TPS| = 30°$ (exterior angle theorem)

Thus, $\dfrac{a}{\sin A} = \dfrac{b}{\sin B} \Rightarrow \dfrac{|PT|}{\sin 40°} = \dfrac{300}{\sin 30°}$

$\Rightarrow |PT| = \sin 40° \times \dfrac{300}{\sin 30°} = 386 \text{ m.}$

Top Tip

Always ensure that you pair up each side with its *opposite* angle when using the sine rule. You may be given the wrong angle as in Q3(a). In that case, be careful to calculate the correct angle.

(b)

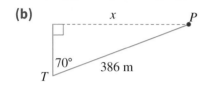

$$\frac{x}{386} = \sin 70° \Rightarrow x = 386 \sin 70° = 363 \text{ m}$$

Q4 (a)

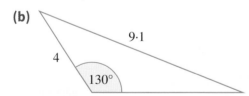

$$a^2 = b^2 + c^2 - 2bc \cos A = 4^2 + 6^2 - 2(4)(6) \cos(130°) = 82·85$$
$$\Rightarrow a = \sqrt{82·85} = 9·1 \text{ km}$$

(b)

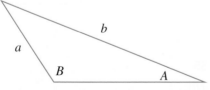

$$\frac{\sin A}{a} = \frac{\sin B}{b} \Rightarrow \frac{\sin A}{4} = \frac{\sin 130°}{9·1} \Rightarrow \sin A = 4 \times \frac{\sin 130°}{9·1}$$

$$\Rightarrow A = \sin^{-1}\left(4 \times \frac{\sin 130°}{9·1}\right) = 20°$$

The bearing can be written as W 20° N or N 70° W.

Q5 (a) $S = \{(2, 4, 6), (2, 4, 8), (2, 6, 8), (4, 6, 8)\}$

(b) According to the triangle equality, the sum of any two lengths must be greater than the third length.

Thus $(2, 4, 6)$ cannot form a triangle since $2 + 4 = 6$. Neither can $(2, 6, 8)$ nor $(2, 4, 8)$ since $2 + 6 = 8$ and $2 + 4 < 8$. Only the lengths 4 cm, 6 cm and 8 cm can form a triangle.

This makes the probability $P = \frac{1}{4}$.

(c)

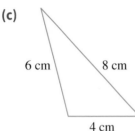
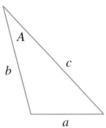

The smallest angle is opposite the shortest side.

$a^2 = b^2 + c^2 - 2bc \cos A \Rightarrow 4^2 = 6^2 + 8^2 - 2(6)(8) \cos A$

$\Rightarrow 16 = 36 + 64 - 96 \cos A \Rightarrow 96 \cos A = 36 + 64 - 16 = 84$

$\Rightarrow \cos A = \dfrac{84}{96} \Rightarrow A = \cos^{-1}\left(\dfrac{84}{96}\right) = 29°$

Q6 (a) Let l be the length of the light beam. Note that the cloud is $2000 - 400 = 1600$ m above the building.

$\sin 60° = \dfrac{1600}{l} \Rightarrow l = \dfrac{1600}{\sin 60°} = 1850$ m, correct to three significant figures.

(b) $\tan 60° = \dfrac{1600}{|YZ|} \Rightarrow |YZ| = \dfrac{1600}{\tan 60°} = 923.76$ m.

$|XY| = 3000 - |YZ| = 3000 - 923.76 = 2076.24$ m.

Let E be the angle of elevation required.

$\tan E = \dfrac{2000}{2076.24} \Rightarrow E = \tan^{-1}\left(\dfrac{2000}{2076.24}\right) = 43.9°$

Solutions to Exercise C

Q1 (a) The triangle ABX is right-angled.

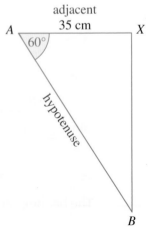

$\cos(60°) = \dfrac{\text{adjacent}}{\text{hypotenuse}} = \dfrac{35}{|AB|}$

$\Rightarrow \dfrac{1}{2} = \dfrac{35}{|AB|} \Rightarrow 2 = \dfrac{|AB|}{35}$

$\Rightarrow 2 \times 35 = |AB| = 70$ cm

(b) From Pythagoras' theorem: $|BX|^2 + 35^2 = 70^2$

$\Rightarrow |BX|^2 = 70^2 - 35^2 = 3675 \Rightarrow |BX| = \sqrt{3675} = 60{\cdot}6$ cm.

(c) The area of the yellow triangle is $A_y = \dfrac{1}{2}bh = \dfrac{1}{2} \times 140 \times 60{\cdot}6 = 4242\,\text{cm}^2$.

The area of the blue triangle is $A_b = \dfrac{1}{2}bh = \dfrac{1}{2} \times 70 \times 60{\cdot}6 = 2121\,\text{cm}^2$.

Thus, the required fraction is $\dfrac{A_y}{A_y + A_b} = \dfrac{4242}{4242 + 2121} = \dfrac{2}{3}$.

(d) Opposite sides are clearly equal in length. We need to show that each corner in the yellow shape is a right angle.

$|\angle ABC| = 120°$, since it is an interior angle in a regular hexagon.

The triangle BCD is isosceles, and $|\angle BCD| = |\angle ABC| = 120°$ $\Rightarrow |\angle CDB| = |\angle CBD| = 30°$ (the sum of the interior angles in a triangle is 180°).

Thus, $|\angle ABD| = 120° - 30° = 90°$.

Similarly, the other three angles in the yellow shape are right angles. Thus, the yellow shape is a rectangle.

(e)

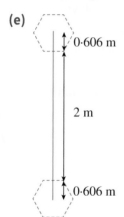

0·606 m

2 m

0·606 m

From the above diagram, we see that the distance shown is $0{\cdot}606 + 2 + 0{\cdot}606 = 3{\cdot}212$ m.

We will now use the cosine rule to find the distance x as shown:

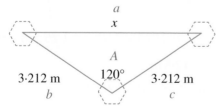

a
x
A
$120°$
$3{\cdot}212$ m
b
$3{\cdot}212$ m
c

$a^2 = b^2 + c^2 - 2bc \cos A$

$\Rightarrow x^2 = (3{\cdot}212)^2 + (3{\cdot}212)^2 - 2(3{\cdot}212)(3{\cdot}212)\cos(120°)$

$\Rightarrow x^2 = 30{\cdot}9508 \Rightarrow x = \sqrt{30{\cdot}9508} = 5{\cdot}5633$ m

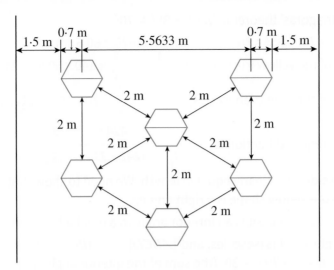

Finally, we see that the total width of the classroom is:
1·5 + 0·7 + 5·5633 + 0·7 + 1·5 = 9·96 m.

(f) The area of one table top is 4242 + 2121 = 6363 cm² (from part (c)).
Thus, the volume of the top is 6363 × 1·6 = 10 180·8 cm³.

Each cubic centimetre weighs 0.75 grams, so the total weight of one
table top is 10 180·8 × 0·75 = 7635·6 g = 7·6356 kg.

The total weight of each table including the metal frame is
6 + 7·6356 = 13·6356 = 13·6 kg to one decimal place.

Q2 (a) In a scalene triangle the three sides all have different lengths.

(b)

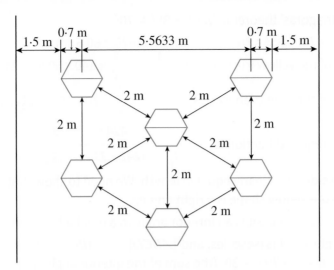

The scale factor $k = \dfrac{9}{7\cdot2} = 1\cdot25 \Rightarrow |DE| = k|BC| = 1\cdot25 \times 8 = 10$ m

$\Rightarrow |FG| = k|DE| = 1\cdot25 \times 10 = 12\cdot5$ m.

(c) Using the cosine rule we get $a^2 = b^2 + c^2 - 2bc \cos A$

$\Rightarrow |BD|^2 = (8)^2 + (9)^2 - 2(8)(9) \cos(60°) = 73$

$\Rightarrow |BD| = \sqrt{73} = 8\cdot544$ m.

(d) Let $x = |OB|$.

$$k = \frac{|OD|}{|OB|} = \frac{x + 8\cdot544}{x} = 1\cdot25 \Rightarrow x + 8\cdot544 = 1\cdot25x$$

$$\Rightarrow 8\cdot544 = 0\cdot25x \Rightarrow 8\cdot544 \div 0\cdot25 = x = 34\cdot176 \text{ m}$$

(e)

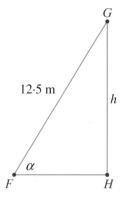

To find the height, h, we need to know the angle α. Since FG is parallel to BC, $\alpha = |\angle CBD|$, which we will use the sine rule to find.

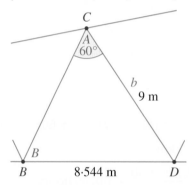

$$\frac{\sin B}{b} = \frac{\sin A}{a} \Rightarrow \frac{\sin \alpha}{9} = \frac{\sin 60°}{8\cdot544} \Rightarrow \sin \alpha = 9 \times \frac{\sin 60°}{8\cdot544} = 0\cdot91225$$

$$\Rightarrow \alpha = \sin^{-1}(0\cdot91225) = 65\cdot818°$$

From triangle GFH, $\sin \alpha = \dfrac{h}{12\cdot5}$

$$\Rightarrow h = 12\cdot5 \times \sin(65\cdot818°) = 11\cdot40 \text{ m} < 11\cdot6 \text{ m}.$$

Yes, the plan meets the condition.

Q3 (a) **(i)** $|\angle BKA| = 360° \div 6 = 60°$

(ii) Area $= \dfrac{1}{2}ab \sin C = \dfrac{1}{2}(30)(30)\sin(60°) = 389\cdot7 \text{ km}^2$

(iii) Area of sector $= \pi r^2 \left(\dfrac{\theta}{360°}\right) = \pi(30)^2\left(\dfrac{60°}{360°}\right) = 471\cdot24 \text{ km}^2$

$$\frac{389\cdot7}{471\cdot24} \times 100 = 82\cdot7\%$$

(iv) $a^2 = b^2 + c^2 - 2bc \cos A = (30)^2 + (30)^2 - 2(30)(30)\cos(60°) = 900$

$\Rightarrow a = \sqrt{900} = 30$ km.

(v) The triangle KAB is an equilateral triangle.

(b) **(i)** $P = 2\pi r = 2\pi(30) = 188\cdot496 \approx 188$ km

(ii)

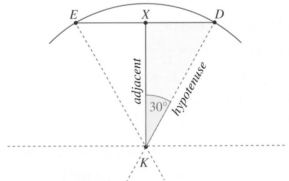

(iii) $|\angle FDC| = 90°$. The angle in a semicircle is a right angle.

(iv) First find $|FD|$.

Pythagoras' theorem $\Rightarrow |FC|^2 = |FD|^2 + |DC|^2 \Rightarrow 60^2 = |FD|^2 + 30^2$

$\Rightarrow |FD| = \sqrt{60^2 - 30^2} = 51\cdot96$ km

$$\text{Time} = \frac{\text{total distance}}{\text{average speed}} = \frac{51\cdot96 + 30}{80} = 1\cdot0245 \text{ hours}$$

(c) **(i)**

Since the triangle KED is equilateral, $KX \perp ED$ and KX bisects $\angle EKD$.

$$\cos(30°) = \frac{\text{adjacent}}{\text{hypotenuse}} = \frac{|KX|}{30} \Rightarrow |KX| = 30\cos(30°) = 25\cdot98 \text{ km}$$

(ii) Suppose KX and FD cross at the point P as shown below.

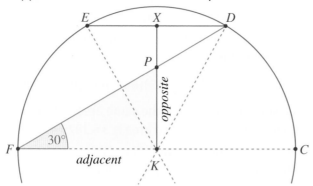

Consider the triangle DKF. It is isosceles, so the two acute angles are equal. Since $|\angle DKF| = 60° + 60° = 120°$, they must both equal 30°.

The triangle KFP is right-angled.

$$\tan 30° = \frac{\text{opposite}}{\text{adjacent}} = \frac{|KP|}{|KF|} = \frac{|KP|}{30} \Rightarrow |KP| = 30 \tan 30° = 17{\cdot}32 \text{ km}$$

$|XP| = |KX| - |KP| = 25{\cdot}98 - 17{\cdot}32 = 8{\cdot}66$ km

Q4 (a)

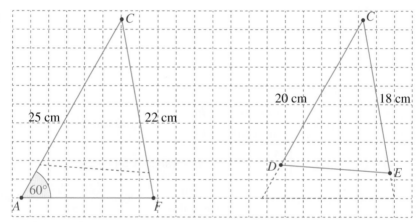

(b) Using the sine rule:

$$\frac{\sin(\angle CFA)}{25} = \frac{\sin 60°}{22} \Rightarrow \sin(\angle CFA) = 25 \times \frac{\sin 60°}{22} = 0{\cdot}9841$$

$$\Rightarrow |\angle CFA| = \sin^{-1}(0{\cdot}9841) = 79{\cdot}8°.$$

(c) $|\angle ACF| = 180° - 79{\cdot}8° - 60° = 40{\cdot}2°$

(d) Using the cosine rule:

$$a^2 = b^2 + c^2 - 2bc \cos A = (20)^2 + (18)^2 - 2(20)(18) \cos(40{\cdot}2°) = 174{\cdot}0669$$

$$\Rightarrow a = |DE| = \sqrt{174{\cdot}0669} = 13{\cdot}2 \text{ cm.}$$

Q5 (a) **(i)** $360° ÷ 3 = 120°$

(ii) $A = \pi r^2 = \pi (65)^2 = 13\,273 \text{ m}^2$

(iii) Consider the triangle formed by joining the centre and the ends of two adjacent blades.

$$A = \frac{1}{2}ab \sin C \Rightarrow A = \frac{1}{2}(65)(65)\sin(120°) = 1829·479 \text{ m}^2$$

Three such triangles have the same area as that of the required triangle. Thus, the required area is $3 \times 1829·479 = 5488 \text{ m}^2$.

(iv) We need to multiply the number of minutes the turbine operates by 15. It only operates for 31% of 25 years.

25 years is $25 \times 365 \times 24 \times 60 = 13\,140\,000$ minutes

31% of this is $13\,140\,000 \times \dfrac{31}{100} = 4\,073\,400$ minutes

Thus the number of rotations is

$15 \times 4\,073\,400 = 61\,101\,000 = 6·1101 \times 10^7$.

(b)

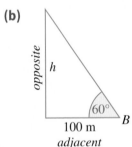

$$\tan 60° = \frac{\text{opposite}}{\text{adjacent}} = \frac{h}{100} \Rightarrow h = 100 \tan 60° = 173 \text{ m}$$

(c) **(i)** $\tan B = \dfrac{154}{100} = 1·54 \Rightarrow B = \tan^{-1}(1·54) = 57°$

(ii) Percentage error $= \dfrac{\text{error}}{\text{true value}} \times 100 = \dfrac{(60° - 57°)}{57°} \times 100 = 5·3\%$

Q6 (a) **(i)** $|ED|^2 = 10^2 + 1·95^2 = 103·8025 \Rightarrow |ED| = \sqrt{103·8025} = 10·2 \text{ m}$

(ii) $\cos \angle AEB = \dfrac{12}{14} \Rightarrow |\angle AEB| = \cos^{-1}\left(\dfrac{12}{14}\right) = 31°$

(b) **(i)** $|\angle DEB| = 180° - 31° - 11° = 138°$ (straight angle)

(ii) Given two sides and the included angle, we use the cosine rule to find the third side.

$|BD|^2 = 14^2 + 10·2^2 - 2(14)(10·2)\cos(138°) = 512·282$

$\Rightarrow |BD| = \sqrt{512·282} = 22·6 \text{ m}$

Questions to Practise

If you have a difficulty with a question do the following.

- Write the page number and the question number in the boxes provided.
- Practise the question. Each time you practise, tick a box.
- Usually, five ticks will indicate that you have mastered the difficulty.

This is a very efficient study method.

Page Number	Question Number						Page Number	Question Number					
		☐	☐	☐	☐	☐			☐	☐	☐	☐	☐
		☐	☐	☐	☐	☐			☐	☐	☐	☐	☐
		☐	☐	☐	☐	☐			☐	☐	☐	☐	☐
		☐	☐	☐	☐	☐			☐	☐	☐	☐	☐
		☐	☐	☐	☐	☐			☐	☐	☐	☐	☐
		☐	☐	☐	☐	☐			☐	☐	☐	☐	☐
		☐	☐	☐	☐	☐			☐	☐	☐	☐	☐
		☐	☐	☐	☐	☐			☐	☐	☐	☐	☐
		☐	☐	☐	☐	☐			☐	☐	☐	☐	☐
		☐	☐	☐	☐	☐			☐	☐	☐	☐	☐
		☐	☐	☐	☐	☐			☐	☐	☐	☐	☐
		☐	☐	☐	☐	☐			☐	☐	☐	☐	☐
		☐	☐	☐	☐	☐			☐	☐	☐	☐	☐
		☐	☐	☐	☐	☐			☐	☐	☐	☐	☐
		☐	☐	☐	☐	☐			☐	☐	☐	☐	☐

Page Number	Question Number						Page Number	Question Number					
		☐	☐	☐	☐	☐			☐	☐	☐	☐	☐
		☐	☐	☐	☐	☐			☐	☐	☐	☐	☐
		☐	☐	☐	☐	☐			☐	☐	☐	☐	☐
		☐	☐	☐	☐	☐			☐	☐	☐	☐	☐
		☐	☐	☐	☐	☐			☐	☐	☐	☐	☐
		☐	☐	☐	☐	☐			☐	☐	☐	☐	☐
		☐	☐	☐	☐	☐			☐	☐	☐	☐	☐
		☐	☐	☐	☐	☐			☐	☐	☐	☐	☐
		☐	☐	☐	☐	☐			☐	☐	☐	☐	☐
		☐	☐	☐	☐	☐			☐	☐	☐	☐	☐
		☐	☐	☐	☐	☐			☐	☐	☐	☐	☐
		☐	☐	☐	☐	☐			☐	☐	☐	☐	☐
		☐	☐	☐	☐	☐			☐	☐	☐	☐	☐
		☐	☐	☐	☐	☐			☐	☐	☐	☐	☐
		☐	☐	☐	☐	☐			☐	☐	☐	☐	☐
		☐	☐	☐	☐	☐			☐	☐	☐	☐	☐
		☐	☐	☐	☐	☐			☐	☐	☐	☐	☐
		☐	☐	☐	☐	☐			☐	☐	☐	☐	☐
		☐	☐	☐	☐	☐			☐	☐	☐	☐	☐
		☐	☐	☐	☐	☐			☐	☐	☐	☐	☐
		☐	☐	☐	☐	☐			☐	☐	☐	☐	☐
		☐	☐	☐	☐	☐			☐	☐	☐	☐	☐
		☐	☐	☐	☐	☐			☐	☐	☐	☐	☐
		☐	☐	☐	☐	☐			☐	☐	☐	☐	☐
		☐	☐	☐	☐	☐			☐	☐	☐	☐	☐
		☐	☐	☐	☐	☐			☐	☐	☐	☐	☐
		☐	☐	☐	☐	☐			☐	☐	☐	☐	☐

Page Number	Question Number						Page Number	Question Number					
		☐	☐	☐	☐	☐			☐	☐	☐	☐	☐
		☐	☐	☐	☐	☐			☐	☐	☐	☐	☐
		☐	☐	☐	☐	☐			☐	☐	☐	☐	☐
		☐	☐	☐	☐	☐			☐	☐	☐	☐	☐
		☐	☐	☐	☐	☐			☐	☐	☐	☐	☐
		☐	☐	☐	☐	☐			☐	☐	☐	☐	☐
		☐	☐	☐	☐	☐			☐	☐	☐	☐	☐
		☐	☐	☐	☐	☐			☐	☐	☐	☐	☐
		☐	☐	☐	☐	☐			☐	☐	☐	☐	☐
		☐	☐	☐	☐	☐			☐	☐	☐	☐	☐
		☐	☐	☐	☐	☐			☐	☐	☐	☐	☐
		☐	☐	☐	☐	☐			☐	☐	☐	☐	☐
		☐	☐	☐	☐	☐			☐	☐	☐	☐	☐
		☐	☐	☐	☐	☐			☐	☐	☐	☐	☐
		☐	☐	☐	☐	☐			☐	☐	☐	☐	☐
		☐	☐	☐	☐	☐			☐	☐	☐	☐	☐
		☐	☐	☐	☐	☐			☐	☐	☐	☐	☐
		☐	☐	☐	☐	☐			☐	☐	☐	☐	☐
		☐	☐	☐	☐	☐			☐	☐	☐	☐	☐
		☐	☐	☐	☐	☐			☐	☐	☐	☐	☐
		☐	☐	☐	☐	☐			☐	☐	☐	☐	☐
		☐	☐	☐	☐	☐			☐	☐	☐	☐	☐
		☐	☐	☐	☐	☐			☐	☐	☐	☐	☐
		☐	☐	☐	☐	☐			☐	☐	☐	☐	☐
		☐	☐	☐	☐	☐			☐	☐	☐	☐	☐
		☐	☐	☐	☐	☐			☐	☐	☐	☐	☐
		☐	☐	☐	☐	☐			☐	☐	☐	☐	☐
		☐	☐	☐	☐	☐			☐	☐	☐	☐	☐

Page Number	Question Number					Page Number	Question Number				
		☐	☐	☐	☐	☐			☐	☐	☐	☐	☐
		☐	☐	☐	☐	☐			☐	☐	☐	☐	☐
		☐	☐	☐	☐	☐			☐	☐	☐	☐	☐
		☐	☐	☐	☐	☐			☐	☐	☐	☐	☐
		☐	☐	☐	☐	☐			☐	☐	☐	☐	☐
		☐	☐	☐	☐	☐			☐	☐	☐	☐	☐
		☐	☐	☐	☐	☐			☐	☐	☐	☐	☐
		☐	☐	☐	☐	☐			☐	☐	☐	☐	☐
		☐	☐	☐	☐	☐			☐	☐	☐	☐	☐
		☐	☐	☐	☐	☐			☐	☐	☐	☐	☐
		☐	☐	☐	☐	☐			☐	☐	☐	☐	☐
		☐	☐	☐	☐	☐			☐	☐	☐	☐	☐
		☐	☐	☐	☐	☐			☐	☐	☐	☐	☐
		☐	☐	☐	☐	☐			☐	☐	☐	☐	☐
		☐	☐	☐	☐	☐			☐	☐	☐	☐	☐
		☐	☐	☐	☐	☐			☐	☐	☐	☐	☐
		☐	☐	☐	☐	☐			☐	☐	☐	☐	☐
		☐	☐	☐	☐	☐			☐	☐	☐	☐	☐
		☐	☐	☐	☐	☐			☐	☐	☐	☐	☐
		☐	☐	☐	☐	☐			☐	☐	☐	☐	☐
		☐	☐	☐	☐	☐			☐	☐	☐	☐	☐
		☐	☐	☐	☐	☐			☐	☐	☐	☐	☐
		☐	☐	☐	☐	☐			☐	☐	☐	☐	☐
		☐	☐	☐	☐	☐			☐	☐	☐	☐	☐
		☐	☐	☐	☐	☐			☐	☐	☐	☐	☐
		☐	☐	☐	☐	☐			☐	☐	☐	☐	☐
		☐	☐	☐	☐	☐			☐	☐	☐	☐	☐
		☐	☐	☐	☐	☐			☐	☐	☐	☐	☐

Page Number	Question Number						Page Number	Question Number					
		☐	☐	☐	☐	☐			☐	☐	☐	☐	☐
		☐	☐	☐	☐	☐			☐	☐	☐	☐	☐
		☐	☐	☐	☐	☐			☐	☐	☐	☐	☐
		☐	☐	☐	☐	☐			☐	☐	☐	☐	☐
		☐	☐	☐	☐	☐			☐	☐	☐	☐	☐
		☐	☐	☐	☐	☐			☐	☐	☐	☐	☐
		☐	☐	☐	☐	☐			☐	☐	☐	☐	☐
		☐	☐	☐	☐	☐			☐	☐	☐	☐	☐
		☐	☐	☐	☐	☐			☐	☐	☐	☐	☐
		☐	☐	☐	☐	☐			☐	☐	☐	☐	☐
		☐	☐	☐	☐	☐			☐	☐	☐	☐	☐
		☐	☐	☐	☐	☐			☐	☐	☐	☐	☐
		☐	☐	☐	☐	☐			☐	☐	☐	☐	☐
		☐	☐	☐	☐	☐			☐	☐	☐	☐	☐
		☐	☐	☐	☐	☐			☐	☐	☐	☐	☐
		☐	☐	☐	☐	☐			☐	☐	☐	☐	☐
		☐	☐	☐	☐	☐			☐	☐	☐	☐	☐
		☐	☐	☐	☐	☐			☐	☐	☐	☐	☐
		☐	☐	☐	☐	☐			☐	☐	☐	☐	☐
		☐	☐	☐	☐	☐			☐	☐	☐	☐	☐
		☐	☐	☐	☐	☐			☐	☐	☐	☐	☐
		☐	☐	☐	☐	☐			☐	☐	☐	☐	☐
		☐	☐	☐	☐	☐			☐	☐	☐	☐	☐
		☐	☐	☐	☐	☐			☐	☐	☐	☐	☐
		☐	☐	☐	☐	☐			☐	☐	☐	☐	☐
		☐	☐	☐	☐	☐			☐	☐	☐	☐	☐
		☐	☐	☐	☐	☐			☐	☐	☐	☐	☐

Page Number	Question Number						Page Number	Question Number				
		☐	☐	☐	☐	☐			☐	☐	☐	☐	☐
		☐	☐	☐	☐	☐			☐	☐	☐	☐	☐
		☐	☐	☐	☐	☐			☐	☐	☐	☐	☐
		☐	☐	☐	☐	☐			☐	☐	☐	☐	☐
		☐	☐	☐	☐	☐			☐	☐	☐	☐	☐
		☐	☐	☐	☐	☐			☐	☐	☐	☐	☐
		☐	☐	☐	☐	☐			☐	☐	☐	☐	☐
		☐	☐	☐	☐	☐			☐	☐	☐	☐	☐
		☐	☐	☐	☐	☐			☐	☐	☐	☐	☐
		☐	☐	☐	☐	☐			☐	☐	☐	☐	☐
		☐	☐	☐	☐	☐			☐	☐	☐	☐	☐
		☐	☐	☐	☐	☐			☐	☐	☐	☐	☐
		☐	☐	☐	☐	☐			☐	☐	☐	☐	☐
		☐	☐	☐	☐	☐			☐	☐	☐	☐	☐
		☐	☐	☐	☐	☐			☐	☐	☐	☐	☐
		☐	☐	☐	☐	☐			☐	☐	☐	☐	☐
		☐	☐	☐	☐	☐			☐	☐	☐	☐	☐
		☐	☐	☐	☐	☐			☐	☐	☐	☐	☐
		☐	☐	☐	☐	☐			☐	☐	☐	☐	☐
		☐	☐	☐	☐	☐			☐	☐	☐	☐	☐
		☐	☐	☐	☐	☐			☐	☐	☐	☐	☐
		☐	☐	☐	☐	☐			☐	☐	☐	☐	☐
		☐	☐	☐	☐	☐			☐	☐	☐	☐	☐
		☐	☐	☐	☐	☐			☐	☐	☐	☐	☐
		☐	☐	☐	☐	☐			☐	☐	☐	☐	☐
		☐	☐	☐	☐	☐			☐	☐	☐	☐	☐
		☐	☐	☐	☐	☐			☐	☐	☐	☐	☐

Page Number	Question Number					Page Number	Question Number				
		☐	☐	☐	☐	☐			☐	☐	☐	☐	☐
		☐	☐	☐	☐	☐			☐	☐	☐	☐	☐
		☐	☐	☐	☐	☐			☐	☐	☐	☐	☐
		☐	☐	☐	☐	☐			☐	☐	☐	☐	☐
		☐	☐	☐	☐	☐			☐	☐	☐	☐	☐
		☐	☐	☐	☐	☐			☐	☐	☐	☐	☐
		☐	☐	☐	☐	☐			☐	☐	☐	☐	☐
		☐	☐	☐	☐	☐			☐	☐	☐	☐	☐
		☐	☐	☐	☐	☐			☐	☐	☐	☐	☐
		☐	☐	☐	☐	☐			☐	☐	☐	☐	☐
		☐	☐	☐	☐	☐			☐	☐	☐	☐	☐
		☐	☐	☐	☐	☐			☐	☐	☐	☐	☐
		☐	☐	☐	☐	☐			☐	☐	☐	☐	☐
		☐	☐	☐	☐	☐			☐	☐	☐	☐	☐
		☐	☐	☐	☐	☐			☐	☐	☐	☐	☐
		☐	☐	☐	☐	☐			☐	☐	☐	☐	☐
		☐	☐	☐	☐	☐			☐	☐	☐	☐	☐
		☐	☐	☐	☐	☐			☐	☐	☐	☐	☐
		☐	☐	☐	☐	☐			☐	☐	☐	☐	☐
		☐	☐	☐	☐	☐			☐	☐	☐	☐	☐
		☐	☐	☐	☐	☐			☐	☐	☐	☐	☐
		☐	☐	☐	☐	☐			☐	☐	☐	☐	☐
		☐	☐	☐	☐	☐			☐	☐	☐	☐	☐
		☐	☐	☐	☐	☐			☐	☐	☐	☐	☐
		☐	☐	☐	☐	☐			☐	☐	☐	☐	☐
		☐	☐	☐	☐	☐			☐	☐	☐	☐	☐
		☐	☐	☐	☐	☐			☐	☐	☐	☐	☐
		☐	☐	☐	☐	☐			☐	☐	☐	☐	☐

Page Number	Question Number						Page Number	Question Number					
		☐	☐	☐	☐	☐			☐	☐	☐	☐	☐
		☐	☐	☐	☐	☐			☐	☐	☐	☐	☐
		☐	☐	☐	☐	☐			☐	☐	☐	☐	☐
		☐	☐	☐	☐	☐			☐	☐	☐	☐	☐
		☐	☐	☐	☐	☐			☐	☐	☐	☐	☐
		☐	☐	☐	☐	☐			☐	☐	☐	☐	☐
		☐	☐	☐	☐	☐			☐	☐	☐	☐	☐
		☐	☐	☐	☐	☐			☐	☐	☐	☐	☐
		☐	☐	☐	☐	☐			☐	☐	☐	☐	☐
		☐	☐	☐	☐	☐			☐	☐	☐	☐	☐
		☐	☐	☐	☐	☐			☐	☐	☐	☐	☐
		☐	☐	☐	☐	☐			☐	☐	☐	☐	☐
		☐	☐	☐	☐	☐			☐	☐	☐	☐	☐
		☐	☐	☐	☐	☐			☐	☐	☐	☐	☐
		☐	☐	☐	☐	☐			☐	☐	☐	☐	☐
		☐	☐	☐	☐	☐			☐	☐	☐	☐	☐
		☐	☐	☐	☐	☐			☐	☐	☐	☐	☐
		☐	☐	☐	☐	☐			☐	☐	☐	☐	☐
		☐	☐	☐	☐	☐			☐	☐	☐	☐	☐
		☐	☐	☐	☐	☐			☐	☐	☐	☐	☐
		☐	☐	☐	☐	☐			☐	☐	☐	☐	☐
		☐	☐	☐	☐	☐			☐	☐	☐	☐	☐
		☐	☐	☐	☐	☐			☐	☐	☐	☐	☐
		☐	☐	☐	☐	☐			☐	☐	☐	☐	☐
		☐	☐	☐	☐	☐			☐	☐	☐	☐	☐
		☐	☐	☐	☐	☐			☐	☐	☐	☐	☐
		☐	☐	☐	☐	☐			☐	☐	☐	☐	☐
		☐	☐	☐	☐	☐			☐	☐	☐	☐	☐